D1065228

WHO OWNS AMERICA?

by
Walter J. Hickel

G.K. HALL & CO.

GKH Boston, Massachusetts
1972

Library of Congress Cataloging in Publication Data

Hickel, Walter J 1919-

Who owns America?

In large print.
1. U.S. — Politics and government — 1969-
2. U.S. — Civilization — 1970-   I.   Title.
E855.H5 1972   917.3   77-38949
ISBN 0-8161-6018-X (1. print)

Who Owns America?
by Walter J. Hickel

Copyright © 1971 by Walter J. Hickel

Published in Large Print by arrangement with Prentice-Hall, Inc.

Set in Photon 18 pt Times Roman

To Ermalee

Contents

Introduction

I've written this book for the young of all ages, the young of thought who refuse to be locked into the past, who do not fear the challenge of change and who anticipate the hope of the future.

We are at a time in our national history when mistrust of the responsiveness of government to the popular will has reached a critical point—a point at which increasing numbers of Americans feel denied and even robbed of the power to influence public policy; a point at which the cry is "return it to us." This mood is not the property of any age or class, and it can be a good and healthy thing if those in government will listen. But if no one will listen, the lack of communication causes frustration and fear. Fear leads to hate, and hate leads to violence.

What Americans want "returned to us" is

a sense of care, a sense of ownership. We want renewed assurance that we have some control over our physical assets and our spiritual destiny. We want to know that the important decisions affecting our life styles, and our very existence, will not be made by an anonymous "them" who may have no suitable consideration for our wishes. The public is asking for a larger role in the direction of its fate.

We live in an exciting time with the opportunity to lay new foundations for individual liberties and national vitality. In this time of great opportunity we need great leadership. We need fearless men to unite and lead us. But, unhappily, the years of the past decade have been years of increasing frustration marked most noticeably by additions to the vocabulary of polarization.

It is not enough to know what is right. The challenge is to act.

On January 27, 1969, three days after I had been sworn in as America's thirty-eighth Secretary of the Interior, I learned that the Union Oil Company's offshore Platform A in the Santa Barbara Channel, a little more than three miles off a

2

particularly attractive beach, had "blown out." An ominous oil slick had formed and, growing larger by the hour, was threatening the total coastal environment of one of the most handsome ocean-front cities in the United States.

The chair in my new office at Interior was a "hot seat" before I ever got to sit down in it. I was physically exhausted by a five-day inquisition to which I had been subjected by the Senate Interior Committee—one of the stormiest confirmation hearings the Senate had ever held on the nomination of a Cabinet officer. I was a controversial figure and a marked man before I did a thing.

Initially I was not sure what my legal authority was in the Santa Barbara situation. Yet I acted—and on my own. Whatever decision had to be made, I was determined to avoid a conglomeration of compromises. You never win anything that way. The sale of twenty oil leases just beyond the three-mile limit in the Santa Barbara Channel flagrantly violated the will of the people of California, expressed as long ago as 1955. Their idea was to preserve a small part of the Santa Barbara Channel as a marine sanctuary. Then both fish and people could have enjoyed the highest and best use of the water.

When I flew over the Santa Barbara oil slick, the ugly smear on the water below made it obvious to me that man's decision had been wrong. But this was only a small part of the whole problem of ownership in America. Was this a wise use of this part of the ocean? Who determines the answer to that question? Who owns the beaches in Santa Barbara and elsewhere? Who owns the fish, the ducks and the pelicans?

Why are the rivers no longer blue, as when the early explorers first saw them? Who owns the water running down out of the mountains to the sea? It belongs to no individual. Although we have the right to use it privately, we do not have the right to abuse it privately. The beaver family that builds a dam knows where and when to stop, because it takes and uses only what it needs. Yet man does not seem to know.

Who owns the air? Who owns the millions of acres of public land that remain in the United States, and the nearly one million square miles of Continental Shelf?

Who owns America?

Sometime in the 1960's a political and economic era came to an end in this country. The rough-and-tumble of economic survival and growth failed to provide the satisfaction that was supposed to come with the accumulation of glitter. We discovered that economic prosperity without due consideration for the needs of the mind and spirit left us with a society where the "good life" was measured in tangibles rather than those intangibles, such as friendship and service, that can make life a joy to live.

We need a truly national approach to government, and we must have men in government who will have the courage to accept responsibility for planning and implementing the policies that will lift us as a nation into the next century. This government must be visionary in nature and be prepared to "return to us" both the physical things that only national government can give back — clean rivers and unpolluted air and land — and those human things of hope and heart.

The subject is the living of life, and it is

not a regional or parochial thing. It cannot be sustained by a government based on the principle that mixing together regional and special interests will produce a truly national policy.

Theodore Roosevelt, the father of enlightened environmental policy in this country, was the first President to see this problem in its entirety. The problem, even in his time, had to do with the obligation of ownership, and the public's residual interest in *any* ownership. He understood this, but very few others have.

History shows the United States has enjoyed its healthiest times when the people felt involved, and neither afraid of government nor ignored by it. People — our job is people! The problems in America are created by the failure to inform the people or to listen to their pleas. Let's seek out the naked truth.

It is clearly time to reaffirm that "we" and not "them" are the new voices of America, and that "we" and not "them" really own America.

BOOK 1

How to Become an Endangered Species

"Conservation" is really "appreciation."
I am not for conservation for conservation's sake.

CHAPTER 1

A Naked Man

I had flown home to Anchorage for the 1968 Thanksgiving holidays, having been in the State capital of Juneau since Richard Nixon's election as President. My mind was not on getting a job in Washington, D.C.; I was Governor of Alaska, and I was totally involved with the 1969 legislative program for the State. Around eight o'clock on the Sunday morning after Thanksgiving, our housekeeper, Viola, came upstairs and said, "The President is on the phone." I clasped my head in my hands and said with anguish, "God, help me!"

I picked up the telephone. The President-elect's message was brief and to the point: "Wally, after great consideration, you are the one I have chosen to be Secretary of the Interior. You are the man to do the job. The announcement won't be made until after the first week in December, and I would appreciate it if this could be kept as confidential as possible."

We ended the conversation. After I hung up the phone, I wept. For twenty-eight years Alaska had been my total life. Now my life was changing. That phone call from Richard Nixon was the first link in a chain of events that were to change my life forever, change the lives of many others around me and perhaps bring a change in the whole approach to the living of life in America.

Perhaps I should have guessed what was coming, because there had been two earlier calls. Three days before, on Thanksgiving morning, John Mitchell telephoned and said, "Wally, the President is considering you for a Cabinet post."

"John, I'm not playing games," I replied. "I don't want to come back there."

"We know that," he said. "That's why we want you."

"But John, there's so much to be done here."

He was persistent: "Don't you have the State in pretty good shape so that you could leave it?"

"It's in pretty good shape now," I agreed.

Mitchell, who was soon to become Nixon's Attorney General, proceeded to wrap up the conversation. "Wally," he said, "I have a meeting with the President in the next couple of hours. Could I at least tell him that you will keep an open mind?"

"John, I keep an open mind on everything."

The next day, for no apparent reason, Vice President-elect Spiro Agnew called. He wanted to know how my family was and whether we had had a good Thanksgiving. It was nothing more than a neighborly conversation between two men who had been acquainted as Governors and who had worked together during the 1968 campaign.

Three days after the President's call, I flew to Palm Springs for the Republican Governors Conference. I had been asked to make a presentation concerning what I conceived to be the proper relationship between the Department of the Interior and the various states. I maintained a "low profile," if Wally Hickel can ever do so. The Nixon team seemed to want to keep a very tight lid on the fact that I was to become Secretary of the Interior.

At Palm Springs, Carl McMurray, one of my assistants, was invited to a small reception given by Dita Beard, congressional liaison in Washington for International Telephone and Telegraph. Naturally Carl was in on the secret, and only after he arrived at the party did he learn that the purpose was to celebrate the pending nomination of Maryland Congressman Rogers C. B. Morton as Secretary of the Interior. Dita and her friends were excited about the prospect of having in this post an Easterner familiar with the corridors of Capitol Hill.

I remained in California through December 8 and then flew to Seattle, where I holed up at the Olympic Hotel for two days. Because of the speech I had made at Palm Springs on State-Interior relationships, reporters in Juneau were beginning to scent the truth. They started beating down my office doors, only to be told that I was in Seattle to do some Christmas shopping.

On the morning of December 11, the news of my appointment was out in the Eastern press, although there was still no official confirmation. That morning a television crew spotted me at Seattle-Tacoma International Airport and demanded to know why I was going to Washington. For lack of a better answer, I said, "To do some more Christmas shopping."

In Washington, my family and I checked into the Shoreham Hotel a few hours prior to the President-elect's evening television show, at which he planned to introduce all the members of his Cabinet.

The television show itself was a proud occasion—not just for the Hickels, but for many Alaskans, who for the first time were represented in the Cabinet of a President of the United States.[1] All of us felt relaxed and

[1] *Ironically, Alaskans did not see the show "live." Transmission facilities were inadequate.*

comfortable; it really was a joyful occasion. The President-elect's manner was exceptionally gracious as he introduced us one by one with a fine sense of style and timing, speaking without notes for precisely twenty-nine minutes. He was generous in his remarks about me: "You can see that his eyes are looking over the horizon to things unseen beyond. He's going to bring a new sense of excitement, a new sense of creativity, to that department."

I would have felt a good deal less comfortable had I been aware of something that had happened to Alaska that same day. As the broadcast ended and the Cabinet designees were shown to another area of the Shoreham for formal photographs, my press aide, Joe Holbert, hurried up with Don Larrabee, Washington correspondent for the Anchorage *Daily Times*. Larrabee said, "Governor, Senator Bartlett died about three hours ago."

I went to tell the President-elect. I was immediately faced with making one of three choices. I could remain as Governor of Alaska. I could step down and permit my successor as Governor, Secretary of State

14

Keith Miller, to appoint me United States Senator to succeed Bob Bartlett; or I could go through with my commitment to join the Nixon Cabinet. I am fairly sure that I was the first Cabinet-designee ever to be faced with such a three-way choice.

The President-elect asked, "Wally, what are you going to do?" I did not hesitate. I dismissed from my mind everything except the fact that Nixon wanted me to serve. My decision was politically more risky than the options of remaining as Governor or going to the Senate. I stuck with my decision to accept the Cabinet appointment.

I explained this to Bonnie Angelo of *Time*, and she said, "Governor, it sounds like you've already caught Potomac fever."

"Bonnie," I said, "you can bet that's one disease I'll sure as hell never catch."

I made the decision because I was a great believer in Dick Nixon. His Inaugural Address was a great document of hope, and I referred to it almost every time I was scheduled to make a speech of my own as Secretary of the Interior.

1. A Meeting on Park Avenue

I had been acquainted with Dick Nixon since early 1952, but I had little personal contact with him until December 1967. At that time I flew to New York and went to the Park Avenue building where both Nixon and Governor Nelson Rockefeller maintained apartments.

The former Vice President and I talked for nearly two hours. The subject of politics never came up. We did not discuss Nixon's possible race for the presidency in 1968, or even any of the problems facing me as Governor of the young State of Alaska. We talked principally about the concern I had for the fiscal situation in the United States. I was convinced that our rising high-interest rate policies were heading the nation toward disaster. I said that if the cost of interest were allowed to keep climbing, we would become a nation of "renters of money." At one point Nixon said, "Wally, run that one by me again."

I repeated the expression to Nixon and reminded him that in certain foreign countries, long-term interest rates had been pushed to highs of more than 20 percent. People could not achieve equity in what they were acquiring, and there was an inevitable degrading of society and its standards. As our conversation drew to a close, Nixon said, "Wally, you really belong in the United States Senate."

In March 1968, John Sears, a campaign organizer who had taken a leave from Nixon's legal firm, came to Juneau. He asked if I would serve as co-chairman, along with Governor Tim Babcock of Montana, of the Nixon campaign in the Western states. I agreed, but I told John: "This point must be absolutely clear. I have no interest at all in any job other than what I'm doing here in Alaska." However, I said we would need some help with regard to the Interior Department. The truth was that Alaskans had had an enormous amount of trouble with Interior, not only in the territorial days but after Alaska became a State.

I also explained to Sears that the new Department of Transportation was very important to the State of Alaska, and that I had been trying without success to interest the federal government in updating and expanding the Alaska Railroad, the only federally owned rail system in the nation. In the vast area of Alaska that lies north of Fairbanks, there is literally no surface transportation. We had a chance to open up the area carefully and correctly, and we were pushing for a railroad north as the finest kind of conservation — something I still believe should happen. I had found a sympathetic man in Secretary Alan Boyd during the Johnson Administration.

I was not to see Dick Nixon again until he asked me to meet with him in Milwaukie, Oregon, in May 1968, just before the Oregon Republican primary. We met in Nixon's suite at the Ramada Inn just outside the city limits of Portland. We ordered steak dinners sent to the suite, but somehow the steaks never got eaten; they were only nibbled at. Nixon had two glasses of dry Vermouth; I had two Scotches, and so did Bob Ellsworth, a former Kansas Congressman who was serving as Nixon's national political director.

We again discussed fiscal policy, and I

18

got onto one of my favorite subjects—how high interest rates and the general nature of the tax structure made it possible for speculators to make a lot of money out of slums. Nixon seemed taken aback and asked, "Why would you know anything about that?"

Then the conversation became more political, and I said emphatically: "Dick, I am certain that you're going to be the next President of the United States. When that happens, we've got to keep the Republican Party progressive." He agreed, turned to Ellsworth and said, "Bob, the top of the ladder starts here."

2. Two Hats and Ten Surrogates

I wore two hats during the Nixon campaign: Western regional co-chairman and one of ten men named by Nixon to serve as "surrogate candidates." Directed by the Pierre Hotel headquarters in New York, the ten of us spoke officially and personally for the Republican candidate.[2] It was an effective campaign weapon, for it put ten surrogates and one Nixon on the road at once to multiply our campaign punch. Nixon's advice to me was, "Wally, find a place, go there, have something to say when you get there, and then go on television."

I doubt there ever was such a well-organized or more effective campaign. We would get the word from the Pierre Hotel that it would be a good idea if we could make a four-day series of appearances in Indianapolis, Dayton, Grand Rapids and Houston, for example. Leapfrogging ahead of us, a team of two Nixon advance men would line up the press, the hotel rooms and the locations for each speech. The airline connections were arranged so that we just had enough time to fly in, make the speech, do the television show — and then on to the next stop. If the commercial airline schedules were inadequate and we needed a jet out of Grand Rapids at four in the

[2] *The other surrogates: Governor John Volpe of Massachusetts; Senator Howard Baker of Tennessee; Senator Mark Hatfield of Oregon; Congressmen F. Bradford Morse (Massachusetts), Clark MacGregor (Minnesota), William E. Brock*

morning, all it required was a telephone call from our advance man. The aircraft would be running up its engines when we rolled up to the terminal.

If I have an obsession, it is always to be positive. My campaign for Dick Nixon reflected this. I campaigned *for* Dick Nixon and the philosophy of government he said he wanted to bring to America. I was a Republican Governor in a State with a heavy majority of Democrats, so my speech-making was concentrated in areas known to be oriented to the Democratic Party or to labor unions.

As the campaign neared its end, we got an alert from the Pierre Hotel that Nixon wanted the surrogate candidates and their wives in New York on election night, November 5. The night did not go smoothly. Hubert Humphrey had come on strongly in the last two weeks of the

(Tennessee), Donald Rumsfeld (Illinois) and George Bush (Texas); Bud Wilkinson, former University of Oklahoma football coach and chairman of the Lifetime Sports Foundation.

campaign, and the amount of the vote for George Wallace of Alabama was a big question mark. It soon became apparent that this was going to be a long night.

The combination of California and Illinois in the Nixon column settled the result, although the Electoral College tally was closer than we had expected: 301 for Nixon, 191 for Humphrey, 46 for Wallace. When the President-elect and Pat Nixon came down to the main ballroom of the Waldorf-Astoria on Wednesday morning, a physical feeling of joy and optimism surged through us all. I turned to my wife, Ermalee, and said: "Won't it be great to be in Alaska and be Governor with Dick Nixon as President? I'm sure that now we will be able to solve many of the problems we've been working on."

Then President-elect Nixon's telephone call on the Sunday following Thanksgiving turned everything around. As Secretary of the Interior, I would have responsibilities that were both new and national.

3. Not for Conservation's Sake

Herbert Klein, President-elect Nixon's Director of Communications, and his assistants had arranged a series of press conferences to be given by the new Cabinet designees. Mine took place on December 18 in Federal Office Building No. 7. Klein could probably get through the rest of his life quite comfortably without any memory of this press conference. In view of what happened afterward, so could I.

I explained—or at least tried to explain—that the decision to conserve a natural resource should be based on reason and good judgment. The problem is to use a resource without abusing it.

I thought I was making this point in a rational manner, but I managed to say all the wrong things. When I remarked, rather casually, "I think we have had a policy of conservation for conservation's sake," I had no idea what a sensitive nerve I was hitting. Indeed, the first press reaction was mixed. Tom Stimmel of the *Oregon Journal* National News Services thought that I had "breezed through . . . with confidence, gusto and instant answers." But Ted Lewis of the New York *Daily News* considered the same "instant answers" and decided that "foot-in-mouth disease has broken out in Nixon's Cabinet a month before it can be sworn in." I think they were both right.

The harshest condemnation of me was to be found on the editorial page of the powerful *New York Times*: "President-elect Nixon's choice for Secretary of the Interior . . . has confirmed the worst fears of those who regard the restoration and conservation of a ravished continent and purification of its polluted air and water as priority business for this generation of Americans." The *Times* also dispatched one of its top Washington correspondents to Alaska "to get the real story on Wally Hickel."

The seriousness of all this did not sink in immediately; in fact, I found some ironic humor in the criticisms leveled at me. I remembered my personal battles in Alaska, long before I served in public office, on behalf of conservation and open-space causes. It seemed that I was always getting into some sort of fight. In 1965, when the

City of Anchorage decided to build a giant five-story parking garage adjacent to the City Hall, in one of the few remaining downtown areas of open space, I thought this would be a serious mistake. Alaskans cherish their open spaces, and I did not want my city to follow the pattern that has made so many of our cities into concrete forests. I had been a member of the City Planning Commission, but my downtown friends kept saying, "Wally, this is one you're going to lose." They did not reckon on the women of the Anchorage Garden Club. The issue went to a vote; the garage was not built.

The press conference had taken place on a Wednesday. The next day, December 19, I flew to New York to confer with the Nixon people. One of the men on their list for Interior Under Secretary was Russell E. Train. He was actually referred to me by Peter Flanigan, a Nixon counselor. Among other things, Train had been an Eisenhower appointee to the United States Tax Court, president of the Conservation Foundation and, under President Johnson, a member of the National Water Commission. He had also prepared a position paper on conservation for Nixon. Later the press came to suspect that Train had been pushed forward as an orthodox conservationist who could be a kind of "flak vest" for me, but talk about Train actually began before I realized how many branding irons were being heated to work me over.

From New York I flew home by way of Seattle. Carl McMurray stayed in Washington and kept me posted by telephone, and during the pre-Christmas weekend I realized that my confirmation could develop into a serious situation. I sent my secretary, Yvonne Esbensen, to Washington on December 27 and flew back myself on January 2, 1969. Meanwhile, *The New York Times* reporter E. W. Kenworthy sent up to get "the real story" on Wally Hickel, was not getting much. I always said that Kenworthy had come to Alaska to hang Wally Hickel, but couldn't find enough rope.

Back in Washington, I began meeting with the Senators concerned, including nearly all of the Interior Committee plus Senator Muskie of Maine and Senator

Kennedy of Massachusetts. I told Ed Muskie, "Senator, when you get to know me, you and I are going to be on the same side on this whole fight over the environment and pollution." Ted Kennedy's only observation was that he would "wait and see."

A significant exchange took place on January 3, the day after my return, with Senator Henry ("Scoop") Jackson of Washington, chairman of the Interior Committee. I had known Scoop for many years, and he was familiar with my numerous activities in Alaska, including the statehood fight. He appeared to be uncomfortable and nervous. He said, "We're going to have a thorough hearing and bring everything out into the open."

"Fine," I said. "I have nothing to hide."

A thorough hearing. Did this mean I was going to be subjected to an inquisition? Possibly. At least, this was going to be more than just another hearing.

But I meant it when I said I had nothing to hide. There was only one thing for me to do: strip myself naked. If we were to have an exposure, let it be a full and honest one. I insisted to my staff that I would appear before the Interior Committee without notes. Why would I need notes? All I had to do was to tell the truth. But I still had not fully assessed the attitude of some men who had already determined that I was guilty even if proven innocent.

4. Digging in for Battle

By now the sixteen-inch guns were firing, and they all seemed to be aimed at me. Heavily critical mail, inspired by press reports and by unfriendly sources on Capitol Hill, was flooding the Senate Interior Committee and my transition office at Interior. I still cannot blame the thousands of Americans who protested my nomination as Secretary of the Interior. If I knew nothing more about Wally Hickel than what I read in the "Washington Merry-Go-Round" columns devoted to me by the late Drew Pearson and his partner, Jack Anderson, I would have been yelling and writing anticonfirmation letters myself. The Pearson column, initially at least, did more than anything else to generate opposition to me. Each time Pearson (or Anderson) launched an anti-Hickel balloon, its language would be picked up and repeated by other journalists and by members of Congress. If Pearson (or Anderson) attributed some impropriety to me, this was immediately assumed to be fact.[3] Some samples:

January 6, 1969: "The new Secretary of the Interior . . . believes that the national domain, including even game refuges, is for business development. His motto for Alaska is more oil wells and less reindeer."

January 14, 1969: "Hickel is an oil and gas man. Until he became Governor he was chairman of the Anchorage Natural Gas Company, which freezes natural gas and sells it to Japan."

January 14, 1969: "Hickel was elected Governor with the active support of oil companies. [He] waged a well-financed

[3] *During the hearings, some "Washington Merry-Go-Round" allegations were used as interrogation questions by Senators who did not bother to paraphrase or alter the precise language that had been published.*

campaign with a lot of expensive Madison Avenue gimmicks, and the oil donations are reported to have been around $400,000."

I felt like framing some of these and sending them to branch managers of oil companies in Anchorage. I was not an oil man, and everyone in Alaska knew it. Before I became Governor I had been chairman of the Anchorage Natural Gas Company, a public service group put together in 1959 to distribute natural gas to homeowners in Anchorage. All we did was buy gas and sell it to people in Anchorage who needed it, thereby sharply reducing heating costs. Our company certainly would have been flattered by the suggestion that it somehow had the ability to freeze natural gas and transport it for sale to a nation more than 3,000 miles away.

As for my "huge campaign slush fund," the average contribution to my 1966 campaign was $29. My so-called "oil money" totaled $800 raised in a drive started by the retail station operator who serviced my car.

Of course, Pearson and Anderson were not alone in opposing my confirmation. The

Los Angeles *Times* said, "He'll make Spiro Agnew look like a real sophisticate." Senator Walter F. Mondale of Minnesota said that my philosophy "did violence to essential conservation principles." In a letter to the Washington *Post*, Anita T. Sullivan of Gainesville, Virginia, complained that the President-elect "has chosen a flotilla of foxes to guard the chicken coop." In *The Christian Science Monitor*, columnist Joseph C. Harsch suggested that Mr. Nixon should get a good copy of the Teapot Dome scandals and send it to me by special messenger. Alistair Cooke, the expatriate Briton who has a wide audience in the Manchester *Guardian*, thought my appointment "recalled to some members of the Senate committee . . . the rueful confession of the late Mayor LaGuardia of New York: 'I don't often make a mistake, but when I do, it's a beaut.' "

Carl McMurray and Roger Cremo, an Anchorage lawyer who came to Washington to act as my legal counsel during the hearings, had begun compiling information on the questions we thought would be asked by the Senate Interior Committee. As it turned out, we could have saved a lot of time researching this subject; the questions asked of most new Cabinet officers in the past appeared to have been rather tame. They resembled polite conversation more than interrogation, and obviously this hearing was going to be different. We started putting together a financial statement to submit to the Interior Committee.

Then President Johnson invited me over to lunch on January 9, six days before the hearings were due to begin. I went to the White House and we sat down in the Oval Office. We never did have lunch. We talked about the confirmation problem. Mr. Johnson said: "Governor, I really don't like what's happening to you. It's wrong. I want to help you. They're organizing against you. They should give a man a chance. They're condemning you before you really have had an opportunity to perform."

Then he said, "I'd like you to go down and see Senator Long and Senator Russell and Senator Anderson." He called in an aide and said, "Call the Senators and tell them the Governor will be down to see them."

I saw Senator Russell Long of Louisiana first. He said: "Governor, I have twenty-three votes for you. The President says you're okay." He said the Interior Committee was going to take me on, but he did not care about that—he had twenty-three votes.

Then I went to see Senator Richard Russell of Georgia. This great Southern gentleman, a kind and fatherly man, said: "Yes, I know that the President wants you to see me. I understand the situation and I too don't like what is going on. It isn't quite right. They've gone too far. I will help."

Finally, I saw Senator Clinton Anderson of New Mexico. His health was very bad. He said: "I was supposed to be chairman of this Senate committee, but I gave it up to Senator Jackson. I'm sure that he will be fair, but I will watch. I don't think it is fair to do what I think is going to happen. I think everything will be okay."

The Nixon staff provided some assistance. Ken Belieu, one of Bryce Harlow's assistants, was assigned to help me, along with two members of Herb Klein's staff to deal with the press problem. But I shall always be especially grateful to President Johnson for giving me support for no reason except the fact that he did not like what was going on.

The tensions and frustrations were mounting. All alone in my room at the Sheraton-Park Hotel, I kept saying to myself: "I can't figure out what the problem is. How do I prove that all these crazy accusations are false?" I was having sleepless nights. At three o'clock on the morning of Monday, January 13, I called Bill Tobin, managing editor of the Anchorage *Daily Times*. I said, "Bill, I need help." He replied, "I'll see what I can do."

5. *'Just Tell That Bear . . .'*

To make room for television cameras and floodlights, my hearings had been moved into a room much larger than the one normally used by the Interior Committee. This was Room 1202 in the New Senate Office Building. The show started at five minutes past ten o'clock on Wednesday morning, January 15. As it turned out, it was to last through Wednesday, Thursday, Friday and Saturday, then—with Sunday off—into the middle of Monday morning, January 20, the date of Mr. Nixon's inauguration. Senator Jackson presided.[4] I walked into the glare of television floodlights. Scoop Jackson, a Democrat who had been offered the job of Secretary of Defense in the Nixon Cabinet and declined said, "Governor Hickel, the Committee on Interior and Insular Affairs welcomes you to the hearing this morning. . . . The Department of the Interior is often called our 'Department of Conservation'—and I can think of no higher duty incumbent on those who administer the Department than the conservation of our great resources." *[Hadn't President Theodore Roosevelt said this sixty years earlier?]*

[4] *Committee members present included Senators Anderson, Bible, Church, Moss, Burdick, McGovern, Nelson, Metcalf, Gravel, Allott, Jordan, Fannin, Hansen, Hatfield, Stevens and Bellmon. Also*

Senator Jackson continued: "Certainly history will show that the Senate has accorded the President, particularly a newly elected President, wide latitude in the choice of those who will serve the country as members of the Cabinet. Nevertheless, this committee and the Senate must meet our constitutional obligations, and therefore this is not a perfunctory proceeding. At a minimum, I expect it to be an enlightening and educational experience for us all."

The words were innocent, but I knew from the tone of his voice and the look in his eyes that the gloves were off. I was presumed guilty of charges that I knew were false.

I was introduced to the committee by Ted Stevens of Alaska, whom I had appointed to the Senate less than a month earlier, following Bob Bartlett's death. Stevens said in part: "Sometimes I feel that many people

present were Jennings Randolph, chairman of the Senate Public Works Committee, and Edmund Muskie, chairman of the Public Works Subcommittee on Water Pollution.

think Alaska is still in the 19th century, a vast wilderness dotted with villages and filled with ferocious animals. [*As if on cue, several senators stared at me.*] We have wilderness areas. These are areas that would dwarf the country from here to Maine and New York to Chicago and still leave 100,000 acres untouched. . . .

"Alaska is not an average state, and I think everyone here will agree that it would take more than average men to govern this new State. . . . One of the concerns of this hearing will be conservation. Alaska is a land where conservation is a watchword. There is no smog and little pollution in Alaska, and if it is humanly possible to prevent, there never will be, because Alaskans know and value pure air, pure water and virgin country. But we also realize the need for industry and the economic prosperity that industry brings.

"There are no more conservation-conscious people in the United States than those of Alaska. Governor Hickel has guarded our resources well, and he will do more for the nation, for I believe he will restore the joy of living to an environment which stimulates freedom."

Mike Gravel, the Democratic Senator from Alaska, was reserved in his introductory remarks. He said, "I would like to be particularly brief and I would like to associate myself with the comments of the distinguished senior Senator from Alaska and merely wish the distinguished Governor of Alaska well at this hearing."

Now I had to make an opening statement. I tried to stress that I would welcome any discussion with the committee about Alaska problems and about my past policies as Governor. But I wanted to distinguish between the vastly different responsibilities that rested upon a Governor and those that would rest upon me as Secretary of the Interior. I wanted the committee to know that my aim would be *prevention of* instead of *reaction to* deterioration of the environment. I felt that patchwork government would not work; I felt that we needed to anticipate the effects of economic growth and new technology so that we could protect and enhance our environment.

I told the committee that all decisions I

made would be governed by the broad national need and interest: "I believe that with realistic environmental quality programs, adequate financing and strong enforcement of the law, progress will be made in protecting our land, water and air. You may be interested to know that I am the only Governor of the fifty states who has ever seized an ocean-going vessel for dumping oil wastes in coastal waters."[5]

Senator Jackson made it clear that my initial questioning would cover three particularly sensitive areas: 1) my attitude concerning the proposal of several New England Senators to establish a free port and oil refinery at Machiasport, Maine, to allow the import of foreign oil outside the restrictions of the established quota system; 2) my opposition to the freeze on State selection of federal land in Alaska

[5] *As Governor, I directed the State to file a $200,000 damage suit against the tanker Rebecca, leased by the Maritime Overseas Corporation, following the arrest of the vessel for illegally discharging oil-laden ballast into the waters of Cook Inlet.*

imposed by my predecessor, Secretary Stewart Udall[6]; 3) what Jackson called "the widely circulated press report that you have personal ties with the oil industry."

I explained that the opposition I had voiced against the free port of Machiasport was the only valid position I could take as Governor of Alaska, and that as Secretary of the Interior I would have to look at the question in terms of broad national interests.

Jackson kept the floor and asked me to clarify my views on conservation and environmental quality. He referred to the "conservation for conservation's sake" remark that had caused a knee-jerk reaction both at the Sierra Club and in the editorial rooms of *The New York Times*. This was a

[6] *The terms "freeze" and "withdrawal" are often used interchangeably but incorrectly. Udall first froze applications for title on federal lands in Alaska on December 8, 1966, effectively stopping the State from selecting its own. This coincided with my replacing a Democratic incumbent as Governor. Then, while I was flying from*

question I welcomed, and I answered it:

I think that really at the turn of the century we had the country going from an agricultural society into an industrial society, and in many cases, for the lack of guidelines on the management of environmental control, somewhat desecrated the earth. Nobody likes that. Nobody wants that. It was wrong. But it was wrong for the reason that it was difficult to restore; but likewise, government did not assume the responsibility that I think it should, to set those guidelines that are so necessary.

Now, as an overall policy, I am for conservation, for the wise utilization and

New York to Seattle on the night of December 11, 1968, the story broke that Udall had "withdrawn" all unreserved lands in Alaska from settlement, including lands on which people had lived for two or three generations. Udall actually signed the order on January 17, 1969, three days before he left office.

conservation of our resources. I would say that when I made that statement, I was thinking of areas in my own country where there are millions upon millions, and I am not stretching this, board feet of timber that are just rotting because they have never been harvested. I do not think that is a wise use of natural resources.

Then Jackson brought up the thorny question of the "withdrawal" of public land in Alaska, an issue (in Jackson's words) "of tremendous importance and complexity." He said, "You are quoted as saying, 'What Udall can do by executive order, I can undo.' " I had made that statement about three-thirty or four o'clock in the morning after getting off an airplane at Seattle-Tacoma International Airport. The press was pushing me for a comment, and that is when I made the statement.

THE CHAIRMAN: "Did you intend, by that statement, that you would undo the executive order?"

GOVERNOR HICKEL: "I made that as

I was trying to get away from the reporter."

THE CHAIRMAN: "Sometimes that is kind of hard." [Laughter.]

Senator Alan Bible, a Democrat from Nevada, put the questioning on a lighter plane toward the end of the Wednesday morning session when he said, "I first want to say that I believe that you have attracted more attention to Alaska than anything that has happened since statehood, and for that at least I compliment you." There was more laughter in the room, and a little less tension. As in the case of Alaska, Nevada's lands are largely federally owned, and Senator Bible's questioning was generally sympathetic. Then Senator Muskie, whose presence was somewhat unusual since he was not a member of the Interior Committee, challenged my opposition to the free port and the oil refinery for New England. Under the Johnson Administration, responsibility for oil import policy had been shifted from the White House to Interior, and if it stayed in

Interior the monkey would be on my back. Muskie said: "You may be in the position of having to lean over backward to favor New England against the oil industry in order to avoid any accusation of bias. Now, what is your reaction to that?"

"Senator," I said, "would you allow me to be just a little humorous at this moment and say I wonder if I couldn't toss this back to the White House like they tossed it to Interior. I know I can't, and I don't want to be facetious."

There was still more laughter, and Muskie then questioned me on water pollution — or "degradation." When I mentioned an untrue report that I had allowed the dumping of ammonia in Alaska waters, Senator Gordon Allott of Colorado, seeing a chance to demolish one of the charges thown up against me by Drew Pearson, asked Muskie to yield. Allott read into the record the specific charge that I had permitted the Collier Carbon and Chemical Company to dump three and one-half tons of ammonia into Cook Inlet every day, thus constituting an intolerable treat to marine life. Pearson's information was wrong, and

Allott knew it—the plant was not even completed. Allott asked, "Governor, what would you say as to the veracity of this statement?"

I replied, "It is a sin to tell a lie."

It had been a civilized morning, and the questions I had been asked were expectable and natural. I had not been challenged—yet—on my personal integrity. Because of the television lights and the tension, I was wringing wet from perspiration, so I went back to my hotel and changed clothes and ate a sandwich all in the same motion.

After lunch, Senator Frank Church of Idaho asked if I had been a welterweight boxer, and upon being told that this was true, he remarked, "Governor, I want you to know as we begin the second round I don't think anybody has laid a glove on you yet." Church, Clifford Hansen of Wyoming and Frank Moss of Utah questioned me on policy matters such as wilderness legislation, keeping the national parks open for recreation, salmon fishing and the proper size of a protected moose range.

Moss's questioning had a touch of hostility in it.

Then I had a celebrated exchange with Senator George McGovern of South Dakota. He quoted from a column written earlier in the Anchorage *Daily News* by Joe Rothstein, who was now Senator Gravel's executive assistant. The column charged: "In league with the canned salmon industry and other powerful American business interests, the Governor brought the full power of the State of Alaska to bear on a pitifully few Native fishermen, whose only offense was seeking out new and more profitable markets for their fish." Referring to an incident that had occurred on the Kuskokwim River near Bethel, Alaska, Rothstein continued: "Governor Hickel's involvement in what was essentially a private transaction between Alaska Native fishermen and a Japanese trading company can best be described as outrageous."

The contract was privately written and I had had nothing to do with it. When I began getting reports and letters indicating that the vast majority of Native and non-Native fishermen in the area was opposed to this foreign exploitation, I learned that the contract included a curious clause. The whole contract was null and void if the Governor did not give his consent. I could see a situation developing in which we would just catch the fish, take them out of a net and put them into a ship. Without local processing, that would be the last we saw of a valuable resource. Eventually there would be no fish but a lot of unemployed Native fishermen. So I refused my consent.

Then Senator Church threw me another haymaker. He produced a letter from two Anchorage men charging that the State of Alaska, encouraged by me as Governor, had improperly issued a commercial fishing permit in the Tikchik Lakes area of western Alaska.

It was brought out that an Alaska Air National Guard plane used to supply equipment to the fishery operators had broken through the ice when it landed on Nuyakuk Lake in February 1967. Now we were getting into the area of straight smear; the implication was that I had ordered or condoned the misuse of a government aircraft.

I remembered the incident, but I was certain I had not ordered that aircraft to the Tikchik Lakes area. I explained that this general practice was neither rare nor necessarily wrong in the remote areas of Alaska where there is no conventional transportation. A private firm will sometimes hire a National Guard aircraft to do a job, and pay for it at normal commercial rates. But what was the truth of this particular situation?

The hearing adjourned for the day. I was glad, for we had a long night's work ahead.

Dripping with perspiration again, I went back to the Sheraton-Park and called a masseur to give me a rubdown while I started telephoning. The urgent priority was to take advantage of the five-hour time difference—it was shortly past noon in Anchorage—and start gathering information.

I called Alaska's Adjutant General, Major General C. F. Necrason, and asked him why the airplane had been flown to the Tikchik Lakes area. That was the easy part. General Necrason went back to his records and sent a telegram reminding me that I had not approved the mission because I had no authority to do so. The company in question, Eagle River Cold Storage, then had requested the assistance of Alaska Senator Ernest Gruening's office in getting Pentagon approval. The mission was approved on a "reimbursable" basis, meaning that the company had to pay.

The Kuskokwim River fishing case was more difficult, because a genuine local argument was involved and the whole file had to be assembled. Roger Cremo was still involved with putting together my financial statement, so Carl McMurray and an Anchorage friend, Carl Brady, started telephoning people in Alaska to get all the correspondence and legal data. This process of assembly was going to take some time, and we obviously were not going to have all the answers the following morning.

I do not think any of us got more than two hours of sleep that night, but I still felt on top of the situation. In fact, I never quite lost that feeling. Senator Dirksen must have sensed that when it was suggested he go down to the hearings because "the Governor needs help." Dirksen drawled:

"The Governor doesn't need help. I would like to tell a story about the farmer out in the back country who was out in the field one day when a neighbor came to him and said, 'John, you'd better get home immediately because there's a bear in the cabin with your wife.' And John replied, 'Well, that bear is just going to have to look out for himself.' "

6. Moral Support from Home

Washington started to fill up with Alaskans. Bill Tobin must have passed the word pretty widely that "Wally needs help." They showed up in a body for the Thursday morning hearings, and shortly before the luncheon break, Ted Stevens found an opportunity to introduce them and read their names into the record.

I was glad to see them, and I shall always be grateful for their moral support, particularly when it became obvious during that second morning session that this was turning into a test of physical endurance. This time the television lights were put directly in front of me, and I could barely see. The lights were so strong that some of the newsmen behind me were wearing sunglasses.[7] I read into the record the telegram I had received from General Necrason. Senator Jackson was a little curious about whether the company had ever paid for the plane, but Senator Allott pointed out that the problem of reimbursement had not been mine as Governor. The order for the mission had been approved at the federal level at the request of a member of the Senate Interior Committee. Senator Moss took me on again concerning the complicated question of Native land claims, and a lot was put into the record without adding much to the public knowledge.

Then Senator McGovern went back to the Kuskokwim River fishing dispute. A $150,000 suit had been filed against me by

[7] *Afterward I was glad I had had the television exposure. The wide coverage given by the National Educational Television network to the hearings was especially helpful in showing millions of Americans the facts of the case.*

the fishing cooperative that had made the original contract with the Japanese, and the story appeared in the Thursday morning Washington *Post*. The suit alleged that I had taken my action in this case with reckless disregard for fishing treaty rights. The Senator seemed to feel that in effect I had been behaving as my own State Department in a sensitive area of foreign policy. Actually, my own Attorney General, G. Kent Edwards, had thought at the time that the Japanese might be violating the International North Pacific Fisheries Treaty. But the Japanese delegation that visited me in my office in Juneau had only one question: Had I given my consent? I had not given my consent, and that voided the contract. But Senator McGovern was not about to let the question go; we still had to assemble the whole Kuskokwim River file for the records, and that was to take the rest of the week.

Ted Stevens joined Gordon Allott in leading the counterattack. Ted had a battery of Alaskans in the room to cheer him on. He read into the record telegrams I had received, in the middle of 1968, from fishermen who objected to a Japanese freezer ship coming in to purchase and process salmon. He also read into the record a long letter from Dr. Clayton Polley of Juneau, a dentist who had lived in Alaska fifty-two years and was a respected sportsman and conservationist. He enumerated thirty-four things that I had done as Governor of Alaska that ought to recommend me to people who considered themselves conservationists. These included: I had vetoed a bill that would have legalized the hunting of muskox; I had launched a study effort aimed at preserving Indian totem poles at their historical locations throughout southeast Alaska; I had ordered the *arrest of a ship* for polluting Alaska waters; I had backed the transfer of 70,000 silver salmon eggs to stock Lake Michigan with that species of fighting game fish; I had induced General Charles A. Lindbergh to address a special joint session of the Alaska Legislature[8] on the subject of

[8] *This was General Lindbergh's first public speech in ten years.*

conservation; I had supported and signed a bill to set aside the McNeil River in perpetuity as a sanctuary for brown bears; and I had eliminated the bounty on wolverines and hair seals.

Under a normal set of circumstances, the hearings might well have ended right there. But they did not. I went to the Sheraton-Park, changed clothes again, snapped at a sandwich and came back to Capitol Hill for the Thursday afternoon round. Now it was the turn of Senator Gaylord Nelson, Democrat of Wisconsin, to take me on.[9]

Questions do become repetitive in Senate hearings, and Senator Nelson reraised the question of what I had meant by "conservation for conservation's sake." I answered it again: allowing the timber to rot was not conservation. I was not criticizing Secretary Udall but the general tone of Interior policy going back the early 1940's.

[9] *Senator Nelson voted against my confirmation but later told me he was sorry he had done so. We became friends and, in the environmental area, allies.*

Nelson asked about my view of the scientific value of a wilderness, and I replied: "I think it is great . . . I think the value of a wilderness area or open spaces is for people to walk and see a broad scope of just what it is all about."

Then he asked me a 1,345-word question that took up a little more than two pages of the written record. It was more of a stirring speech than a question. He mentioned the lack of immediate attention paid to Rachel Carson, author of *Silent Spring*. He quoted from a letter written by the inventor William P. Lear, who believed that a steam-powered automobile was now feasible, using fuel costing a fraction of what gasoline costs at the pump. He spoke of "the crunch [that] will come when the federal government is arraigned against the biggest enterprise in America, General Motors, and the rest of the auto industry who have great stakes in the internal combustion engines, against the oil industry who have great stakes in selling gas, not ten-cent kerosene. . . ."

For twenty minutes I had been wondering what the question was, but now the Senator put it. He asked me if, as Secretary of the Interior, I would have the guts to say to the industry: "You are going to convert or you are going to meet the standard of exhaust emission, or you aren't going onto America's highways. Are you prepared to make that kind of fight?"

I replied, "Yes, Senator, but it probably would take me fifteen rounds if I was in good shape."

I have often wondered how things would have worked out if I had had the chance to go the full fifteen rounds. As it happened, I went about eight rounds before my manager — the President of the United States — hit me over the head with my own stool and threw in the towel.

The Thursday hearings were adjourned at four o'clock in the afternoon. I think this was the day that Roberta Hornig, a reporter for the Washington *Evening Star,* buttonholed Carl McMurray in the hallway and asked him about a West Coast report that my oldest son, Ted, was an executive for the Union Oil Company. McMurray said: "He's a service attendant at a Union Oil station, if that's what you mean. He's making money to go to school."

I shook hands with my fellow Alaskans who had come down to stand by me, then headed for the Sheraton-Park to change. I was completely exhausted, but we had some more telephoning to do to get the full file on the Kuskokwim River fishery fight on the committee record.

It was that night that I told my wife, Ermalee: "This just isn't fair. It just isn't fair." Twenty-four hours elapsed before she understood what I meant.

7. Tanning My Hide

It was the morning of the third day — Friday, January 17, 1969 — that almost wrung me out. There was a goading quality to the questions thrown at me. In this case my principal attacker was Senator Lee Metcalf, a Montana Democrat. I had been warned by one of my aides that he would be a hostile questioner, and he was. Some of the exchanges went like this:

57

SENATOR METCALF: "Do you have any of those stock options in Alaska Interstate?"

GOVERNOR HICKEL: "I have no stock options in Alaska Interstate."

THE CHAIRMAN (Senator Jackson): "The Senator may have been out of the room, but I did, I believe the first day, ask the Governor about this matter."

SENATOR METCALF: "I wasn't out of the room."

THE CHAIRMAN: "Oh. You were present."

SENATOR METCALF: "I was present. I heard some of his answers. I wasn't quite satisfied."

SENATOR METCALF: "Did you put Alaska Interstate into trust?"

GOVERNOR HICKEL: "It is in trust too, all my things are in trust. [I put all my holdings in trust when I became Governor in 1966.] Whatever they want I will do, and I don't know what more I *can* do."

SENATOR METCALF: "I have been concerned about your interests in the consumer and what happened to the consumer of natural gas in the franchise that you still have in Anchorage. . . . That is, the sale of natural gas through the Anchorage Natural Gas Corporation to the franchise that you enjoy and exercise and still have a million-dollar interest in."

GOVERNOR HICKEL: "Senator, those figures could be right. I am not that conversant with them. . . . We did cut the heating rate. . . . I do know in those early years there were substantial losses. Possibly it is tied into equity because there isn't a lot of capital in Alaska. . . . And so the rates were cut, and I was happy. So I think it is a general attitude, and I see no conflict. What would the Senator want me to do? I will do whatever you wish."

SENATOR METCALF: "I am glad to hear you say that you will divest yourself of all this. . . . I want to point out a record where apparently you had two objectives. One, as Governor of the State, you were responsible for the appointment of a regulatory commission such as you have in Alaska. Second, as the owner of a franchise and a man who has stock in trust in this Alaska Interstate and Anchorage Corporation, you have used or you have gone to the side of high, extraordinarily high, and exorbitant profits rather than protect the interests of the consumer."

GOVERNOR HICKEL: "I don't buy that!"

THE CHAIRMAN: "Suppose the Governor responds to the last question, and then we will recess until two o'clock."

SENATOR METCALF: "I am delighted to recess now and maybe the Governor can come back after lunch and respond."

We used some rather rough language in the territorial days of Alaska, but until that Friday morning nobody had come that close to insinuating that I had used the office of the Governor of Alaska for stealing purposes. I had deliberately stripped myself naked; now what did they want? My hide, flayed, tanned and nailed on the door of Room 1202? It was indeed time for lunch and another change of clothing, although I had to keep reminding myself in the taxicab: *Keep it cool. . . . Don't lose your cool. . . . Don't lose your cool. . . .*

It must have been about this time that some of my Alaska supporters began telling me, "You ought to tell the whole bunch of them to go to hell." They did not mean that, of course; they were just trying to help me. If I had actually started packing my bags, they would have been as ashamed of me as I would have been ashamed of myself.

Senator Metcalf may have had second thoughts over lunch, since the first thing he did when the hearing resumed was to put into the record a memorandum from Ted Stevens that officially shot down the Drew

61

Pearson charge that I had permitted Collier Chemical to discharge intolerable amounts of effluent into Cook Inlet. Then he went back to my earlier connection with Anchorage Natural Gas, back to the whole subject of public power and my attitude about it. As a Montana Senator, Metcalf had a legitimate concern for public power, but he was in a blind alley when he voiced suspicions about the men I had appointed to the Alaska Public Service Commission. They not only were not "political cronies" —I could not even remember their names offhand. He failed to comprehend the problems of a young State. He did say, "You are going to be responsible for at least saving for us in the Northwest a continued low-cost public power." And I replied, "I believe in it."

We also had the documents on the Kuskokwim River dispute, and we put them into the record. They included the text of a decision by United States District Judge Raymond E. Plummer, which held that I had acted reasonably and within the limits of the law. Senator McGovern, who had made the most of this matter, did not comment, but Senator Church was beginning to come around. "You have responded to the questions of the committee with civility and good temper. I commend you for that. . . . I want to wish you well." Senator Jackson observed that I had "held up very well" and excused me from the glare of the television lights, although he asked me to stay while other testimony concerning my qualifications was put into the record.

Representative Dean McCarthy of New York seemed to think I would have made a good Secretary of Commerce. Former Senator Gruening, a fellow Alaskan and a Democrat, backed me nobly. David Brower, executive director of the Sierra Club, opposed me: "His own past statements have sent a wave of apprehension across the country." Brower did not stand up too well under questioning by Ted Stevens ("I don't know that. I have never been to Alaska myself"). A delegation from the Alaska Federation of Natives endorsed me. Lehman Brightman, a Sioux and Creek Indian from South Dakota, opposed the appointment of "Mr.

Pickle Hickel" who would give the country away and build dams on it and drain all the oil out of it.

This went on until ten minutes past five. Whoever drained oil out of the country, I was fully aware that a lot of oil had been drained out of me. Yet, when I walked into the Sheraton-Park that Friday night, I told Ermalee again, "This just isn't fair." She said: "Wally, why do you keep saying that? I think you're handling yourself pretty well."

I managed a grin. "Ermalee, you don't get the point. It isn't a fair fight because there aren't enough of *them.*"

8. *A Ten-Dollar Lease*

Saturday morning, the fourth day of the hearings, began with an executive session of the Interior Committee. I was not present, although I was available to be called for questions concerning my financial statement. It was at this executive session, without my presence, that I ran into another spot of trouble I had not anticipated. This concerned a ten-dollar oil lease I had taken out in 1953 and had long since allowed to expire because I was in the construction business and not in the oil business. In the territorial days we called these "pick 'em out of the hat" leases. It was a kind of federal grab bag. All you needed was ten dollars and proof that you were an American citizen at least twenty-one years old to play a game of lottery — but without guarantee that you would ever be able to use the land, since Alaska, as a State, would make its own land selections later. Chairman Jackson was worried about this and wondered if the committee should put everything over until Tuesday, the day after Nixon's inauguration. Senator Mark Hatfield of Oregon objected: "It appears to me we have oral confirmation answering our questions that have been raised most recently. To wait until Tuesday, until we can get written confirmation, seems to be a little out of keeping with what we have been willing to accept through three days of many things, by [Hickel's] oral testimony."

Senator Metcalf, who less than twenty-four hours earlier had verged on calling me a thief, concurred: "Here is a man with many charges and . . . if a hearing means anything at all, it means he comes before us and we take his word." It was a curious turnaround by Metcalf.[10] Senator Anderson was getting impatient: "I think we ought to go ahead and vote as soon as possible. I have seen enough of this situation. People make certain charges and do not sustain them."

The hearings went back into public session. Chairman Jackson brought up the matter of the lease, which had expired in 1963. The problem that bothered Senator Jackson, and some of the others on the committee, simply did not exist. Neither did the problem of my relations with the New York Life Insurance Company, although Senator McGovern thought it did. He suspected that I had made a deal with New York Life to reduce health insurance benefits paid Alaska State employees in return for a loan to finance the expansion of a shopping center in Anchorage. We were

[10]*Because of the disputatious nature of the public hearings, the full record of the committee's executive sessions was made public, which is not the usual practice.*

able to document that my loan from New York Life was negotiated well before I was elected Governor. There was no deal. We later terminated the State's contract with New York Life, put it out for bid and got a better contract with another company.

Without a lunch break, the committee went into executive session—this time with me present. Senator Anderson was getting still more impatient: "Why do we not just approve him?" Chairman Jackson replied: "We cannot just approve him. We have to go over his financial statement this afternoon."

We went over the statement. It indicated that I had assets amounting to about $5 million. The list of companies of which I had to divest myself included "Clark's Painting and Decorating." When we got to that I thought, "My God! Here I am, a person who started out with my hands, and I am being asked to sell a little company that I started with a personal friend, literally a one-armed paperhanger who had lost an arm in an automobile accident." There wasn't any conflict; this was clearly apparent. I continually said I would do whatever they wanted me to do. Yet the interrogation went on, and on, and on.

The executive session wound up at three-thirty in the afternoon, and I remember Senator Church saying something like "Gentlemen, maybe this time we've gone too far." One of my Anchorage friends certainly thought so. This was Andy Milner, a contractor who weighs over 200 pounds and could probably fold railroad ties for his morning workout. That Saturday afternoon, while I was doing a television interview, Andy spotted Senators Mike Gravel and Scoop Jackson heading for an elevator and hurried after them. As the elevator door started to close, Andy stopped it with one hand, then reached in and grabbed Gravel with his other hand. I did not witness the exchange, but a lot of other people did. Andy said: "Mike, they've been hammering at Hickel about the federal filing thing. Why haven't you said anything? You know everyone in Alaska did it."

Gravel replied, "I never did."

"Then you were either too stupid to do it

or you didn't have the ten dollars," Milner shot back.

By now Jackson was peering out of the elevator, possibly looking for a policeman, and Milner let go. The elevator door closed, and it was all over.

In fact, everything was nearly all over. On Monday morning, Inauguration Day, when the committee reconvened in executive session, Carl McMurray, Roger Cremo and I sat outside the door, expecting to be called for questioning. But by now even most members of the committee were getting disgusted with the repetition of empty charges. So we were never called in that morning at all. The vote was 14 to 3 to report my nomination to the Senate favorably. The negative votes were cast by Senators Nelson, McGovern and Moss.

The great comic W. C. Fields once made a motion picture called *You Can't Cheat an Honest Man,* and as Senators came out to offer their congratulations, I thought to myself, "How do you *prove* you're an honest man?" Scoop Jackson answered that question when he told the press, "All the charges against Wally Hickel just blew up."

The Senate confirmed me three days later by a vote of 73 to 14. That night, January 23, my suite at the Sheraton-Park was full of happy Alaskans. I was both exuberant and exhausted, so I said, "I'm going to take you folks to dinner." They all went away to change, but I started to lose interest in dinner. When they came back an hour or so later, I was walking around the suite literally naked, except for a bath towel. We ended up ordering from Chicken Delight. I never did get dressed. I ended the ordeal the way I had entered into it — a naked man.

I left a living and found a life.

CHAPTER **2**

Search for a Country

I never was much of a joiner, and I am not even sure how I got into the Republican Party. Nor do I really know how I came to be a member of President Nixon's Cabinet for twenty-two months. I am a free-thinking and impatient man, and I do not always go by the book. I understand well enough the right of the President to fire me; he has the inherent privilege to fire anyone at the Cabinet level. What I do not know is why he ever hired me. Perhaps no one looked closely enough at me or my kind of Republicanism.

Back in Kansas, my father was a Republican of sorts, but he tended to look at the man rather than the party. I have always done more or less the same. As a boy

71

of nine, I passed out "Hoover pencils" in 1928. I was sure that Hoover would win, but I was really for Alfred E. Smith. This had nothing to do with Smith's brown derby, or with the fact that I had been born into a Roman Catholic family. It never occurred to me to connect deep religious convictions with politics. I simply liked Al Smith. I am sure my father voted for Hoover in 1928, and I suspect he did the same in 1932, when Franklin Roosevelt was elected President. My father viewed the New Deal with mixed feelings; he disliked the Agricultural Adjustment Act, which the Supreme Court ruled unconstitutional in 1935, but he favored rural electrification. No wonder: living outside Claflin, Kansas, we hardly knew what electricity was.

It is a mild wonder that I ever became a Republican at all when I started to be politically active. Had I been born fifty years earlier, I almost certainly would have been an outspoken Populist. When I was born on August 18, 1919, in Claflin, Kansas, historians had not gotten around to assessing the very considerable influence of Populism on American politics, and as a small boy I would not have known what a Populist was. But the people's grievances which the Populists represented over a period of twenty years, when America was emerging from its 19th-century rural condition into a new century of technology, were very real to a Kansas boy in the early 1920's. Wartime prosperity was only a memory then, and farmers by and large never did share properly in the synthetic prosperity of the Coolidge years.

I would not have known then where to find a book about these grievances, but as a child I did understand that they all involved one central problem: the scarcity of "cash money." It was a mysterious thing. Money was somehow bound up with the availability of a precious metal called gold. Obviously there was a lot of money in existence, but it always seemed to be held by a few people. When I asked my mother about this, she would say, "We're not poor, we just don't have money." I accepted that. Somebody had it, but very little of it was lent at low interest rates, and practically none to tenant farmers. The Homestead Act of 1862, which became law under Abraham Lincoln, was intended to create a whole new class of land owners, but it didn't work out that way. There never was that much public land to begin with, and by the time my father was born in 1893, there was little, if any, in Kansas. So my father, like many others of his generation, became a tenant farmer.

1. *It Rained Mudballs*

My first boyhood memory, and it is so clear and distinct, is of a team of mules. The names of the mules were Pete and John. They were backed up to the edge of the house, the "great house" in which I was to live for the next seventeen years, to haul some furniture that belonged to the Frank Grizells, the owners of the farm, with whom we had been living. This must have been 1922, when I was about three years old. The Grizells moved into the town of Claflin, a German-American community two and one-quarter miles away, which had a population of about 800. It was almost exactly in the middle of Kansas, and it was on the main line of the Missouri Pacific Railroad, which ran from Kansas City,

Missouri, to Pueblo, Colorado. The nearest town of any size, Great Bend (population about 10,000), was twenty-five miles to the southwest on the Santa Fe. We heated the Grizell house and cooked our meals with wood and coal; for light, we had two-mantled Coleman lamps, which burned ordinary low-octane white gasoline, plus those old-fashioned kerosene lamps. The house was not wired for electricity until 1938. I do not recall when we first got a telephone, but naturally it was a hand-crank wall instrument on a party line, which was great for those days.

The local mercantile store would give the general call, which was seven long rings. Housewives throughout the area would pick up the phone to hear that Buehler's had peaches on sale. Similarly, everyone knew that the code for the Hickels was one long and two short. There were very few secrets in those days; I was raised on a bugged telephone.

My parents were both first-generation Americans. My mother's parents, whose surname was Zecha, emigrated from southern Germany about 1890, and my mother was born in Odin, Kansas, in 1894. Nearly everyone in the area was of German ancestry, and until the middle 1930's, the grade school in Odin conducted classes in German for half of each day. My grandparents on the Hickel side had left southern Germany a decade or so before the Zecha family did, and my father, Robert Anthony Hickel, was born near Claflin.

My grandparents never did learn to speak English, and my oldest sister, Gertrude, was handicapped by the mix of German and English when she first went to school. Perhaps that is why my parents stopped speaking German in our home. I understood the language fairly well as a small boy, but I have a difficult time with it now.

There were ten children in our family. I was the oldest boy. My sisters Gertrude and Catherine were four and two years old, respectively, when I was born. Seven other children were born in the "great house."

The Grizell family was kind to us in the Depression 1930's, when kindness meant a great deal. But to me it was unthinkable that the Grizell place, the castle in which we ten children were reared, was not truly "our" home. How could you buy something that was already owned? Even if Dad had owned his own land, how could four sons hope to acquire a farm apiece?

I often asked my father why he did not buy a farm. He always answered by explaining the impossibility of borrowing money. Even as a boy I thought that there was something totally wrong. Dad was a good farmer, a successful one. I would say to Dad that there must be some way to get our own land, but apparently there wasn't any way. It finally dawned on me that we would never own the home we were living in. Somehow it could never be for sale — to us. This was a crushing realization.

The three quarter-sections of land Dad farmed included 400 acres of wheat and 80 acres of pasture for a dozen or so milk cows and twenty to thirty horses. It was a dawn-to-dusk existence. It may sound now like a hard life, but I did not think of it in those terms when I was a small boy, and neither did thousands of other American boys who grew up in about the same way: up at dawn, start doing chores as soon as you were old enough, gather the eggs without breaking too many, pull your weight during the day, go to bed when the chickens went to bed.

I was milking cows when I was five years old. I was in the field behind four head of horses and a gang plow when I was eight. I had a little red wagon that I tied to the tug of one of the horses before I took the team into the field. I remember distinctly the afternoon one of those fearsome Kansas thunderstorms came up. I had always been afraid of lightning, and I knew that iron attracted it. The lightning was violent that day, and the rain was coming down in torrents. I unhitched the horses by crawling down the tongue of the plow, then across the backs of the horses to put up the tugs. I hooked on my little red wagon and headed for home, a mile away, at a full gallop. The little wagon was zigzagging crazily behind the horses, and I was scared to death. In my terror I was urging the horses on, and the harnesses were sliding off the sides of their bodies as I approached the house.

As I was nearing home the rain let up; finally it stopped altogether. By the time I reached my mother standing in the yard, the sun was shining brightly and she asked me what was the matter. I told her my story as an eight-year-old would, a tale of the rain and the lightning, and the more I talked the brighter the sun shone. I said, "Mom, Mom, it was really lightning." She said, "Son, don't panic. Have no fear." I turned the horses around and went back to my plowing. Years later I could well analyze the strength of her doing what she did. I have had many occasions to remember those words: *Son, don't panic. Have no fear.*

When we finally got a tractor, in 1928, I drove it at the age of nine. A year later, I started driving my brothers and sisters to school in a Model T Ford. This was only during the wheat-planting season when my father did not have time to drive the children himself. My parents, just by giving me the work to do, instilled in me an attitude of confidence. The greatest thing I got out of my childhood was not formal schooling but religious training and a sense of confidence in whatever I had to do. Mother used to say, "Walter knows no fear."

My father knew no fear either. For several years he managed the Saturday night dances at the Knights of Columbus hall, which meant that among other things he was a kind of chief bouncer. When I was nine or ten years old, I was present when he was umpiring a baseball game—one of those Sunday afternoon ball games that were such great events in all the small towns in our area. After one close decision, a large man called Dad a son-of-a-bitch. My father calmly walked over and said: "Sir, you can call me any names you like, but you can't call my mother a name. I want you to apologize." The man refused. My father whipped him thoroughly, walked back and finished umpiring the game. On the way home he asked Elmer and me not to say anything about the incident to our mother. He apparently did not realize that he had a black eye that Mom was bound to notice immediately—and did.

Early years do form a person, and these were good years. We grew more than enough food to eat, and we never lacked for essentials like clothing. We had a lot of parties. The women divided up the cooking in their own way, and there was always plenty of homemade sausage in the German tradition. It was usually Dad who made the home brew, and he took pride in it.

My parents were the greatest couple on earth. It was the combination of the two. They were strict, but strictness and guidance are sometimes confused as strength and stubbornness are sometimes confused. They were strict in teaching the right things, but they convinced us of the wisdom of not doing them in the wrong way. My parents' relationship and their enthusiastic love of life meant a great deal to all of us Hickel children and had an enormous influence on all of our lives. They both had a great sense of humor. My God, how my mother laughed! She just shook all over.

We had a saddle pony named Billy, but one pony did not seem enough for four boys. One day my brother Elmer and I, on our own, decided to saddle up a working horse named Prince. We were so small that we had to use a block and tackle to get the saddle on his back. If I had had enough sense just to get on Prince bareback, everything would probably have been all right. But Prince objected violently to the saddle. To make matters worse, I had found a rusty old spur and fastened it to the heel of my shoe. I had seen all the cowboy shows and this seemed the right thing to do. When I got into the saddle and dug in that spur, Prince bucked and I went flying through the air. I was lucky not to break my neck.

Another day Elmer and I used the saddle pony to rope a steer. We got the rope around the steer all right, but we couldn't get it loose. I hung onto the steer while Elmer ran back to the house to get a butcher knife and cut the rope. We didn't say anything until Dad came in a day or so later wondering why a steer was running around in the pasture with a piece of rope around its neck. Elmer and I had to tell him the story. Dad was not amused.

It seems to me now that I had a great deal of personal freedom on that tenant farm in

Kansas. My mother especially, and sometimes my father also, allowed me to do things that they did not allow the other children to do. I remember hearing my mother say something to the others that I probably should not have overheard. They were asking why Walter could do such-and-such and they could not. She said, "Well, Walter's different." And I suppose I was different. Certainly they thought so in Washington forty years later.

I remember going down to a little creek to sit on the bank and dream. I would walk the pastures and always look west or northwest—never east or south. I was fascinated by the glories of spring, for it literally did have a wild, fresh beauty. I would run out to pick the May flowers and listen to the singing of the meadowlarks. One time I remember talking to a meadowlark for what seemed hours but in reality was probably a few minutes. I had a feeling of genuine communication: I would talk, and the meadowlark would talk back to me.

I loved every bit of the natural state. There were still opossums and badgers to trap, along with a few muskrats. When the dew was on the fields, there was a sort of mist on the ground. Then I would go to plow in the fields, and as I watched the soil turn over it all seemed so great — *so human.* The gulls would follow me and squawk, and every once in a while their droppings would fall on my head and I would swear at them in a boy's cussword language.

I loved to climb — to see. There weren't any hills in central Kansas, so I climbed the highest fence I could find, and after that to the top of the barn, to look again. When I was about four years old, I climbed the farm's windmill, which was about forty feet high, and found myself on a little platform. How I managed to crawl around on that platform I cannot remember; had I ever thought to look down, I probably would have fallen and killed myself. My mother saw me up there and was panic-stricken. Dad came running from the barn, and I heard him tell Mom, "Don't frighten him." He called to me: Keep looking up! Keep looking up!" As my father climbed up the windmill, I quietly slipped over the edge of the platform to meet him, always looking up, and Dad got me down. But the only reason I had climbed that windmill was to look as far west as I could see. The land was so flat that they used to say, "If I had strong enough eyes I could see the back of my head."

Then came the 1930's, the Depression and the dust bowl years. You had to live in that dust bowl to understand it. You were dimly aware that the land around you was dying. "Darkness at noon" was a literal happening. You could not see the sun. You would see this stuff coming out of the North like an ugly thunderstorm. One minute there would not be a cloud in the sky, then suddenly you could not see anything. You couldn't drive because the dust drifted about in great clouds, like windblown snow. I have seen rain come down in the form of mudballs—millions and millions of little mudballs. Remember the old radio joke about the fellow who looked up twenty feet and saw a jackrabbit digging a hole?

I couldn't have been more than twelve when I decided to find my life outside

Kansas, even though I did not cross a state line until my high school class went to Kansas City, Missouri, for its Senior Day trip. By then I had learned simple facts about oceans and mountains and all the things that were to be explored outside Kansas. I was curious. I used to think about all the great countries of the world where I might want to go, because there was no room or opportunity in Kansas for me to do the things I wanted to do. Of course, I knew by then that we would never own our own farm, but I had the vision that some day I was going to own a string of houses that stretched as far as I could see across the Kansas flatland.

I wondered why the farms were blowing away. I knew that something had upset something if Mom had to hang wet bed-sheets over the windows to keep out the dust.

I used to wonder, also, about this frantic effort to plow up the Western prairie. There seemed to me such natural beauty in the pastures where I ran, and in the buffalo holes that caught the water when it rained. When someone plowed up one of these pastures it bothered me a little bit. I could not put my finger on the problem, because we were farmers and this seemed the right thing to do. To grow more wheat, of course, you had to plow up more land.

That is what we did, and that is what upset nature's balance. There weren't any dust storms when the Indians lived by themselves in Kansas, Oklahoma, Nebraska and the Dakotas. The upset dated back to World War I, when we started plowing up the prairies to sow grain for the Allied armies of western Europe. The topsoil had been held together for thousands of years by buffalo grass and a few trees. The plow jarred it loose from its subsoil underpinnings. Having made a lot of money by selling grain during World War I, the farmers kept right on in the same way, on a much bigger scale, during the 1920's. This is how we not only depressed the agricultural economy but came close to destroying the land of what came to be known as the dust bowl.

It was only after I became an adult and was able to look back at the things that bothered me as I sat on a Kansas creek bank, that I came to realize we had done all these things for a short-term monetary reason. I had actually been thinking about the whole environment without knowing what the word meant. What we did to the prairies was not "right," although the reasons we did it are at least understandable. We must never do anything like that again.

All I really knew then, sitting on that creek bank, was that I had to find myself a country.

2. No Tenants in the Tetons

I was a poor scholar, but I was rich in curiosity and enthusiasm. I graduated from Claflin High School with something below a C average. I remember an algebra teacher named Merle Hoover who used to become disgusted with my lack of academic achievement. He told me once: "Walter, you can do anything you set your mind to do—you've shown me that. I just can't get you interested in schooling." He was right. I was impatient, and I was interested in knowledge, not grades.

Whatever I did outside the classroom, I threw everything I had into it. In football I played quarterback and halfback, but at 135 pounds I was too light to be very good, even in those days when hardly anyone on a high school team weighed as much as 200 pounds. I did better in track. During my senior year we put together a mile relay team that set a state record. We did it at the Salina relays. I was leadoff man and handed the baton to my cousin, Martin Miller, who was nearly blind without his glasses. Clasping the baton, Martin turned and ran off the track into the crowd. Willing hands pushed him back. By that time he was in last place. In my excitement I started shouting at him and running along beside him on the infield. He passed everyone on the way. In fact, I ran Martin's full quarter mile beside him, stride for stride. The judge thought I was illegally pacing him until he learned that it was I who had run the first leg of the race.

Going to college had not entered my mind. I was too anxious to move on — "to find a country." In 1937 I took off with two young friends named Clarence Mullenix and Bob Brust—we were all seventeen at the time—to see the great West and part of Canada. We started out in a 1936 Chevrolet from which we had removed the back seat to make room for smoked bacon, home-canned food, oil for the car, bedrolls and tents. We also had a cigar box with $87 in it to be spent on absolute necessities such as gasoline for the car and food we could not take with us.

As long as I live I shall never forget my first sight of the Rockies as we approached them from the east. These were the first mountains I had ever seen. We went up through Rocky Mountain National Park, the Tetons, into Yellowstone then into Glacier National Park, into Canada and back home by way of Idaho and Utah. We camped one night along Cottonwood Creek in the Tetons, and I never got over the wonder and excitement of having found the space and beauty of something all people *owned*. We knew nothing of public land in central Kansas. But Yellowstone, Glacier, the Tetons: these were owned by all

Americans, and I, Wally Hickel, the son of a tenant farmer, had as much title to these natural wonders as the richest banker on Wall Street. They were *ours* — what beauty, what vision someone had to do all this!

Thirty-one years later, after I became Secretary of the Interior, I rode horseback along Cottonwood Creek. I easily found the spot where Clarence and Bob and I had camped overnight, and the whole excitement I had as a young boy came over me again. But now, as Secretary, my real responsibility was to 200 million Americans, to see that this wonderful place was wisely used for future generations.

Everything I did in those early days was a means to an end, and this included the boxing I did after my return from that first Western trip. I had never been inside a boxing ring, and all I knew about the sport was what I had learned from watching newsreel films of Joe Louis and other professionals. I didn't even have boxing gloves. But I had heard about the Golden Gloves tournaments, and they sounded like opportunities for at least limited travel. My mother made me a punching bag out of ticking used for making pillows. I filled it full of wheat and hung it in the granary where the harvest hands slept. I knew nothing about the fine points of footwork, and there was nobody around to teach me. I just went at that bag with my bare hands: jab, hook and cross. And when I broke open the bag with a solid punch and the wheat spilled out, I had won my fight for the day and I would take down the bag and Mom would patch it up again.[1]

The 1938 State Golden Gloves tournament was to be held in Salina, about seventy-five miles northeast of Claflin. At 142 pounds, five pounds under the welterweight limit, I was a little too big to be a lightweight and a little too small for the welterweight class. So I entered the tournament anyway as a welterweight. I

[1] *In January 1969, when the storm warnings about my confirmation hearings were building up to danger proportions, a young man named Tom Holley was assigned to my office to answer the mail—most of which opposed my confirmation. He ran into one letter that read: "Dear Sir, Are you the*

went to Salina in a Model A Ford with a pair of borrowed basketball shorts, an old car blanket for a robe and a pair of tennis shoes. I probably was as frightened as any kid on earth, but I was not going to let anyone know that. I won my first fight by a decision, my second by a knockout and I got to the final round on a forfeit. I won the fourth fight by a decision, and I was the Class B Golden Gloves welterweight champion of Kansas.

I was not quite nineteen when I went into the insurance business. Dad and I went to the county seat, and he gave me a power of attorney to make it possible for me to write policies and legally commit big insurance companies to liability. I made as much as $300 a month — in 1938, when $100 a month was considered a good living wage. I was getting a great informal education. I mixed

same Wally Hickel that used to kick the hell out of people behind Jones's barn every Saturday night in Claflin, Kansas?" Tom Holley had never met me then, but he answered: "You're damn right I am. Come visit me, and I promise not to hit you."

with older people, all kinds of people, including bankers and politicians. I was exposed to everything, and I learned the bad and good of it all. I had the freedom to make my own decisions.

I could have stayed in Claflin and undoubtedly made a living in insurance, but that was not enough. I wanted to look at another section of the country. Along with my cousin Martin Miller, who has remained a great personal friend all my life, I decided to go to Florida. Martin and I, along with two other friends, drove through Oklahoma and Arkansas and stopped in New Orleans to attend the National Eucharistic Congress and see 25,000 candles lit simultaneously for an open-air midnight Mass. We then drove on to Florida, always looking and searching.

I still had not found what I was looking for, but I was certain that it lay westward beyond the Tetons. I had to see the Pacific Ocean; my first experience in the Tetons had fired me up to go all the way to the West Coast. In the back of my mind was Australia. By the summer of 1939 it was apparent that Mom and Dad were going to be moved from one farm to another, and that the "great house" on the Grizell place was going to be torn down.[2] It was time for me to move, too.

I got out of the insurance business without telling anyone what was really on my mind. In January 1940 I signed up for a regional Golden Gloves tournament in Hobbs, New Mexico. I took a train to Dighton, Kansas, without telling my parents I was not coming back. It seemed easier to make the break that way. At Dighton I joined Scotty McLean, a fine, tough old Scotsman who coached the Kansas Golden Gloves boxing team that was going to Hobbs. After the Hobbs tournament he was going on to California where two of his sons lived. I telephoned home and asked my parents to send my clothes to Hobbs and also to send me $25, because I was going on to California with

[2] *Thirty years later, when I was Secretary of the Interior, my youngest brother, Bob, said to me: "If you had stayed in Kansas they'd never have torn that house down. You'd have figured a way out of it."*

Scotty McLean. Scotty drove me from Dighton to Hobbs, and when I got there I found my clothes and the money, which represented a great sacrifice to my father at the time. I hid $10 deep in my billfold and earmarked the rest to take me to California. It was a long time before I broke that ten-dollar bill.

I went to the finals of the tournament and lost the regional championship by a decision. That didn't bother me much. Winning or losing a boxing match was not that important to me; getting to California was, along with the Pacific Ocean and what lay beyond that ocean's horizon.

I felt a physical thrill when we crossed the border of California, but that was nothing compared to my emotions when I finally saw the Pacific Ocean itself, which I had been dreaming about so long. It seemed to me the frontier of the world. I saw the whole Pacific basin as a front door, not as a back door.

I stayed with Scotty McLean's two sons in Maywood, an eastern suburb of Los Angeles, and I had one more amateur fight in California. This took place in Jeffries

Barn near Burbank. It was named for Jim Jeffries, the former heavyweight champion. Jim Jeffries himself was there that night and I had the pleasure of meeting the man who some oldsters thought had been the greatest champion of them all. I was matched with a tall, strong welterweight named Jackie Brandon. I had seen Brandon fight twice, and both times he won by a knockout. I didn't see how I could possibly beat him. He had every physical advantage over me — height, weight, reach and experience.

In the first round he hit my nose and broke it. Scotty McLean was in my corner, and I told Scotty that I was going to quit because I couldn't see. Scotty said: "Hang in there, hang in there. You'll hit him with your right and you'll kill him."

I changed my boxing style to protect my broken nose. The fight was for four two-minute rounds, and I had never gone four rounds before. Then, in the fourth round, I hit Jackie Brandon with my right. I hit him so hard that I raised him completely off the floor of the ring and literally had to pull my glove away to let him fall. I hovered over him wondering if he was really down.

He was down all right—and out.

I had won the fight, but I had not come all the way to California to fight Jackie Brandon or anyone else. I had fought Brandon as a part of "passing through." I envisioned Japan; I envisioned everything on the rim of the ocean horizon, everything that I had ever dreamed about.

Obviously, getting to these places was not going to be easy.

3. Voyage No. 280

My first destination choice was still Australia. I went down to the White Steamship Company in Los Angeles and talked about how I could get to Australia. I had made a friend, Ted Adlam, who was a British subject and had no problem about going to Australia. I had a problem. I was not yet twenty-one years old, and I could not get a passport on my own. I would be twenty-one on August 18, 1940, and I was willing to wait. Two days after my birthday, I inquired again. I was told that I could apply for my passport and my visa to

Australia, but it would probably take three or four months.

That seemed like a lifetime. I asked where I could go without all these formalities — these passports and visas. Somebody named off a long list of places: the Philippines, Guam, Wake, Hawaii, Panama, Puerto Rico, the Virgin Islands. Then, at the very last, I was told that I could go to Alaska.

I asked, "How far up in Alaska can you take me?"

"If you had come in here two weeks ago, we could have taken you to Nome, but now as far as we can take you is Seward."

I didn't know where Seward was, but I said that I would go there. I bought a steerage ticket from Seattle to Seward for about $41. And Ted Adlam and I started out.

We drove to Santa Barbara because Ted's parents lived there, then got on a train and wound up in Salem, Oregon, where we ran out of money. Ted said there was a Ronald Jones family in Salem that his parents knew, and he called them. Mrs. Jones came down to the railroad station in a big black car; I think it was a Lincoln. She took Ted and me to their house, which was probably the finest home I had ever visited up to that time. Ted and I stayed there a few days. Upon leaving, I asked Mrs. Jones if she would lend me $20 because Ted and I needed money. She gave me the money, and we boarded the train for Seattle.

Twelve years later, when Eisenhower's Secretary of the Interior - designate Douglas MacKay, then Governor of Oregon, was considering appointing me Territorial Governor of Alaska, I visited MacKay in Salem with a delegation of Alaskans. I asked MacKay if he knew anyone named Ronald Jones. It turned out that Ronald Jones had been a State Senator and was quite an influential person. Governor MacKay told his secretary, "Get me Madge Jones." Mrs. Jones came on the line and MacKay said: "Madge, you can't guess whom I've got in the office. He's an Alaskan and he says he owes you twenty dollars." After the meeting, J. L. McCarrey, Jr., then an Anchorage lawyer and later a federal judge, drove me out to the Jones's home. I gave Mrs. Jones a twenty-dollar bill, which she asked me to autograph.

In Seattle, Ted Adlam and I transferred to the Alaska steamship Company's S.S. *Yukon.* This was the *Yukon's* voyage No. 280, departing Seattle on October 26, 1940.

The *Yukon* was a one-stack oil burner displacing 8,250 tons. We slept in dormitory bunks; not much space went to waste in steerage. The food was adequate but definitely plain; many years later I heard that the bread baked for steerage passengers was kept in the refrigerator longer than the bread for first and second class so it would be slightly tough and those of us in steerage would eat less of it. In fact, it became a kind of game to sneak into first or second class and get a better meal. I did this several times but I was always caught and thrown out. A kind woman named Enid King used to sneak food to me on the side, and I later paid her back by chopping wood for her in Anchorage.

The *Yukon* was a happy ship. During the voyage I encountered a young man named

Taylor who advised me not to stop in Seward but to go on to Anchorage. He had a brother there, and he told us about a cabin in Anchorage where we could sleep. Another passenger, realizing my financial circumstances, gave me a sleeping bag. We got off the boat at Seward on the cold Friday night of November 1, 1940. We were a little late because we had made an unscheduled stop at Prince Rupert in British Columbia to pick up and deliver to Ketchikan, Alaska, 278 passengers aboard the southbound S.S. *Alaska*, which had hit a reef off Elliott Island during a big blow the preceding Saturday night.

Ted and I were nearly broke, and that night Ted slept on a bench in the railroad depot. I slept on the floor of the hotel room of a man I had met on the boat. The next morning I set out to borrow some money. The third man I asked gave me ten dollars. I do not remember his name, but the following August I recognized him on the streets of Anchorage and repaid him with a twenty-dollar bill. I had used his ten dollars to buy a fifty-cent order of hotcakes, asked for two plates and split the order with Ted.

Then with our remaining money we bought two railroad tickets to Anchorage. That is how I arrived in Anchorage with thirty-seven cents in my pocket. Within an hour or so I had two cents left. I had gone up to Lucky's Market and spent the rest on a loaf of bread and some bologna, which Ted and I shared.

We found the cabin Mr. Taylor had mentioned. That cabin was literally my home for a couple of months, although it had a door that would not close. The site of the cabin is now downtown Anchorage, at the corner of Fifth and B, but then it was in the wilderness.

No matter. To me, this was "the place." I had found my country

Alaska is a great country, made up of great people.
Alaskans cannot fail, because they're doing a job
they love for a country they love.

CHAPTER **3**

Home

I knew that Alaska was going to be "my country" before I stepped off the S.S. *Yukon* in Seward. I knew that just by feel. Traveling by sea for the first time in my life, I was rarely out of sight of land, but the land I saw looked like nothing I had ever seen in Kansas. For seven days we sailed past virgin country: forests, towering mountains and great fjords. The physical impression was overwhelming. It was all so great, so free and so fresh.

The open plains of Kansas seemed very limited in contrast to all that I saw in one week aboard the *Yukon*. The challenges of a new country were literally busting out all over. In seven days my thinking pitched ahead at least twenty years. I envisioned great opportunities for any man who wanted to use and care for this property, not just exploit it and then go away. While I was still at sea, I was acquiring pride of "ownership," and if I had legally owned all of the Territory of Alaska, with deeds to prove it, my pride could not have been greater. Actually I, as an individual, *did* own some of Alaska. Of the Territory's 586,412 square miles, an area more than twice the size of Texas, less than one percent was privately owned at the time. The rest was public land, a staggering expanse that an awed American soldier, seeing it for the first time during World War II, described as "miles and miles of miles and miles." I owned as much of that expanse as any other American—just as I also "owned" a piece of the Tetons and Yellowstone.

As far as the rest of the United States was concerned, Alaska was as foreign as any foreign country could be. In 1940, the year Adolf Hitler conquered France and blitzed Great Britain, most Americans, in the East at least, felt more kinship with Europe than with their fellow countrymen who had settled in Alaska. For most of the Western world, 1940 was a year of fear and pessimism.

This was not the case in Alaska, which then had a population of 72,000. The only atmosphere I can recall from 1940 was one of optimism. And in my case the feeling was a little more than optimism. It was pure happiness, a feeling that every new day was going to be the greatest day of my life. At no time was there ever a fleeting thought in my mind that I had made the wrong choice in picking a new home.

1. Staking A Claim

Anchorage in 1940 was a closely knit community of 3,500 people surrounded by moose and fish. There were few automobiles, hardly any roads leading out of town and only eight blocks of pavement. Only one street could really be called paved — Fourth Avenue, where much later I built the Captain Cook Hotel. Originally, Anchorage was what its name suggests: a primitive port of call for trading vessels sailing into the inlet named for the British explorer James Cook. It took on the character of a small town about 1914, following a decision, encouraged by President Wilson, to build a 471-mile railroad from Seward to Fairbanks by way of Anchorage, mostly using the same equipment that had built the Panama Canal. By the time I arrived in Alaska, the wild days of the turn-of-the-century Gold Rush existed only in the memories of ancient sourdoughs propping up saloon bars, although a lot of gold was still being mined — $26 million in 1940, as compared to $9.7 million seven years earlier.[1] Most of this action was in the Fairbanks area, 351 rail miles to the north, but I was less impressed by gold mining than I was by a totally new geographical perspective. I was living in a wider world, a world extending to within two and one-half miles of the Soviet Union, a world inhabited by people who did

[1] *This was partly due to President Franklin Roosevelt's devaluation of the dollar in 1933 by raising the price of gold from $20.67 to $35 an ounce.*

not feel bound by the habits of social class and who had rediscovered the old frontiersman's ethic of trust and faith. It was a world in which a young man had to work, but such a man could make his way.

I got my first job in Anchorage washing dishes at the Richmond Cafe on Fourth Avenue. At first I worked for my meals, but soon Mrs. Richmond, a wonderful woman who took a lively interest in ambitious new Alaskans, was paying me a dollar an hour. For a long time I chopped wood once a week for my shipboard friend Enid King, who always gave me an extra meal. Every once in a while she would drive by the little cabin where I was living to see how I was doing. She lived in a duplex on the property where I now have my office. One night when I was chopping wood, a man named Keith Lesh delivered groceries to her. Enid King and Keith Lesh were married,[2] and Keith

[2] *Enid Lesh died in 1956. Keith Lesh remains one of my closest friends. My traveling companion to Alaska, Ted Adlam, married in Alaska, had one son and died of a brain tumor in 1948.*

wound up owning what was then the biggest grocery chain in Alaska.

I had been in Alaska about a month when I got a job helping clear out a pole line to a new Army base that was being laid out a couple of miles from downtown Anchorage — Fort Richardson. This created a problem. I didn't own any clothing suitable for outdoor work in an Alaska winter. It was a little like borrowing that ten dollars on a street in Seward; I had to look for a place that would charge a purchase and trust me.

The first two stores turned me down. I stopped at a third store, where a man heard me out as I described my predicament. He said, "Young man, you need some help." Without further discussion he told me what I needed in the way of working clothes, then outfitted me completely. The cost came to $72. I signed nothing. The man simply said, "Pay me when you get the money." His name was Ike Bayless, and I did pay him. The great feeling at the time came from the knowledge that this man had confidence in me and knew that I would pay when I got the money.

After the pole line was cleared, I got a job in the boiler works of the Alaska Railroad, which had its main offices in Anchorage. I was in the boiler works when I heard that they were looking for a welterweight to match with a professional named Jimmy Bays, and for a $125 purse. The fight was to be tucked in between dogsled races during the February 1941 Fur Rendezvous, which is Alaska's annual community social with a touch of Mardi Gras. Jimmy Bays had, or once had, a rating in *Ring* magazine, so on the record I was out of my league. This was certainly not Golden Gloves competition.

I begged for the chance to fight Bays anyway, not only because I needed the $125 but because I thought I could beat him. Again it was one of those situations in which, looking at the form sheet, there seemed to be no way I could win. I trained religiously in my off hours, mostly skipping rope and shadowboxing. My ring work was not all that rusty, since I had knocked out Jackie Brandon in California less than a year earlier. But I had to be the underdog; the Anchorage *Daily Times* repeatedly spelled my name "Hinkel."

I decisioned Jimmy Bays in six rounds in the old Community Hall, later torn down, and the few people who bet on me may have made more money out of the fight than I did. I was satisfied with the $125 purse, which was the most money I had had in hand since arriving in Alaska. I fought only one more time, and I lost the decision without caring much. Looking back, I suppose I was a good enough welterweight to have become a championship contender with proper coaching, but boxing to me was only a means to an end. I looked upon my early jobs in Anchorage the same way. It was all a part of staking a claim in "my country."

I never made more than subsistence money at any of these jobs—probably $175 a month at most. But I was acquiring more confidence every payday, and by September 1941 I felt sufficiently sure of myself to get married to Janice Cannon, who came from a pioneering family.

The marriage was happy but tragically short. I took Janice back to Kansas in December 1941 to meet my parents and family. We had planned to spend about a month on the trip, but Pearl Harbor changed all that. We were advised that it would be several months before we could get passage back to Alaska. Janice was never to return.

I got a job in Wichita as an inspector for Beech Aircraft in the rapidly expanding aircraft industry, and our son Ted was born in the spring of 1942 in Kansas. In the fall of that year I moved to Denver to become an inspector for the Army Air Corps procurement division, but that job was also short-lived. Janice became seriously ill in early July 1943, and she died about a month later in the Mayo Clinic at Rochester, Minnesota. Janice's mother came down from Alaska and took Ted home. I made my way back to Alaska on another ship.

2. Her Money

Pearl Harbor changed the course of all American lives, and it upgraded the importance of a whole Territory in one day. Politicians whose entire knowledge of Alaska came from the jingles of Robert Service and the stories of Jack London looked at a map and became aware that substantial chunks of American real estate, both on mainland Alaska and in the Aleutian chain, lay closer to Japan than to Washington or New York. It requires some stretch of the imagination today to recall that the Japanese actually bombed Dutch Harbor on the island of Unalaska and that Japanese soldiers for about a year occupied the Aleutian Islands of Kiska and Attu. Anchorage was no longer an easy-going little community with cabins that had doors which would not close; it was on its way to becoming the biggest city in Alaska, just as Fort Richardson was on its way to becoming a half billion-dollar military installation with enormous strategic importance.[3]

I spent the rest of World War II as a flight and maintenance inspector, based at Fort Richardson. Now and then I went to Fairbanks, which was a contact point for

[3] *Old Fort Richardson, to which I had helped clear a pole line in late 1940, became Elmendorf Air Force Base in 1951. A newer Fort Richardson adjoins Elmendorf now.*

Soviet pilots shuttling American-built military aircraft across Siberia to the German battlefront. The Russians all seemed to have cameras slung around their necks, although we Air Corps personnel were forbidden to take pictures of anything having to do with the military.

In Anchorage young Ted and I lived with Ted's maternal grandparents, the Cannons. I still owed a considerable amount of money on medical bills, so I worked nights as a bartender in an Anchorage saloon called the South Seas. I was not exactly a bouncer, but I did have to keep order occasionally. The atmosphere was a little different from that of the Knights of Columbus Hall in Claflin, Kansas, where my father had been both dance manager and bouncer.

I had also started dating a girl named Ermalee Strutz, the daughter of another pioneering Alaska family. As a young girl she had worked in one of the small fish canneries on Cook Inlet, and she was a secretary at Fort Richardson when I met her during World War II. As we talked about getting married, we agreed to save our money independently. By April 1945 she had a little more than $1,000 in the bank, and I borrowed nearly all of it to buy an airplane. I had the wild idea of starting up a postwar air route between Anchorage and Homer on the south peninsula.

I bought the airplane from a museum in Denver. It was a 1929 six-place Verville, powered by a 225-hp Wright J-5 engine. I took a leave from my Air Corps job to bring the plane from Denver, where I went with a friend, John McCormick. We both had private piloting licenses and about sixty hours of flying time apiece, although neither of us had ever flown more than fifty miles from Anchorage or flown anything bigger than a light plane with a 65-hp engine.

In Denver I proceeded to wreck the airplane on takeoff. I told John McCormick, "From here on out, you do the flying." The wings, the propeller and the tail section were demolished, and the repairs took several weeks. When we finally got the plane in the air, we headed for Alaska in a manner that was both unusual and risky, for any airplane built in 1929 — and only seven Vervilles were ever built — had rather primitive instruments. We made a routine stop in Rapid City, South Dakota, then headed for Sheridan, Wyoming, which we calculated to be a two-hour flight. After three and one-half hours I said, "John, Sheridan has got to be around here somewhere." Finally John looked out the window and said, "There it is." We landed, but we were in Billings, Montana. Somehow we had missed the whole state of Wyoming.

We also missed our checkpoint at Lethbridge, Alberta, during a driving rainstorm, found a highway and followed it to the nearest city, which turned out to be Edmonton. This was during World War II, and there was a lot of American military in Edmonton. Two jeeps, bristling with machine guns, escorted us to a parking place; after all, we were unexpected arrivals in a foreign country. I asked to see the American officer in command, who turned out to be a three-star general. I told him my story and he said, "Son, let me see that plane."

He took one look at my Verville and said, "If you have the guts to fly it, I have the guts to help you." Then he sat down and wrote a letter for me. It said that any time I needed help, the military along the way was to give it. I said, "General, I'm sure you'll never have to help us."

About an hour out of Edmonton we lost one magneto. The engine was running so roughly that we could hardly stay in the air. We looked at our road map and spotted Lesser Slave Lake; surely we could land on the beach. But that was impossible, because the beach was too rocky. Then we found an old railroad and followed it, thinking that if the engine quit, we could put the plane down on the railroad tracks. After four hours and twenty minutes we wound up at our original destination, Grand Prairie, to discover that Black Widow fighter planes had been out looking for us for two hours. And we were out of gas.

We put seventy-two gallons into an eighty-gallon gas tank and flew to Fort Nelson. There we were weathered in. After three days we got out of Fort Nelson but wound up flying blind in the clouds in a box canyon. I literally ate a No. 2 pencil—chewed it up. I was praying all the time, and I made a deal with myself and God that if we landed safely I would never

117

again try to fly a plane. When we got back to Fort Nelson, I walked away and hitchhiked a ride to Anchorage on an Air Transport Command plane, then sent someone back to Fort Nelson to pick up our Verville. I later sold the plane, but when I got to Anchorage I was broke, and I had to borrow another twenty dollars from Ermalee. It is no wonder that to this day she jokes that I had borrowed so much from her that she had to marry me "for her money." We were married the following November 22.

Ermalee was perfectly designed for me. She has the kind of sophistication that makes her feel equally at home at a Washington white-tie dinner party or in an upcountry Alaska village. Her manner is as delicate as a butterfly, but she also is tougher than a boot. She has to be tough to live with me. I'm not intolerable, but I can be awfully impossible. She must have thought so in February 1947 when she was in the hospital awaiting the birth of our first child, Robert, and I walked in to announce that I was through working for wages and was going into the construction business.

Ermalee asked, "How? How, when we have to borrow money to pay for the baby?"

I said, "It's all set, Erm. I have thought it all out."

Strictly speaking, it was not "all set." But I had "thought it out." I believed in Alaska. I believed that the newly built Alaska Highway would open up great new traffic to a Territory bound someday to become a State. Moreover, the jet age was just around the corner, and Anchorage was the logical stopping point for foreign carriers that would soon be opening up the short polar air route linking the Far East to the capital cities of Europe.

I bought three lots, one of them with a basement on it in Spenard, an Anchorage suburb, and began building homes. I saw this as a time to build the things Alaska so obviously was going to need a decade later. For me, the road to business success lay in that direction. But I also wanted to build things that took into account a man's heart and mind and the need to satisfy his soul as well as his stomach.

3. Carpentry, Plumbing and Dynamite

Shortly after we were married, Ermalee and I moved into a partly finished frame house I had bought. We completed the house ourselves. It was then that I began learning a lot about carpentry, plumbing and electrical wiring. In the middle of 1947, about six months after Robert was born, I sold the house and moved into one of the homes I was building in Spenard. I had the feeling then that I had found my direction.

In March of the following year I had completed the Spenard project, and our second son Wally was born on March 22. I said to my wife, "Erm, we're going on a trip. I'm going to think this out." She had never been to the continental United States — what we called "Outside."

One month to the day after Wally was born, we started out. With three young children we boarded the S.S. *Aleutian* and took the seven-day trip to Seattle, where I had a new car waiting. We took a four-month trip covering all of the Western and Mid-Western states and as far south as Texas. And we visited my family in Kansas.

My father was getting ready to move from his third tenant farm, and I decided it was time to stop all this. Dad was now in his middle fifties, and he had had enough wheat farming for one lifetime. I told him, "Dad, you're going to buy a house." He and Mom did buy a house in Claflin and moved into it. It was very important to me that they own their own home at last.

Another purpose of my trip was to get one of my brothers, Vernon, to return to Alaska with me. He was nineteen at the time. He came back in the car with us and has worked with me ever since.

We drove home via the Alaska Highway, and I saw tremendous opportunities for tourism. We arrived home August 22, four months to the day after we left. Although fall was approaching, I wanted to get started. So I did. I formed a partnership with a famous old-timer and friend of mine, Emil Phiel. In two years we built forty-eight rental units, which we owned jointly. This was the start of the Hickel Construction Company, with a management consisting mostly of me, and assets of a pickup truck for transport and a checkbook for accounting purposes.

We did not have many specialists in Alaska in those days, so it was imperative that I be fairly handy about doing anything and everything. I considered myself a quick learner, so I had no qualms about literally handling dynamite. I learned one day in the dead of winter that the culvert was frozen solid beneath the driveway leading to one of the duplexes we were building. I picked up a fellow do-it-yourselfer and croquet-playing friend, Mitch Abood, an Anchorage insurance man whose ancestry was a mixture of Irish and Arabic, and who many years later played the Jewish lead in an Anchorage production of *Fiddler on the Roof.* Surely, between us, we could handle a simple problem like a frozen culvert.

We drove out to the scene of the trouble in my new pickup truck, surveyed the situation and decided that three sticks of dynamite ought to be just about right. We hacked out a hole at one end of the frozen culvert, inserted the dynamite, lit the fuses and ran like county sheriffs.

The explosion cleared the culvert very neatly. But that wasn't all. When the blast went off, the culvert became a kind of gun barrel. A huge chunk of ice shot out like a projectile, through the air and straight into the side of my new pickup truck. After that I left blasting to the experts.

By 1951 I was working with another famous old-timer, Carl Martin, on a forty-unit housing development we called Martin Manor. The following year I undertook on my own a ninety-six unit project in Anchorage's Simondson Subdivision, and started construction of my first tourist-related project, the Travelers Inn. People were beginning to call me a plunger, a gambler eventually bound to roll snake eyes. I might have appeared to be plunging, but I always had a project thought out in my mind before I started it. If the project felt right, I went ahead; if it did not feel right, I dropped the whole thing.

I never tried to do anything someone else had already done. I always looked for problems that had not been answered, needs that had not been met. I felt that Alaska, as it developed and qualified for statehood, would be "home" to three basic kinds of people: 1) a contented working force, 2) a smaller group who would go into business and be satisfied with a basic, steady income, 3) a small minority I called, even then, "the searchers." Searchers are people who are curious. The effective searcher combines the best of the dreamer and the doer.

In 1953, when I opened the Travelers Inn, Alaska had not yet been exposed to the phenomenon of the modern motel with its variety of facilities. I discussed my idea first with the bankers; they turned it down cold. But I knew I was right. Alaska was ready for what I had in mind, so I went ahead and bought the land. I had the motel finished before I could get the financing arranged. The Travelers Inn was an immediate success, and the bankers were the first to offer congratulations.

We did it again in Fairbanks. In 1955 a group of Fairbanks residents known as the Fairbanks Hotel Association wanted a modern hotel facility. They said they had faith in my ability to build it and would lend me $200,000 to get the job done. They planned to get this money by issuing bonds, and they sold $218,000 worth of bonds to nearly 600 individuals in Fairbanks, in denominations as small as ten dollars. I pledged, on my part, to retire the bonds within five years. With $218,000 in hand, I said, "I'll build it," but I knew I would really have a problem financing it. I needed at least $750,000.

As I walked down the streets of Fairbanks, my accountant, Frank Molitor, asked me, "How are you going to finance it?"

I replied, "I'm going to charge it."

A reporter who was following us said, "Sincerely, Mr. Hickel, how *are* you going to finance it?"

I stated flatly, "The Seattle First is going to finance it." My quote appeared in print. The Seattle First National Bank had never heard about it. However, they helped put up the money. The Fairbanks Travelers came out twice as big as the one in Anchorage. On October 15, 1960, when the bonds were due, we threw a party in the banquet room to pay off all the Fairbanks people who had initially given us their money and their trust. We had accepted the responsibility of fulfilling the people's wishes and needs.

I felt the same way when I built the Northern Lights Shopping Center, the first in Alaska, on the outskirts of Anchorage; I wanted to fulfill a need. I am also an enthusiast for originality. Alaska had never had an escalator, either public or private, so I decided to put one in the shopping center. It was hauled from Chicago in December 1959 on two forty-foot flatbed trucks up the Alaska Highway. One truck got lost for ten days. The bankers were upset about the whole idea: "You can build a staircase for $500."

The escalator cost me $90,000, but it was worth it. You could get on the bottom of it in Anchorage and arrive at the top in Spenard because the city limits went right through it. We put up one sign at the bottom "Leaving Anchorage, Arriving Spenard" and another top "Leaving Spenard, Arriving Anchorage." The kids were so wild about it they rode it all day.

In 1954 I started a new home as a base for a growing family. Three years later we moved into our rambling two-story home near Cook Inlet in Anchorage's

Turnagain-by-the-Sea area. It was a good house for a big family. Besides Ted, who was then fifteen, Ermalee and I had four younger sons: Robert, Wally Jr., Jack and Joe. We had a going-to-bed routine called "piling on," in which the four small boys climbed on my back, hanging on to me and hanging on to each other as I staggered up the stairs.

I always told them that everyone has to have a base: "Travel the world over, and no matter where you settle, this place will always be your home.'"

4. Sparring in a Larger Ring

Everything depends on the caliber of our leaders in government, and I thought that the trouble in Alaska by 1950 was that nothing seemed to be happening. We were governed by the Department of the Interior, but nobody in Washington appeared to know where or who we were.

In those days the Anchorage Republican Club had to scramble hard just to come up with enough names to fill the ballot in territorial legislative elections. So I didn't object when my name was listed in 1950 as a candidate for the territorial House of Representatives. I did not campaign; the only thing my poster said was "Alaska First." I shed no tears when I failed to survive the primary.

During that same year I did get involved — and rather emotionally — in another local campaign. I worked to help send an Alaskan farmer, poet and member of the territorial House to the territorial Senate. His name was Gerrit Heinie Snider, a Dutch immigrant and a cherished friend to this day. It was easy to work for Heinie. His opponent was the Mayor of Anchorage, Z. J. Loussac, and important political figure and a leading vote-getter in the primary. In October 1950 I delivered a pro-Snider radio commercial eight times over three Anchorage radio stations. My language was pretty rough. I believe that words like "bungler" and "political plague" were about the mildest observations I made regarding the Mayor. My oratory was certainly not gentle, and I really do not know how much it had to do with getting Heinie elected. But he did get elected in what was considered an upset, and he went to Juneau as a territorial Senator. Mayor Loussac and I came through this confrontation with considerable mutual respect, and in later years we became good friends.

My next political chore was to line up a speaker for the Lincoln Day Dinner of the Anchorage Republican Club in February 1951. I wanted Herbert Hoover. I called Guy Gabrielson, then chairman of the Republican National Committee, and told him that this was the kind of name we needed. He told me there were difficulties involved. But I wanted Herbert Hoover.

Arthur Langlie, then Governor of Washington, heard about my problem and asked me to come over and see him. I was already in Seattle trying to sort out the matter. I spent about an hour with Governor Langlie, and he convinced me that getting Hoover would be nearly impossible because of the former President's age and the long distances involved. After all, the dinner was to take place in the dead of Alaskan winter.

Langlie spoke with the National

Committee, and when I called Gabrielson back he gave me the names of two young Republican Senators who had been elected in the off-year Republican sweep in November 1950. Either would be available to come to Alaska. One was Herman Welker of Idaho. The other was Richard Nixon. I asked Gabrielson, "Who's Nixon?" So it was Welker who came to Alaska in February 1951.

The Senator did a good job for Alaskans, assuring them that "your Senators from Idaho have been and are now firmly committed to the fact that you deserve your place in the Union." He meant statehood, which by now was a priority issue in Alaska.

5. But on What Terms?

Practically everyone living in Alaska was for statehood, and a lot of people wanted it so badly that they did not care too much about the wording of the organic law Congress had to write and pass to make Alaska the forty-ninth state. I cared, because I was concerned not only about statehood — I was for that all along — but about how our resources would be used. This issue made me a controversial figure in Alaska politics.

In early 1952 a statehood bill actually got passed by the House of Representatives in Washington. It was not a good bill. Basically it would have given Alaska statehood in name only, leaving more than 94 percent of the State's 375,296,000 acres of land in the hands of the federal government. The House bill would have turned over to the State only 23 million acres of land; I felt that Alaska should retain at least 100 million acres, to be selected over a suitable span of years. I told Ermalee: "Come on, let's go to Washington. We have got to get that bill rewritten or at least get it recommitted in the Senate."

Robert B. Atwood, who was chairman of the Alaska Statehood Committee and also publisher of Alaska's largest newspaper, the Anchorage *Daily Times*, was already in Washington. I telephoned Atwood at his hotel and told him I was working to recommit the bill. He said, "All the opponents of statehood are trying to do the same thing." I said: "Bob, that is not my point. I am *for* statehood, but I am sincerely against this bill. We need a better one."

Ermalee and I stayed with Senator Welker at his home in Spring Valley, Maryland. It was during this visit that I met another Senator who lived in Spring Valley. Welker and I were in one of the Senate halls when he spotted a person unfamiliar to me. "Here's a man you should meet. Wally, this is Dick Nixon." We shook hands.

I also talked to Vice President Alben Barkley, a warm and human man. He understood my problem but was actually for statehood on any terms because he — and a lot of other people — assumed that statehood would automatically mean two more Democrats in the Senate.

I put my main case to "Mr. Republican," Senator Robert Taft of Ohio. I told him to give us our lands and we would build not only a great state of the Union, but a great country of the world. He was impressed, and he called three young staff lawyers. He asked me to discuss with them what I thought should be in the statehood bill.

After about a week the lawyers had

completed their work on my suggested amendments. I met with Senator Taft again. He put his hand on my shoulder and said: "Son, you can go home now. I think we have this in good hands."

I was halfway home, making a plane connection in Los Angeles, when I was paged at the airport. I went to the telephone and found myself speaking to I. Jack Martin, Senator Taft's administrative assistant.

Martin said: "Wally, you've got a lot of work to do. We've recommitted the statehood bill by one vote — 46 to 45."

I considered this a great victory, but many Alaskans did not. They thought recommitment meant that statehood was dead. On March 5, 1952, Bob Atwood's newspaper, the *Times*, attacked me in one of the longest editorials it had ever published: "The land problems mentioned by Mr. Hickel are old chestnuts which have been bandied about for years. . . . Mr. Hickel says Alaska . . . would get nothing but the tops of mountains and mud flats. . . . The twenty-three million acres that would be available for the new State are almost equal to the total area of the great State of Indiana. We have never heard Indiana complain that it does not have enough land to operate a state successfully."[4] The *Daily Alaska Empire*, published in Juneau, came to my defense, labeling Atwood's editorial "a rehash of the same old arguments he had been propounding for years, and in the usual irrational pattern. . . . Indiana does not complain. Nor do we expect it to since that State controls 98.7 percent of its total acreage, has a population approaching four million and a per capita income well above the national average."

I was thirty-three when Dwight Eisenhower was elected President in 1952, and some people were pushing for my appointment as the new territorial Governor of Alaska. The choice narrowed down to Elmer Rasmuson, a leading banker

[4] *There was nothing personal about this. It must be remembered that in Alaska, particularly in territorial days, the fellow you called an s.o.b. at three in the afternoon frequently was your cordial dinner host that same evening.*

long prominent in Alaska Republican politics; B. Frank Heintzleman, a Department of Agriculture forester in Juneau; and myself. The appointment went to Heintzleman, who had a public image of being opposed to statehood.

I led a group of eighteen protesting Heintzleman's attitude and some of his appointments. By then I was president of the Anchorage Republican Club. We drafted a letter to Heintzleman, dated December 15, 1953, objecting to a "lack of strong leadership" and a "lack of interest in the Governor's office on the statehood program." We demanded a "positive stand by you" on statehood. After a week had gone by with no comment from the Governor, the committee agreed to release the text of the letter to the press, which correctly interpreted it as a grass-roots revolt.

In 1954 I was elected Republican National Committeeman for Alaska. One of my greatest supporters was Bob Atwood. In April of that year, I had the distinction of heading up a group of Alaskans to confront President Eisenhower on the statehood issue. The delegation included E. L. ("Bob") Bartlett, territorial delegate to Congress and later a Democratic United States Senator, and John Butrovich, a Republican territorial Senator from Fairbanks who did not bother much with the niceties of language. He took on the President with harsh words, and soon the President's face began to flush. Both his face and the top of his head were blushing. When Butrovich finished, Eisenhower looked at me and said, "Well, young man, at least I'm glad *you* think I'm an American." The exchange was smoothed over, and J. C. Morris, an Anchorage insurance man and real estate developer, presented the President a gift of ivory. Eisenhower may have been upset by the tough talk, but he got the statehood message.

During this same visit I got into a widely reported argument with William Strand, who was then director of the Interior Department's Office of Territories and who opposed full statehood for Alaska. This took place at a cocktail party given by Strand in his Washington home for the

Operation Statehood delegation. It started when I asked Strand to consider appointing Mike Stepovich, a man with strong Alaska support, to a federal judgeship at Fairbanks.

"You won't get your man in," Strand told me. "I am going to send a man from Massachusetts for that job."

Then we got into the statehood argument. Strand said that as long as Alaskans failed to "support and defend" Governor Heintzleman's Administration, they would get nothing. Strand favored a "partition" scheme under which only part of Alaska (if any) would become a State. He told me that he would run things for Alaska without any interference from Republicans in the Territory. He said he did not give a tinker's dam about what I thought, and that as Republican National Committeeman-elect, I should go back home and tell my fellow Alaskans that. He also told me that Alaskans could huff and puff all they wanted, but he had three members of the Senate Interior Committee sewed up, and the statehood bill was not about to get anywhere.

It was not exactly a quiet conversation, and a good deal of it was overhead at the cocktail party downstairs. Mrs. Strand came upstairs several times to hush up the fight, but she never succeeded. People downstairs were listening, and that is how the story got into the Alaska press, first in the Juneau *Independent*.

At one point Strand told me that Alaskans must accept partition and that it was my job to see that they did accept it. I asked how anyone could expect to sell Alaskans a scheme that had no purpose and no advantage.

"You don't sell it to them," Strand told me. "You stuff it down their throats."

Strand was actually telling me that he was the dictator of Alaska's future. I was not about to buy this.

In June we took up the matter at a weekend caucus of Alaska Republicans at McKinley Park. We adopted a resolution strongly reprimanding Strand, although we did not mention him by name. We merely called on the Eisenhower Administration to take cognizance of "this detrimental policy."

We were also taking on the fish industry, and the fish industry knew it. On June 18, 1954, the *Alaska Weekly*, a Seattle publication representing everything we disliked about "outside interests," denounced me as that "high-flying Anchorage boy trying to do a man's job. . . . When Hickel elected to engage Strand in a knock-down and drag-out battle within earshot of three dozen or so rubbernecks, the die was cast. He found himself in over his head and chose to fight his way out, both fists flying. The champ won and the amateur ran to Mama licking his wounds. Trouble is, the boys in the neighborhood got wind of the whole thing and are now laughing up their sleeves."

The boys in the neighborhood, whoever the *Alaska Weekly* thought they were, did not laugh very long. Within a few weeks, Bill Strand was fired.

In 1956 I ran again for National Committeeman against Henry Benson, a popular Republican who was then Alaska's Commissioner of Labor and who had never lost an election. The vote was close, but I won. I had not even campaigned, because I was in Washington fighting for the statehood bill. This was during the pre-jet travel age, and I made twelve round trips to Washington that year. My principal memory of 1956 is changing clothes in a Stratocruiser sleeping berth.

Late that year Heintzleman resigned as territorial Governor, and I was endorsed by the Republican State Central Committee to replace him. Eventually I came out for Mike Stepovich, the son of a Serbian immigrant who came to Alaska in the Gold Rush days. Aside from the fact that I was totally involved in the statehood argument, I was sure that Stepovich was the man Fred Seaton, Eisenhower's Secretary of the Interior, wanted to appoint. My instinct was right, and Stepovich was our next Governor.

Besides, there *was* a real argument against statehood that had to be beaten down. Many people in high places were concerned by the "contiguous issue"—the fact that Alaska was physically removed from the rest of the United States. Virginia's powerful Howard ("Judge") Smith, a Democrat who chaired the House Rules

Committee, opposed Alaska statehood. So did Minority Republican Leader Joe Martin of Massachusetts. But on May 28, 1958, statehood passed the House by a vote of 210 to 166.

We still had to get the bill past the Senate. I told Secretary Seaton: "Let me take on the tough ones. I only want to speak to the opposition."

I went to see Senators John Bricker (Ohio), Norris Cotton (New Hampshire), Andrew Schoeppel (Kansas) and Styles Bridges (New Hampshire). Cotton and Schoeppel had both visited me at my home in Anchorage the year before. When they left the Territory, they were still against statehood.

In Washington I based my argument on the total public good. I wanted to stop the abuse of things owned by all Americans—the abuse of the mining interests at the turn of the century; the abuse of the salmon industry; the abuse of everything the territorial status of Alaska made available to the special few. When I saw Norris Cotton I grinned and said, "You s.o.b., this bill is going to pass and I want you to vote for it." He replied, "You s.o.b., if it does, you'll have to give some of your time to public life."

He voted right, then waved his clenched hands in a victory salute to me in the gallery. That was on June 30, 1958. The vote was 64 to 20. Seven days later, President Eisenhower signed Public Law No. 85-508. After a referendum approved the bill by a 6 to 1 majority, Alaska was proclaimed a State on January 3, 1959. We had the right to select for our own use a total of 103,000,000 acres of land—about what I had in mind when I fought to recommit the earlier statehood bill in 1952.[5]

6. 'I've Thought It Out'

Meanwhile, the fact of impending statehood had created turmoil in Alaska Republican

[5] *This selection process was held up by Secretary Udall's orders in 1966 and 1968 which first "froze" and then "withdrew" public lands in Alaska. See footnote, page 40.*

ranks. I and many other Republicans wanted Mike Stepovich to run for Governor in the fall of 1958, but Mike wanted to run for the Senate. I told Mike, "I wouldn't have supported you for territorial Governor if I had not believed you intended to run for Governor when we got statehood." There was a long and stormy session at the Travelers Inn in Anchorage, lasting until three o'clock in the morning. At one point, Johnny Butrovich had tears in his eyes and said, "That young man is using me." But Stepovich persisted in going for the Senate, and Butrovich wound up running for Governor himself.

Both men lost. I am still convinced that if the ticket had been turned around, Alaska would have started out as a Republican State. Our first elected Governor was the Democrat William A. Egan. A State's first elected Administration has tremendous power to direct its destiny, since it has authority to create an entire political machinery from scratch. After the election I told Ermalee, "In my lifetime we may not be able to straighten out Alaska if it heads in the wrong direction."

When Nixon first ran for President in 1960, Alaska had two Democratic Senators, a Democratic Governor and a Democratic Congressman. But we put together a successful campaign and Nixon carried the State. Yet I had a bad feeling in my bones about the 1960 election.

Fulfilling a pledge to campaign in every state, Nixon came to Alaska during the first week of November. The organization was there, but it was Nixon's visit that won the State. On a Sunday night, two days before the nation was due to vote, I escorted Dick and Pat Nixon to their plane at Anchorage International Airport. Pat went up the ramp, followed by the Vice President. I said, Dick, I'll see you in Washington at the Inauguration."

The Vice President took a couple of steps, turned and said, "Yes, Wally. Yes."

I think I can read people, and I walked back into the terminal and told Ermalee, "We've just lost the election because Dick Nixon doesn't think he's going to win."

In March 1964, on Good Friday, the most

severe earthquake ever recorded in North America struck Alaska. In less than five minutes this catastrophe took 117 lives and caused three-quarters of a billion dollars worth of property damage.

I was not in Anchorage at the time. Less than an hour before the earthquake hit, I landed in Tokyo as head of a State Chamber of Commerce trade mission. After I learned of the disaster, a member of the United States Embassy accompanied by a three-star general came to our hotel to see if they could help. I had tried to call home, but could not get through. The general told me: "Wally, call this number at the base in Tokyo. Tell them it's General Hickel calling, and you want to get through to Elmendorf Air Force Base quickly." Within ten minutes I was speaking to an airman at Elmendorf. From a helicopter report the airman told me: "The Turnagain area is devastated. The houses across the street are gone, but your home is standing. General Reeves says, 'Come home.' "

We still had no word about our families. I turned to my friend, Alvin Bramstedt, president of the Midnight Sun Broadcasting

Company, and said, "We've got to get home to our families and rebuild the city." When we landed at the Anchorage International Airport, Al and I got in a car and started toward our homes. We were driving on what we had known as a familiar street when a military guard stopped us. The street was gone. We took another route to my home. No one was there. It was dark, so I went to the Travelers Inn. I found my family there. All were safe.

The authorities had evacuated Turnagain. I knew, however, that the geology of that end of Turnagain was safe. There was a small spring below my home. I checked it and found it still running and unimpaired. I showed the authorities and they let us stay in our homes.

It was a tougher battle as far as downtown Anchorage was concerned. There was even talk about moving the city. The community was frightened, and rightfully so. But in 1958 I had had the first private professional geological report done on a downtown Anchorage area where I was planning to build. I knew that the area still standing was solid. Sixty days after returning to the scene of the disaster, I announced that I was going to build a brand new hotel in Anchorage — the Captain Cook. Some people thought I was crazy. Others stood by my confidence.

In nine months, right through the winter, we put up that hotel. We started digging a hole in the ground in August. It was such a challenging project, right on the site of a tragic disaster, that people from all over the country rallied to help us. Industries cut delivery times and pushed us up their priority lists. We opened the following June 17. What a time schedule! Our first registered guest was a great old-time pioneer legislator named E. B. Collins, whom we had flown in from the Pioneers Home in Sitka. As I wheeled him into the lobby in a wheelchair, he said, "Wally, you've got the finest roadhouse on the trail."

Politically I was not so successful in 1964. The Republican state convention was a debacle. There was a hopeless split between the liberally-oriented Nelson Rockefeller Republicans and the Goldwater conservatives. My position was that Rockefeller could not get nominated and

147

Barry Goldwater could not win. So I stuck with Nixon and was wiped out. It became obvious at the convention that I would not be selected as National Committeeman, so I withdrew.

Then, eighteen months later, I told Ermalee: "I've thought it out. I'm going to run for Governor." I announced on March 3, 1966. All of our intelligence indicated that a majority of Alaskans shared my belief that we had had only token leadership in Juneau for eight years. Several of my closest friends had toured the state from Ketchikan in the south to Nome in the north, and we thought a narrow victory was possible if we worked hard enough.

My announcement was ridiculed. Alaska's Secretary of State, Hugh Wade, declared that I might have spent my $100 filing fee more wisely by purchasing tickets on Alaska's famous "ice pool," a legal lottery in which ticket holders try to guess the precise date and hour when the ice breaks up each spring in the Tanana River at Nenana, south of Fairbanks. But I went to my office at the Hickel Investment Company, told my brother Vernon to take over the business, walked out and never went back.

I was a 9-to-1 underdog to win the governorship. In the Republican primary I was opposed by two popular men, former Governor Mike Stepovich and Bruce Kendall, a former Speaker of the State House of Representatives. The newspapers thought my campaign was a joke, but we sighed up 4,265 volunteers who paid a minimum of one dollar and pledged themselves to work in at least one of ten different areas. There were "Workers for Wally," "Women for Wally," and even "Walkers for Wally," including one crippled fellow, Cliff Weber, who walked the State on my behalf. I covered the State personally by plane, sometimes flying hundreds of miles just to meet five or six Eskimo voters in the northern bush districts. I was determined to get more votes in the August primary than Stepovich and Kendall combined, and I did.

During the whole election, even in the primary, I ran *against* no one. Instead I was running *for* the governorship. After the primary, Mike Stepovich declined to campaign for me, and Bruce Kendall joined the Democratic Party. By two-thirty on election night, Josef Holbert of the Anchorage *Times*, later to become my press secretary in Juneau, was pressing me to concede to the Democratic incumbent, Bill Egan. During the next half hour the tide turned, and I went ahead to stay. Egan considered demanding a recount but dropped the idea, and I was declared the official winner by 1,080 votes.

Two years later, during the Senate fight for my confirmation as Secretary of the Interior, the Associated Press at one point identified me as an "oil millionaire." Nobody seemed to know that during my race for Governor I had been refused permission to campaign on all but one of the oil company drilling rigs in Cook Inlet near Anchorage. In fact, I had no big business or industrial support at all. I had put together a people's campaign and won the election as a free man.

I had an attitude in mind: the people who would serve in the State government had to be people who wanted to *do* a job, not merely get a job. Furthermore, whether you were a Native fisherman in a remote bush village or the president of an oil company, my door in Juneau was open. *Everyone had an audience, but no one had a claim.*

My election as Governor had no apparent national significance. But as I campaigned in 1966, I was impressed by the performance of a man who was campaigning for Republicans on a much larger scale. This was the same man I had supported for President in 1960 and 1964: Richard Nixon. I had great respect for Michigan's Governor George Romney, who made Alaska an early port of call before dropping out of the 1968 campaign. We raced dogsleds during the Fur Rendezvous, and I was accused of throwing the race to Romney. I didn't throw the race; Romney didn't realize that when I yelled "Trail!" I meant "Get out of my way and let me pass!" This was the only race he won in 1968. Then Nelson Rockefeller dropped out too, for the time being, and it all came together. That is why I told Dick Nixon, when we met in Milwaukie, Oregon, "You're going to be the next President."

If you make a decision for the few, generally it is at the expense of the many. But if you make a decision for the general public, it will also benefit the few.

CHAPTER **4**

The Invisible Line

I felt lucky about predicting the results of presidential elections. I had not missed one since 1928, when I was passing out Hoover pencils as a boy in Kansas but secretly rooting for Al Smith, who had about as much chance as Goldwater had in 1964. I even correctly called the Harry Truman upset in 1948. In 1968 the nature of the Republican Party convention at Miami Beach made Richard Nixon's nomination a sure thing; and given the political combinations that already existed or were taking shape, it was almost impossible for him to avoid being elected.

What I had not counted on was going to Washington myself; I had been elected

Governor of Alaska for a four-year term, and I had occupied the office for a few days less than two years when I got that Thanksgiving-weekend telephone call from the President-elect informing me that I was to become Secretary of the Interior.

The Department of the Interior in Washington, D.C., is a great fortresslike building covering an entire city block. It was finished by the Old Curmudgeon, Interior Secretary Harold L. Ickes, in 1937. Interior, with its 70,000 employees throughout the country and a multitude of agencies ranging from the Bureau of Mines to the National Park Service, has always been one of the most heavy-footed and most obscure departments in the federal system. I predicted in a speech that it would be called the romance department of the 1970's and within a year we were to make it come alive.

When I took office in 1969, pollution was no longer a joke; this was made clear by the nature of my confirmation hearings. It was aggravating millions of Americans; frustration and hostility toward government and industry were growing. The nation was desperately looking for leadership, and I decided that we would take that lead.

Pollution control, however, was by no means the private domain of Interior. The public sometimes criticized us for not taking action against air pollution, inefficient solid waste disposal and harmful pesticides. Actually, we had no mandate in these areas. They were assigned to Health, Education and Welfare and the Department of Agriculture. But we did have the Federal Water Pollution Control Administration, and it was principally with this vehicle that we set out to reverse a trend in America.

Interior was created in 1849 to look after the public lands, which were mostly in the central and western part of the United States. As industry began to gain in importance at the turn of the century, it turned more and more of its attention to this department. It was not long before Interior was said — with some truth — to be in the pocket of big business. Public demand was for goods and services derived from the natural resources of America, and the Interior Department was responsible for managing the bulk of those resources. It is not fair to label the developing Interior-industry relationship as an unholy alliance. But as the 20th century progressed, the private interests called more and more of the shots. It began to appear that these interests owned America.

I knew differently. The problem was to restore a just and fair balance in the management of those things owned by 200 million Americans—the public lands, the Continental Shelf and the properties that are privately owned but can be abused in such a way as to infringe upon the rights of others.

Unlike some strong voices being raised, I did not look upon American industry as a collection of predators. Nor did I agree with people who called the conservationists "a bunch of freaks." I was for responsibility on the part of industry for our natural environment, and I was for responsibility on the part of conservationists for all the needs of the public. I was for *balance*, and the challenge was to find and define it.

1. 'Getting Their Attention'

Contrary to my tarred image, I had never been personally involved in the oil business. But I knew the men who were, and I knew the business. I have always had a healthy respect for America's oil men. The men at the top are some of the most talented in the country. The men in the second and third echelons can be some of the roughest and toughest men in the world. I like them and respect them, but I have never been awed by their power and influence. In fact, power and influence on this scale have always concerned me — and should be a national concern. I made this point many times in talks with John Ehrlichman, President Nixon's Chief Counselor on Domestic Affairs.

One thing these tough but able oil men respect is equal toughness. But first you have to get their attention. I got it in 1968 at the Republican National Convention in Miami Beach.

Prior to the convention I had been named to the Resolutions Committee as chairman of the Subcommittee on Natural Resources and Agriculture. In the weeks preceding the convention, the platform and its individual planks were rewritten many times. When we finally got down to the final version, Senator Karl Mundt of North Dakota, a member of the subcommittee, wanted to do yet another draft of the agricultural policy plank. The committee did not object — and it did not object when I asked for the privilege of rewriting the natural resources plank.

My experience as Governor of Alaska, when I had been unable to get the attention of the oil companies concerning an extension of the Alaska Railroad — which would have saved the public millions of dollars and protected the Alaska environment at the same time — made me all the more determined to let them know that a balance was necessary. The needs of all the public had to become the concern of oil men and the concern of all industry. Yet I had not found the "handle" to make them concerned.

I revised the resources plank to put in two short paragraphs calling for a national fisheries policy and a polar development policy, and I added the word "Eskimo" to the section concerning Indians—the first time the Eskimo had ever been mentioned in a party platform. Then I put through the final draft for retyping.

When it came back to me, I noticed that something was missing. There was no reference at all to the controversial oil depletion allowance. The typist had dropped it by accident.

I had not ordered this, because I knew some kind of depletion allowance was needed. However, I did feel that the oil industry should be using more of the money for research purposes. I suddenly realized that I found my "handle" to get attention, so I said nothing.

The plank was approved by the full Resolutions Committee without anyone noticing the omission. It was later spotted by Senator John Tower of Texas. Obviously disturbed, he hurried to the committee chairman, Senator Everett Dirksen of Illinois, and whispered into his ear. "Find out what the Governor wants," Dirksen growled.

Senator Tower came over and asked.

I replied, "I don't want anything."

Tower relayed my comment back to Dirksen, who scowled and repeated, "Find out what the Governor wants!"

The second time the Senator came back, I said, "I want nothing except the oil industry's attention."

Bryce Harlow, who was already one of Richard Nixon's aides, came to me and asked, "What happened?"

"I don't know," I said.

I did know that the platform plank could be altered at this point only with the permission of the subcommittee chairman — myself — or through the presentation of a minority report that would go before the full convention and on national television. I didn't think anyone would want that.

Senator Dirksen seemed very thoughtful when he approached me after an unscheduled adjournment. He said, "If I can arrange a meeting with the major oil company heads within twenty-four hours, will that satisfy you?"

At six o'clock the following evening I walked three doors down from my suite in the Fontainebleau Hotel to Dirksen's suite.

The Senator met me outside his door, saying: "Wally, be as tough as you want to be. I'm with you. They've never been in such a position." As we walked into the room, he said, "Gentlemen, you have a problem, and I'm supporting the Governor."

I proceeded to talk to the representatives of the oil companies. "I will respect the man who disagrees with me after he's heard my argument, but I will not respect anyone who rejects a reasoned proposal out of hand without hearing it through. I don't want campaign contributions: I don't want any personal help; I want nothing but your assurance that you will at least listen to our proposals for developing and protecting Alaska."

They listened and they well understood my point. The reference to oil depletion went back into the platform.

When all this was going on, I had no idea that within a few months I would be Secretary of the Interior and responsible to America for protecting her waters from pollution of any kind—especially oil. Then suddenly I was Secretary, and my first big problem involved oil.

2. Santa Barbara

The Santa Barbara blowout will be remembered as an awakening of the American people. As oil spilled into the Santa Barbara Channel, the nation was given a dramatic illustration of what pollution could do to an area of great natural beauty. Even more important, the behind-the-scenes battle over the Santa Barbara incident, which is less well known, became a turning point in the relationship between government and industry.

Union Oil's Platform A "blew out" on January 27, 1969—four days after I was confirmed. We could not gauge the seriousness of the problem immediately, so we asked for a continuing flow of information. I was dead tired, and so was my executive assistant, Carl McMurray. We had both been going for twenty hours out of twenty-four since the confirmation hearings began on January 15. We were working on adrenalin, not physical energy.

I went to Camp David, the President's retreat, to try to get a couple of days rest. My stay, however, was short-lived.

Carl had remained at the office at Interior; by now he was getting reports from Santa Barbara every half hour. On Sunday morning, February 2, I was called to the telephone. It was Carl. "I hate to do this, but things look bad. Santa Barbara appears to be the kind of thing you would want to take a look at. It's like the flood at Fairbanks."

I said: "I'm on my way. Get me an airplane." By the time I got back to Washington, a White House Jet Star was waiting. So were Ed Weinberg, my holdover Solicitor from the preceding Administration, and Tom Holley, whom McMurray had brought up from the Bureau of Outdoor Recreation to handle our heavy mail load.

I was not sure of my legal authority, and on the way to California I asked Weinberg how I could get at this thing if I needed to shut down the drilling. Weinberg seemed to think I would be on shaky legal ground.

We arrived in Santa Barbara about nine in the evening to find a huge crowd milling around and carrying protest signs, plus newsmen with their notebooks and microphones. Tom Holley had about five copies of a press release, but I don't think he ever had a chance to hand them out. We were driven downtown to the Coast Guard station for a briefing, then made it to our hotel about one in the morning. Fred Hartley, president of Union Oil, was waiting for me. I told him, "Fred, if this is as bad as I've heard, I'm going to shut you down." Hartley said something about my not having the authority.

"Well, by God," I said, "I just gave myself that authority."

The next morning Ed Weinberg and I got into a Coast Guard plane to fly over the oil slick while Tom Holley stayed behind to cope with a swarm of reporters. It took only a few minutes in the air over the Santa Barbara Channel to fill me full of the situation — the oil, the terrible mess, the justified outrage of the people in Santa Barbara. I was also outraged by what I sensed to be bureaucratic resistance on the site to do anything positive about a crime committed against nature. Some people had worked so closely with the oil men for so many years that they simply could not conceive of a Secretary of the Interior doing something drastic about an oil slick.

At that time I thanked God I had known something about the total problem before I got to Washington. Otherwise, I might have overreacted and hurt one side or the other. When the Coast Guard plane landed after the flight over the slick, I was prepared to walk that invisible line of authority.

Tom Holley got aboard the plane and asked me what I was going to do. I said, "I'm going to announce that I'm shutting them down." Holley was afraid I could not do it. "The hell I can't," I replied.

I got off the plane, walked to the microphones and told the newsmen that the slick was even worse than I had been led to believe. It was obvious to me that if the wind shifted, the oil was going to hit the Santa Barbara beach. I said that I intended to call the chief executive officers of the oil companies involved and advised them to suspend operations immediately. The reporters gasped and began to flood me with questions about "How?" I kept saying: "They're not going to operate again, and I'm calling them to tell them that. I'm not asking them; I'm telling them."

We went back to the hotel. I talked to some of the oil company heads directly and got the others on long-distance telephone. By noon Monday I had—or thought I had—voluntary commitments from six oil company presidents to stop drilling in the channel until we could assess the geological damage and find out whether the companies were abiding by the drilling regulations. We made an exception permitting Union Oil to drill a relief well to stop the oil leakage that was already going on because of what happened at Platform A.

Tom Holley typed out a news release himself and handed it out as we boarded our Jet Star for the return flight to Washington Monday afternoon. When we arrived in Washington I went straight home.

On Tuesday morning Carl McMurray went into his office at Interior and learned that many rigs had resumed operations in the channel "under maximum safety controls" and that others were getting under way. Carl informed me when I arrived at my office, and I was furious. The decision to permit resumption of drilling was taken by

Eugene Standley, Chief Interior Department Engineer on the scene.

The immediate problem was to get more geological information. I called in Dr. William Pecora, director of the United States Geological Survey,[1] and got all the information he could give me. It became obvious that if the Santa Barbara Channel rigs were operating in accordance with existing regulations, we had to upgrade the regulations. These were tragically inadequate.

Then I got a call from Fred Hartley, telling me that the other companies had resumed drilling. I already knew that, but I hit the ceiling again. Something had to be done to stop this, but what? What were the limits of *my* authority? I did not know them, and I had to find out.

It was at this point that I started leaning hard on Interior's Solicitor, Ed Weinberg. This went on all day Wednesday February 5, while the citizens of Santa Barbara were

[1] *Now Under Secretary of the Interior.*

getting madder and madder. It appeared to them that I had sold out to the oil companies.

On Thursday morning I told Carl McMurray, "Get Weinberg in here."

Weinberg came, and I asked him again what I could do to stop this business. "Don't tell me that as Secretary of the Interior I can't stop people from polluting the waters. You tell me how to do it."

He said: "I don't know of any way you can do it. They are operating within the lease."

"Well, can I change the lease?"

"You would have to get the oil companies to agree."

"Dammit, can't I terminate the lease? Isn't there any provision in there that says if they are damaging the environment we can just stop the lease?"

Weinberg then came up with precisely the kind of caution I did not want to hear. "You realize," he said, "that the Director of the Bureau of the Budget is not going to take kindly to this. You would be losing money that they have projected against your budget and you would open yourself to a suit from the oil companies to recover the money they've already invested."

"I don't give a damn," I said. "If I have to go talk to the Director of the Bureau of the Budget I will, but I just want to know what I can talk to him about. Tell me what the law is!"

Again Weinberg did not produce anything, so I turned to McMurray and said, "Get him out of here." They left.

Sitting there alone, I was boiling with frustration. I thought, "There's got to be a way." I punched a button and placed a call to Richard Kleindienst, the new Deputy Attorney General. I explained the situation to him. "All I want is some way to stop them right now, and some way to keep them from starting again until I determine that it is safe for them to do so. That's all."

I was so sure that Kleindienst would find what I needed that I told the Interior Department's information officer, Alex Troffey, to get going on a press release immediately. About ten o'clock Thursday night I called Kleindienst again. He said the opinion was ready, and I sent one of the associate solicitors, Raymond Coulter, down to Justice to pick it up.

There *was* a protection clause in the lease giving us the authority we needed. I did not have the authority to close down the drilling rigs because they were polluting the water, but ironically I did have the authority to close them down if they were wasting the oil — which they were. What a sad commentary on the attitudes toward the environment which I inherited as Secretary! I stopped the drilling by executive order even as we were getting out the news release for Friday morning publication.

The next day we began a complete revision of the existing regulations to provide much tougher specifications for offshore oil drilling. But I obviously needed a better weapon to deal with oil spills immediately after they occurred. Cleaning up a spill cannot wait for a court judge to decide who is liable. It has to be done before the pollution kills the wildlife and ruins the beaches. For this reason I demanded that all companies who hold drilling leases on the outer Continental Shelf accept liability for cleanup *even before the cause of a spill is determined.* This became known in short as "absolute liability without cause." It also became one of the most controversial topics in both the executive and legislative branches of the federal government.

Senator Dirksen called when he heard about it and said: "Wally, you're going too far. This could either wipe out the industry or the Administration. It may even be unconstitutional."

I replied, "That's a debatable point, but not if industry accepts it." Then I said to the Senator, "Give me four months to try to sell this and I'll turn the corner."

Don Dunlop, my scientific advisor, was getting calls from people in the oil industry: "What's with this guy Hickel? What's this unlimited liability business? What's that bastard trying to do to us?" Dunlop would say: "Gentlemen, he's trying to be fair with you, but he's firm. He thinks if there's oil on the water, you've got to clean it up. We'll find out later who spilled it. It's that simple."

The following weeks and months I met individually with nearly every major oil company president or chairman of the board in this country, and several from abroad. I explained the situation. Business as usual, as practiced since the turn of the century, was no longer good enough. This was an entirely new ball game. The rewards in the past had come to those who could get the best products to the market fastest and cheapest. With that attitude, the environment was not something to be protected but exploited. Now the priorities in America were shifting. The public would no longer stand for the destruction of the resources and beauty of an area. Protecting the environment must now become part of the cost of doing business.

Is it right to destroy the air and water and land that belong to all of us? This might make a business more profitable, but success that abuses other people's rights is not true success and is not acceptable to the public.

In response to my arguments, I was flooded with facts and figures relating to the economics of oil production. But I explained that in dealing with offshore drilling, economics could not be the only consideration. The companies were paying for the use of something that was not just theirs. They only had a lease on public property.

When I explained the situation to Mike Halbouty, a respected geologist and independent operator from Houston, Texas, his first reaction was that this would break the independent. Operations would become uninsurable; insurance companies would cancel policies. I listened and then asked, "Mike, what are your liabilities now?"

He said: "Well, generally we have a deductible policy. Possibly $25,000 deductible."

"No, Mike. What are your limits of liability?"

"Whatever it costs to clean it up."

"How much?" I asked.

"Whatever it costs to clean it up!" he said. "The only thing we pay is the deduction in the premium."

"Mike, isn't that in essence absolute liability?"

Astonished, he looked at me and admitted, "Yes, I think you're right."

"Mike," I said, "all I'm trying to do is state it so there won't be any argument in case there is a catastrophe on the outer

172

Continental Shelf. I am spelling it out in the language you are saying you have already accepted! The American public cannot take a chance that there could be an argument about who would clean up pollution in case of a disaster, because it might be months before a court could make the decision."

"Absolute liability without cause" was acceptable because it was fair. If all competitors abide by a regulation, then an individual competitor can live with it. If one is favored, the others are weakened or destroyed.

About a month before Senator Dirksen died, he talked to me and said, "Wally, I'm not saying you won a battle, but I am saying I think you've turned a corner."

I replied, "Senator, it's been a tough battle."

It had been tough and it continued to be. I was receiving vibrations from leading Republicans who feared I was jeopardizing a major source of campaign funds. It is at times like this that making a decision for the public good takes guts. It is not the guts of doing or saying it. It is the guts of living with it. I held my ground not to hurt a few but to help all, including the few. In the process we were cleaning up a relationship between business and government. Should the campaign contributor own the person he contributes to? Or should he contribute for fairness in government?

If we had made our decisions at Santa Barbara (or later in the Chevron case) reluctantly, hesitantly or apologetically, we would have been wiped out and the public would have been irrevocably harmed. The oil industry would not have been helped; nor would the Administration. So I made the decision and charged forward with all confidence to say that this was what we were going to do and why.

We went clear over the top, because it was so totally right. When you get down to the naked truth, you let the world know what you are doing and why—and then it becomes acceptable. This, in fact, will strengthen the position of a President or an administration because it builds credibility with the public.

"Absolute liability without cause" is now

acceptable to those in business, and it is totally acceptable to the American people. We began getting letters from people who now felt that someone in government cared, and cared about *all* Americans. The first real test came in February 1970 when an oil spill appeared in the Gulf of Mexico on a lease held by the Humble Oil Company. I called Bill Pecora and said, "Get it cleaned up!"

Government and industry worked together. The best equipment and the necessary manpower were mobilized to do the job, and threatened oyster beds and wildlife areas were saved. Most important was the fact that this incident proved that "absolute liability without cause" worked. It turned out that the oil creating the slick on the Humble lease came not from Humble's offshore operations but from another company's petroleum refinery upriver on the Mississippi.

We heard no more about it. Backed by government regulations permitting third-party legal recourse, the emergency was handled through self-policing and the environment was restored.

The whole absolute liability concept had the effect of prodding the conscience of the oil industry. Before Santa Barbara, oil executives had thought of "spills" only in terms of monetary cost, which was negligible. Not more than $100,000 worth of oil was lost in the Santa Barbara Channel as a result of the Platform A blowout—not a huge sum by oil industry standards. Now the oil men realized that they had been producing offshore for twenty years without adequate consideration for the whole environment.

I was not yet through with the Santa Barbara situation. The California papers implied that I had sold out to the oil companies because limited pumping was resumed on Union Oil's Platform A after the immediate danger had passed and emergency steps had been taken to alleviate the blowout. What they did not understand was that the infamous Platform A *had* to resume pumping. Only the pressure drawdown created by pumping oil could prevent more leakage due to ruptures existing in the substrata and the natural pressure forcing oil upward toward the surface of the seabed. As the furor continued, the press and conservation groups did not know exactly where to stand with regard to what I was doing.

My idea was to do what I felt had to be done and let others judge for themselves. Within the entire field of federal leases that extended from the boundary of State waters at the three-mile limit and out to Santa Cruz Island, drilling and pumping operations remained shut down by our order. We drastically revised and toughened the regulations for offshore oil drilling. We also began initial drafting work on legislation that would be introduced to Congress calling for the federal government to buy back the twenty federal leases beyond the State marine sanctuary in the direction of Santa Cruz.

I never criticized those who attacked me. I did not resent the concern thousands of Santa Barbarans and Californians expressed about the renewed operations of Platform A—in fact, I welcomed it. I was aware of the frustrations they felt. As early as 1955 the people of Santa Barbara had fought against the establishment of offshore rigs on their resort doorstep. I believed they had the right to yell as loudly as they wanted, because they had yelled before the fact.

Putting the truth across proved to be difficult. A group from Santa Barbara flew to Washington to see me on February 19, 1970. They called themselves GOO — "Get Oil Out" — and were led by a number of leading citizens. They demanded that a two-week moratorium be placed on Platform A to prove whether drilling truly prevented oil seepage or whether that argument was a ruse to let Union Oil continue pumping.

The argument was not a ruse; we had had the answer since December 17, 1969, when a minor crack in a pipeline on Platform A's rig caused a three-day stoppage for repairs. Within hours, a sizable oil slick appeared 800 feet east of the platform, originating from fissures in the ocean floor — just as a special advisory panel of geologists and engineers had predicted. When the pumps were reactivated, the seepage stopped.

I laid this evidence before the Santa Barbarans to examine, just as I had put it into a letter to the Los Angeles *Times* dated February 4, 1970. Then I said, "Ladies and gentlemen, I will order the moratorium you are demanding on one condition: that you clean up the water and beaches from the oil pollution that results." The people from Santa Barbara accepted the evidence and returned home with a better understanding of the situation.

Meanwhile, I was getting further and further out on a limb. But when I looked around the public was supporting us.

3. Saving Their Hides

In mid-March 1969 I journeyed into the strangely beautiful and mysterious Everglades, one of our few remaining unique wildernesses. I thought it was time more attention was paid to the plight of the Everglades alligator—not only for the alligator's sake, but in the interest of protecting a life form vital to the ecological balance of this flat tabletop area in southern Florida. At that time it was estimated that poachers were illegally killing the reptiles at a rate of 40,000 a year, selling the hides for $4 to $6 a foot to tanneries outside Florida.

The National Park Service set up a midnight demonstration of poacher patrolling to illustrate the difficulties faced in trying to apprehend the illegal hunters in that remote and dense area. I chose to play the part of poacher. I said, "Give me a five-minute lead and you'll never find me." And they never did. The exercise might have seemed melodramatic, but it attracted national attention to the problem, and the public gave strong support to our efforts to augment the ranger staff to try to stop the illegal slaughter.

My trip drew support for my request to Congress to make interstate shipment of alligator hides illegal as a protection to an endangered wildlife species. It also achieved progress on a ticklish political and economic problem, that of getting enough water for the Everglades to preserve its wildlife and vegetation. In a "summit meeting" at the remote Lost Man's Ranger Station on the Gulf of Mexico, Florida Governor Claude Kirk agreed to help assure the park of sufficient water throughout the year. He concurred that the park should not be at the whim of the Army Corps of Engineers, which controls the water supply from Lake Okeechobee through a network of waterways and canals. The system, built to control floods and to provide water to major agricultural producers in southern Florida, had not adequately taken into account the needs of the park.

But the real significance of my trip to Florida came on March 15, as we lifted off the Gulf in an amphibian airplane and headed for the airport in Miami. As we flew north, I asked the pilot to veer off course to view the jetport being constructed outside of Miami. It was to be the largest in the nation. Miami, one of the great transportation centers of the country, urgently needed such a facility. However, conservation groups and concerned citizens were worried about the chosen location. It was just north of the park. They feared the effects of pollution and the fact that the community which would mushroom up around the jetport and the proposed highway from Miami would serve as a dike cutting off the vital flow of water. As we flew over the site, we could see one runway already complete. The potential long-term damage was obvious.

When I got back to Washington I called Secretary of Transportation John Volpe, a scrappy executive from Massachusetts whom I had known when we were both Governors. Legally this was a matter in John's jurisdiction. There was nothing I could do until the park was actually damaged. Then it would be too late. John understood and really wanted to help.

After months of intensive negotiations, Secretary Volpe and I flew to Miami after winning the President's blessing. In Miami we signed an agreement with Governor Kirk and the Dade County Port Authority. In essence, the agreement stipulated that all concerned parties—the federal government, the State of Florida and the Port Authority—would cooperate in locating a new site for the jetport. In the interim it would be used only for airline training flights, with no further construction or development permitted. I stated at that time, "If it were turned over to Interior, it would be turned back to nature."

The January 1, 1970, *New York Times* called our achievement in the Everglades "an outstanding victory for conservation."

4. *Private Talks with Pearson*

It was after the jetport episode that Drew Pearson came to see me. This was the second time I had met him; our first meeting took place immediately following my confirmation hearings. Mr. Pearson's attitude toward me in his syndicated column had been vicious, pointed and personal. At no time, however, did his writings affect my attitude toward him personally.

It was at the suggestion of my fellow Alaskan, former Senator Ernest Gruening, that I invited Drew Pearson to breakfast after the confirmation hearings. Being an optimist, I jumped at the idea. So Pearson, Senator Ted Stevens, Senator Gruening and I met at my apartment in the Sheraton-Park Hotel.

I found Mr. Pearson very much a gentleman. I had made up my mind that I would not discuss any comments he had made about me. The meeting lasted about an hour and a half, and I talked about all the progressive things I wanted to do in Interior. This quite surprised him, and I realized during the conversation that he wanted to tell me something. I sensed an apology coming, but I did not want him to say the words.

Senator Gruening explained to him my record as Governor of Alaska and my fight for the general public good. Ted Stevens explained our actions together, since he was Republican majority leader in the Alaska House of Representatives when I was Governor. The conversation focused on how we were going to handle the problems that had been raised during my confirmation hearings. In fact, Ted Stevens made this statement: "Hell, Mr. Pearson, you just really don't know how tough Wally Hickel is!"

As we were leaving my apartment and I was walking toward my limousine out front, Pearson grabbed my arm and said, "Well, Mr. Secretary, I'd like to do . . ."

I cut off the conversation, because I did not want Pearson to apologize for anything he had written about me. I really did not want him to be embarrassed. I said, "Mr. Pearson, I thank you for coming to breakfast, and I'll be looking forward to seeing you again." I climbed into my limousine and I heard him say in a low voice, "I'd really like to help."

Then, early in April 1969, Drew Pearson to my surprise arrived in my outer office. He wanted to congratulate me on the actions we had taken not only in Santa Barbara, but on my approach to the alligators in Florida and the Miami jetport. "You're going in the right direction. I want to compliment you." The meeting did not last more than a few minutes.

I next saw Pearson, at his request, on July 14, 1969. It was the most unusual meeting I had ever had with a person in his capacity. He came in and said: "Mr. Secretary, I truly want to help you solve the problems you are approaching. You seem to really care and understand the situation that confronts the American public."

He went on: "Writing the column, that's a simple thing. I will either do that in supporting your causes or I'll go out and

185

talk to the American public. I'll give up what I'm doing now and get on radio or TV or anything you might want done to help get across the message. I really want to do this. It's something that just feels like . . ." he hesitated. ". . . something I not only want to do, but I have the ability to help."

His voice had a lot of compassion in it, and there was no doubt that he really meant what he said. I was deeply moved and only thinking about his wanting to help. He said, "After you've given this plan some thought, just tell me what you want me to do and I'll do it no matter what it would cost me personally."

I was never to see him again. He died on September 1.

5. Prosecuting the Polluters

There really are very few new laws needed to straighten out the environmental problems we have in America. So often a law is an excuse *not* to do something, and the great weakness of government is that those who sit in the decision-making chairs are surrounded by layers of reasons not to do something.

I am unimpressed by those who feel that laws alone can change our society. Only men can change it, and if their intention is right they can usually find the means of change in laws already on the books. It would have been easy to waste our time drafting and fighting for legislation designed to eliminate all water pollution.

Instead, we dusted off the 1899 Refuse Act for the teeth we needed to straighten out the nation's water problems. That was law enough. All that was lacking was guys with guts. The laws are there. What is needed is the men — men with an attitude.

On September 4, 1969, I backed up my warning that the government would "prosecute those who pollute" by ordering hearings on charges against a municipality, four steel companies and a mining firm accused of polluting waters. We threatened court action against the City of Toledo, the Interlake Steel Company on the Maumee River, the Republic Steel Corporation, the Jones and Laughlin Steel Company on the Cuyahoga River and the United States

Steel Corporation—all intrastate cases in Ohio. The mining firm was Eagle-Picher Industries Inc., in Baxter Springs, Kansas—an interstate case since Oklahoma water was involved. Both the Maumee and Cuyahoga rivers in Ohio are tributaries of Lake Erie, one of America's most abused and polluted bodies of water. The Maumee was so bad that the slugs that live on the bottom and survive on garbage were dead, and the Cuyahoga had so much oil in it that it actually caught fire.

The industries and some of the hometown newspapers were furious. So was Ohio Governor Jim Rhodes. He came to see me with a group of businessmen, and they were nearly violent. I gave it to them straight. Is it right, I asked, to accept those things of public trust as ours to plunder? Answering my own question, I continued: "No! You've got to clean it up!"

Hearings were held. Those violating water quality standards were given 180 days to present acceptable plans to eliminate pollution; otherwise I would go directly to the Attorney General to arrange court actions to be filed by the Justice Department.

The hearings were informal, and they proved all over again that the public *wants* to be included. People want to know what is happening. They want the chance to express their concerns about a problem, or their approaches to an answer. Once this is done, solutions are found. This was true in the case of the City of Toledo and the industries mentioned. Within the time span I set, all of them came to us with intelligent plans to meet water quality standards.

6. *The Shrimp Boats Are Coming*

Mendel Rivers, the powerful Congressman from South Carolina, was the man the White House said would stop whatever I wanted to do at Santa Barbara. He is now either in heaven or in hell, and I hope it is heaven because I gave him hell. We crossed swords when a German company planned to establish a major petrochemical complex on Hilton Head, South Carolina, one of the most beautiful locations on the Eastern seashore. This was a factory that would provide needed employment and chemical products for the Southeastern United States. I had no complaint with the company's intentions. But when the designs and engineering plans were studied by our technical staff, it was evident that the Badische Analin and Soda Fabrik (BASF) planned to discharge effluent into the waters and build a navigation canal that would threaten the marine life of Hilton Head.

This issue came to our attention when the citizens of the area rose up in protest. They picketed and pleaded for someone in government to notice what was happening. The oyster beds and the shrimp were in danger, and one of the most important estuaries in terms of wildlife management was threatened. To me, it was a classic case of developing one resource at the expense of others.

I wrote to Hans Lautenschlager, the president of BASF, on March 26, 1970. I said in part:

The area in question is a splendid estuary, virtually free of pollution. . . . Our scientists and engineers advise that it is technically feasible to construct a plant with no effluent. This would completely protect the existing water quality of the area. This Department would strenuously oppose any action which would result in degradation of that water quality. . . . Construction of proposed navigation channels to serve your plant could damage the estuarine environment by destroying fish and wildlife habitats. . . . This Department will oppose strenuously any proposal for channel dredging which would cause environmental damage or which would cause a significant increase in environmental hazards.

The same day I wrote to Robert McNair, Governor of South Carolina:

Over and above my statutory responsibilities, I am very much concerned personally with the need expressed by the President that the task of cleaning up or preserving our environment calls for a total mobilization by all of us and involves governments at every level.

I had no legal power to prevent the plant from being built improperly, but I felt it my duty to let the company know that if the plant did pollute once it was operating, it would have to answer to me.

Within days, Mendel Rivers was on the telephone. He explained that he had as much concern for the environment as I, and that he knew better than I did what was good for his State. But I insisted that the company was not including environmental protection in its cost of doing business, and that the destruction of one natural resource such as oyster beds, in the name of developing another resource, was not going to be condoned by the Department — and did not need to happen.

Shortly thereafter, a shrimp boat left Hilton Head and sailed north for Washington, D.C. On April 27, 1970, I interrupted a heavy schedule to go down to a dock on the Potomac River. As I arrived, the shrimp boat was just pulling up. A crew of both whites and blacks was aboard. They jumped on the pier, shook my hand and said, "We bring the gratitude of the people of South Carolina." They handed me two large cardboard boxes. Inside were 45,000 signatures of local residents expressing their thanks. I was overwhelmed by their gesture, and I heard no more from Mendel Rivers.

7. 'Return It Like You Found It'

The polluters of the past were providing goods and services for the public, oblivious to the environmental consequences of their actions. I cannot blame them. Even twenty years ago the industrial and municipal effluent being discharged into public waters was in most cases too little to pollute. Nature has a built-in system to break up and clear away pollution. But today it is a different story. Many of our rivers and lakes have passed the level of tolerance, and even the oceans are in danger. Today's polluters cannot avoid the issue of environmental responsibility. The additional cost to protect the environment must now and forever be included in the cost of any item.

The Florida Power and Light Company had started building a six-mile canal to discharge "hot water" from its Turkey

Point nuclear-generating plant into the waters lying next to the Miami-Card Sound and the beautiful and often misused Biscayne Bay. The Biscayne Bay National Monument, which lies between Key Biscayne and Key Largo, was jam-packed with marine life and was now threatened with thermal pollution.

This brand of pollution is frequently misunderstood. It comes from overheating water beyond the tolerances of indigenous plant and animal life. Generally a five-degree rise in water temperature is enough to create thermal pollution, and sometimes a rise of one or two degrees will do so. In any event, when water is too warm to support the life systems that live therein, it becomes polluted. This issue has taken on a new meaning with the advent of nuclear-generating plants. These facilities demand enormous quanties of water for cooling purposes. Standard procedure is to take the water of a river, a lake or an ocean, pump it through the plant, let it absorb the heat and return it to where it came from.

Technology has devised ways of avoiding thermal pollution through the use of cooling ponds or towers, both of which are expensive. I believe this expense is acceptable to the consumer. The average person today is willing to pay a few cents more per month for energy if the creation of that power does not pollute the air or the water of his area.

We took Florida Power and Light to court. The reasoning behind our case was simple: You do not own the water; the public does. *We are not saying that you cannot use the water.* We say use it. And we may not even charge you for its use. *But—return it like you found it.* That's the cost of doing business.

8. Protection, Not Punishment

So much seemed to happen in February 1970. On February 11, a Chevron Oil Company rig in the Gulf of Mexico just off Louisiana caught fire. For weeks the fire raged. Finally it was blown out with explosives by the great oil fire fighter Paul ("Red") Adair. The damage caused a significant spill.

As soon as we heard of the fire, I sent a

team of personnel from various Interior bureaus to the scene. An investigation brought out that the fire had been caused because the platform was not equipped with a storm choke. This small device is absolutely critical to a safe operation. In the event of a storm or other calamity, the choke cuts off the oil supply; in this case it would have snuffed out the fire.

This situation was different from the one at Santa Barbara. The latter was a drilling blowout that we followed up with new, strict regulations. The Chevron fire took place on a production rig.

Concerned about the neglect on the one platform, we closed down the whole field and ran a check of safety devices on many of the 7,000 offshore oil rigs in the Gulf. We were staggered to discover that literally hundreds of rigs were operating without chokes. Oil can be pumped out somewhat faster without the choke, which also creates a small maintenance problem. In a great many cases the chokes were apparently taken out of the rigs to make up for production time lost during Hurricane Camille in August 1969. This was negligence of the highest order.

I flew down to take a personal look. In the airplane on the way back to Washington, I told Bill Pecora, "You've got to hit them with a two-by-four to make them believe you." I was determined to prosecute, but it disturbed me that this case might go to court and drag on for months or even years without being resolved.

I called in my new Solicitor, Mitch Melich, and explained my dilemma. Mitch said, "You can always take it to the grand jury." I jumped at the idea. A grand jury has the power of subpoena to assemble evidence and return an indictment for the public to see. I knew that the fight had to be out in the open or it would not be won at all.

At this point I asked John Connally to come to see me. Connally, a former Governor of Texas who later was to become Secretary of the Treasury in the Nixon Cabinet, probably knows the oil industry and its leaders as well as any man in America. He is an astute lawyer, and when I outlined to him the evidence from the Gulf and told him that I was going to prosecute, he agreed with my decision.

I said, "John, go tell your people the story."

I reached Attorney General John Mitchell in Florida and said: "John, get me the best young lawyer you have in the Justice Department. I'm taking Chevron to the grand jury." The case set an historic precedent. Chevron was indicted on 900 counts and was found guilty. The fine was $1 million. But what hurt the oil companies far worse than any fine was the headline treatment the newspapers gave the case. The oil men had abused a public trust.

This was not a case of punishing anybody. It was a case of not permitting an oil company to punish 200 million Americans. It was fascinating to me that the key to victory in all these struggles with America's industrial giants was keeping the facts out in the open where the press and the public could see what was happening. The day of behind-the-scenes government and closed-door leadership is not only out of date but no longer tolerable. The public wants and deserves decisions made in the best interest of all. The public can help them happen. And the oil industry, on the whole, feels the same way.

There were those who disliked our actions. They put pressure on the White House and they put pressure on us. On February 12, 1970, the day after we learned of the Chevron fire, I was meeting with my staff in my office on the sixth floor of the Interior Building. We had just gone through a difficult struggle within the executive branch over the budget and the President's State of the Union message. It was becoming clear that we were not getting the backing we felt we were entitled to from many of President Nixon's top advisors. Cool winds were blowing our way, and we did not fully understand them. Some of my staff began to discuss this. It was obvious they were being frustrated.

I said: "For God's sake, don't get gun-shy! When you get your head squared off, don't overreact. *Go* when we feel something is right. We must be strong, forceful and deliberate. We only make gains when we don't hold off. I say *let's keep moving!*"

That is exactly what we did.

BOOK **2**

Return It to Us

interests. Those interests can be anybody large or small, an individual conglomerate or an individual rancher.

It was Abraham Lincoln's theory that government should only do those things that private enterprise cannot do or cannot do so well. This does not mean total involvement by government in private enterprise, but it does mean guidance and regulation. We have the greatest incentive system ever put together on earth, but free enterprise allowed to run totally free will destroy itself.

The thrust of government must change so that we act positively instead of reacting negatively. We must make an inventory of all those things we own. The task of putting together such a catalogue of assets is entirely possible with the technology we now have available — computer systems, satellites and instant communication. Once the inventory is complete, judgments can be made on what is the highest and best use of all those assets. These judgments must be reached with the help of public hearings to get a balanced understanding of the primary needs of a local area as well as the requirements of the nation as a whole.

The lack of a broad inventory led to the Santa Barbara disaster. Overruling any other consideration, the federal government evaluated the oil-rich Continental Shelf beyond the Santa Barbara marine sanctuary only in terms of income. This is the result of short-term, stopgap decision-making, which in government is usually motivated by the need to balance budgets.

The Department of the Interior is responsible for most of America's resources, both *renewable* items that are alive (such as trees and fish) and *depletable* resources such as oil and ore.[1] At the same time, Interior is in charge of the resources that restore the spirit of man and that must be cared for and conserved, such as the great parks and preserves from the Everglades on the southern tip of Florida to the 9.5 million-acre Arctic National Wildlife Range in the northeast corner of Alaska.

The Secretary of the Interior thus has a dual responsibility for sensible use and

[1] *Major exception: the Forest Service in the Department of Agriculture.*

conservation of these resources. This is as it should be. He is supposed to bring into the office the widest possible perspective in assessing the overall needs of America. It is his obligation to represent the total public need, not only with regard to fuel and raw materials required to feed, clothe, house and transport the people, but with respect for such things as the wilderness and wildlife that contribute to the environment of the heart, the mind and the soul.

1. Parks to the People

One of the realities of modern America is that the wide-open spaces are not accessible to the majority of our citizens. Most of our great national parks are located in the West or the North, out of reach of much of the 85 percent of our population who live in urban areas. Although millions of Americans are able to travel during their holidays to visit these parks, many millions more are restricted in their travels and unable to get there.

These millions need open spaces, and it was with that in mind that I launched a program called "Parks to the People," designed to establish new parks in or adjacent to America's great metropolitan areas. Federal and state lands being used for military and other purposes were surveyed as potential park property. The first two major projects we undertook were Gateway East and Gateway West. Gateway East was the proposed Gateway National Recreation Area just south and east of the New York City limits, a few steps from the door-steps of millions of urban dwellers. Gateway West was a project to incorporate San Francisco Bay with federal properties and turn it into a vast recreation and scenic area.

I will never forget the time Mayor John Lindsay of New York and I walked the beaches of Breezy Point examining the potential of the Gateway National Recreation Area. The date was May 13, 1969. Mayor Lindsay was enthusiastic about the entire concept, and he outlined his ideas for mass rapid transit which, for a minimum fare, would transport the millions who are isolated in metropolitan New York to the open spaces of air, beach and water on Sandy Hook, Breezy Point and Jamaica Bay.

John and I sprinted down the beach, laughing like a couple of kids and drinking in the fresh air coming off the sea. To me, this project was an example of imaginative government at its best, because it would tackle the deepest causes of our urban crisis. *The issue is people.* And the answer lies in those projects that inspire people and bring out the best in them, refreshing their spirits and giving them new perspectives. This Gateway project was also exciting to me because it was attainable. The properties were available and the financing was within reach.

2. A Great Deception

The financing of park and recreation land acquisition was perhaps the biggest piece of unfinished business I found waiting for me when I took over as Secretary of the Interior. The American people have been misled terribly through the legislative game of authorizing without appropriating. A citizen, hearing the announcement that such-and-such national park has been authorized, believes it has thereby been acquired. Often, only the concept of the park has been authorized. No money has been appropriated to pay for it.

The authorizing of parks without appropriating funds has made many land speculators rich, because once the park is authorized, the land values increase sharply, over a period of years reaching a point where they are ten and sometimes fifty times as expensive as when the park was initially authorized. I believe that when it comes to protecting the American people and protecting America's open spaces, authorization should be tied to appropriation, or else long-term real estate contracts should be signed, a down payment made and the balance paid over a period of ten or twenty years.

A perfect example of how not to help the public was the Point Reyes National Seashore in California. When it was authorized for around $14 million, the funding was not appropriated. For this reason the federal government, over the years, ended up paying $38 million for the property. If we had tied appropriations to authorizations or used long-term real estate contracts, the total payment, including interest, would have been about $17 million, thereby saving $21 million. Besides, we would have been able to use the area for the last ten years.

Another scandalous example is the Cape Cod National Seashore, where the land values have increased nearly a hundredfold since legislation was passed to authorize it. In the name of conservation, the public is being raped.

3. Blackouts and Brownouts

Ever since the famous blackout in New York City in the fall of 1966, the American public has been aware that our national sources of energy are not inexhaustible. The massive influx into American homes and offices of electrical appliances — stereos, television sets, electric hair dryers and especially air conditioners—has put an enormous strain on the national energy supply. Major cities have experienced rationing of electricity known as "brownouts," in which factories are forced to limit their hours of production and homes in some areas have their power supply reduced. Experts are now discussing a national energy crisis, and environmental groups have urged consumers to cut down on the use of electricity.

One of the greatest challenges America faces in the 1970's is to provide the power it needs without wasting the fuel reserves of the nation or desecrating the air and water. It is no secret that some utilities are among the worst polluters in the world, with the result that big-city mayors have unhappy people on the one side as a result of air and water pollution, and unhappy people on the other side demanding power for the whole living of life.

One of the unforeseen problems in the nationwide energy situation has been the setback encountered by nuclear-generating plants. Several years ago the emergence of these plants filled the country with optimism. The influx of electricity produced by nuclear power was predicted to be the solution for the diminishing oil supply and the increasingly difficult chore of retrieving coal. Today less than one percent of the nation's needs are met through nuclear production. And the plants that are operating are facing public hostility because of the fears of radiation and the threat of thermal pollution. It is possible that nuclear power plants will be of growing importance in the next decade. But, in the meantime, we must rely principally on fossil fuels such as oil, coal and gas.

Huge areas of the Rocky Mountain states are covered with a slatelike rock known as oil shale. This promises to be one of the great future sources of petroleum products. The problem here is one of inadequate technology. We already have procedures to extract oil from shale, but the environmental fallout would be intolerable. To produce a minimum of a million barrels of oil a day, a refinery would have to process a million tons of shale. The waste product would be close to a million tons a day of dust—dust as fine as talcum powder. This would create an impossible disposal problem and the environment would be desecrated. Therefore, I vetoed plans to begin oil shale production until this problem could be solved.

4. The Alaska Pipeline

During the twenty-two months I served as Secretary of the Interior, a major project facing me was the proposed petroleum pipeline across Alaska. Stretching 789 miles south from the oil-rich fields of the Prudhoe Bay area on the North Slope to the ice-free port of Valdez, Alaska, the project would be the largest private engineering enterprise in the recorded history of man.[2]

The Alaska pipeline was a project *everyone* seemed to have an opinion about. And the opinions were as violent as they were varied. Some of the more stubborn antipipeline spokesmen were certain that the project would wipe out one of the world's last remaining — and certainly one of the most magnificent — primitive areas. At the

[2] *Other projects larger than the $1 billion to $2 billion pipeline, such as the Aswan High Dam in Egypt, were government undertakings and government-financed.*

other extreme was a "damn-the-torpedoes, all-we-care-about-is-getting-the-oil-out" minority. They felt that "the only people opposed to the pipeline are a bunch of little old ladies in tennis shoes who've never been to Alaska and don't know a damn thing about it."

The discovery of oil and gas at Prudhoe Bay in commercial quantities culminated two decades of intensive search on the North Slope by private industry and government. Secretary Udall authorized the original leases on the North Slope in June 1964. Three years later, on April 14, 1967, as Governor of Alaska, I predicted in a speech before the Wall Street Club in New York City that Prudhoe Bay would become the "Number One Wall Street of the North."

I was confident that a reliable and safe way to get that oil to market could be found, and in April 1969 President Nixon established a federal task force to explore ways to do it. This group consisted of representatives from the departments of the Interior, Commerce, Defense, HEW, Transportation and HUD, plus representation from an ad hoc conservation-industry committee, members of the science and technological group of the National Science Foundation, and the Office of Management and Budget.

I directed the task force to assemble a set of environmental stipulations for the pipeline, and I followed this up with the appointment of a technical advisory board to assemble existing and additional data on geological and engineering factors. More than two dozen federal scientists and engineers, all of them professionals with knowledge of Alaska, labored with dedication to accomplish their task. This group was headed by Bill Pecora of the Geological Survey, who recommended the technical stipulations to be met along the entire route. Maximum safety was the cardinal guideline in these deliberations, and Pecora was one of my strongest supporters for the concept that "Yes, we'll build the pipeline, but only when we know we can do it right." Bill is an expert geologist who shared my view that we can have unspoiled beauty along with development if we honor our obligation of ownership.

In the fall of 1969, Pecora sent me the results of our summer-long study of the permafrost problems and what can happen if you try to cross areas of permanently frozen earth with a hot oil pipeline. If you do not design properly to isolate the pipe from certain varieties of permafrost containing a high quantity of water and glacial silt, the permafrost will turn to soup when thawed. It is like putting a hot pipe across a frozen lake.

Pecora's report made it clear that we still lacked some of the answers. I called Bill at his office in the Government Services Administration Building at 19th and F streets, which is linked to Interior by a long underground tunnel. Bill was in my office in less than five minutes. As he came in, I said: "I want to get to the bottom of this. Stay with it, Bill. I want this done right."

There had never been any question that the pipeline could be built safely—if it were built above ground. The oil companies, of course, wanted to build the pipeline in the traditional way — bury it. I said, "Bury it above ground."

This was possible. After inspecting some Canadian experimental work, I thought the best way was to bury the pipe in a "berm" or raised mound of earth, which would separate the bottom of the four-foot pipe from the permafrost by a kind of insulating roadbed, three feet thick. We felt that it probably would not be necessary to put more than one-fourth of the pipeline above ground to protect permafrost areas. But oil companies still resisted elevated construction on cost grounds. We estimated that the overall cost, including maintenance, would be almost identical.

There was still another serious question. The pipeline would terminate at Valdez, which is a highly active seismic zone and therefore earthquake-prone. Would an earthquake cause a major spillage disaster?

The answer was that if the pipeline were elevated in the earthquake zone as well as over the permafrost farther north, seismic dangers could be reduced to a minimum. Valves would be automatically or manually activated to reduce the spill in the event of a pipe break, and dikes could be constructed to channel the flow of oil into containment basins.

The argument was still unresolved when I left Interior. There were many pressures both for and against the pipeline: from preservationists and conservationists, from within the oil industry, and from the folks back home in Alaska. My correspondence showed that a majority of Americans shared my conviction that the pipeline deserved to be built, but only with proper respect for the environment.

In the May 1970 issue of *Harper's*, Lewis Lapham wrote in an article entitled "Alaska: Politicians and Natives, Money and Oil":

The frontier conception of the wilderness differs appreciably from the polite regrets so often heard in New York and Washington. . . . In an Anchorage bar I remember one man saying, "Two years ago it was the hostile, frozen North. Now all of a sudden it's the goddamned delicate tundra."

Ironically, it is both. It *can* be hostile if you are unprepared to cope with the unique conditions of the Arctic. And yet, it is also delicate, as witnessed by the scars left by earlier, less careful explorers.

Our problems in getting an environmentally safe pipeline were compounded by difficulties with the oil companies involved. In the early days of the pipeline proposal, it became evident that Trans Alaska Pipeline System (TAPS), the organization seeking to build the line, was concerned only with getting a permit—not with designing a safe line *first*—before a spadeful of dirt was turned. As one independent oil operator put it during a private meeting in my office in Washington, "It's been a tradition in the business for those guys to go out, in Saudi Arabia, Texas, Kansas or wherever, and build a line, and then go back and fix the problems *after* they occur." We had to turn this attitude around—and we eventually did. But we also had another problem: the organizational tables of TAPS itself, or rather the lack of one.

Organized in the fall of 1968 by three oil companies, Atlantic-Richfield, Humble (a wholly-owned subsidiary of Standard Oil of New Jersey) and British Petroleum, the Trans Alaska Pipeline System was merely a loose consortium, operating under a gentlemen's agreement with no formal corporate structure. This meant we were faced with "decision by committee" — a shortcoming we were all too familiar with in the halls of government. This was an unwieldy situation at best, and it was made more difficult early in 1970 when five more companies joined the consortium — Mobil Oil, Phillips Petroleum, Union Oil of California, Amerada Hess and Home Oil of Canada. (Later, in 1970, Home Oil sold out its 2 percent interest to the others.)

With seven Indians and no chief it was difficult to get anything done, particularly as far as getting technical data was concerned. There was no single spokesman or executive who had the authority to say, "Okay, this is what TAPS will do." By the time all the principals could be telephoned in Texas, New York, California and London, it could take weeks just to get an agreement on what color to paint the toilets in the construction camps.

The situation was finally corrected when "taps" was played for TAPS in August 1970. In its place was created the Alyeska Pipe Line Service Company (ALPS), a legal corporate entity representing seven companies and able to speak for itself.[3]

5. *The Reason Why*

I could understand the fear and concern of many Americans regarding the pipeline project. It would cross the desolate North Slope, the Brooks Range and vast areas of permafrost, spanning more than 300 streams. Like a parachute jump, the job had to be done right the first time. I also considered it totally reasonable and fair that Alaskans should have an opportunity to enrich the land they love and to share its great natural wealth and beauty, both for their own advancement and for the benefits

[3] *Participants in ALPS and their respective shares: B-P Pipe Line Company (British Petroleum), 28.08 percent; Arco Pipe Line Company (earlier Atlantic-Richfield), 28.08 percent; Humble Pipe Line Company, 25.52*

it would bring to the entire nation.

Fear generally comes from the lack of knowledge. And there are a great many Americans who lack knowledge about the Arctic. I dream of the day when man will change his attitude toward the Arctic and polar regions. It has begun. Today we see emerging the same romance and challenge in the North that lured man to explore the rest of the globe. There is vastness, untouched and undeveloped. There is beauty, peace, wealth and opportunity. Hidden in the frozen ground, covered by snow and ice, lies a treasure chest of resources. The natural beauty of the area promises to be one of the great sources for refreshing the spirit of man for as long as the human species inhabits the earth.

In a *Special Report to the People: The Potential and the Promise of the Arctic,* published by the Department of the Interior

percent; Mobil Pipe Line Company, 8.68 percent; Phillips Petroleum Company, 3.32 percent; Union Oil Company of California, 3.32 percent, and Amerada Hess Corporation, 3 percent.

in 1970, I wrote: "To get at that treasure and enjoy the wonder of Alaska without destroying the unique Arctic environment, is one of the great challenges of our generation."

I cherish the beauty of my north country, Alaska's "resource of the heart and soul." And I never would have given the Alaska pipeline my support if I were not absolutely certain, on the basis of facts rather than emotion, that it could be designed and constructed without endangering this resource of beauty. Americans realize that we cannot "stop the world and get off." Nor can we simply turn off the ignition of America. To do so would be to plunge our nation into economic, political and industrial darkness. The key is to do the job right.

6. A Clean Land

When the obligation of ownership of our public properties is taken seriously, the government can begin to take an overall look at the pollution problems facing our country and get to the root of them. As I became more deeply involved in solving the water pollution problems of America, I began to realize that in many instances we were trying to deal with symptoms, not causes. Primary and secondary treatment of sewage in every municipality in the country is urgently needed. Tertiary treatment, in which the effluent entering the system leaves so pure that it is drinkable, is a goal we must move toward as rapidly as possible. But even if every municipal sewer pipe in America produced pure water, many of our rivers and lakes would still be polluted.

For this reason I began in the summer of 1970 to spell out a clean-land doctrine. It is in the care of our land that the battle is won or lost with regard to clean rivers, clean lakes and even clean air. A vast amount of pollution in this country is caused by the abuse of our natural resources. You cannot clean up a stream and make it swimmable if it passes through an area where vegetation has been callously bulldozed for a housing project or for poorly planned farming. When nature's natural filtration system is removed, soil and silt are carried by the runoff of rains and irrigation into that stream. We must ensure that strict zoning on stream, river and lake shores is written and enforced so that construction and farming are given adequate guidelines to protect the environment. This is not to stop development, but to make certain it is tied to wise use without abuse of our resources.

This is an issue in which government must take a strong lead, but in which the private individual can play a major part. This was illustrated for me in Anchorage in August 1970. Our city has three creeks running through the middle of it. They are beautiful little streams that start in the Chugach Mountains and run into Cook Inlet. I have always enjoyed them and considered them part of the special character of Anchorage. However, they have begun to be rerouted, funneled through culverts under new highways, and the green areas protecting their banks are disappearing.

Accompanied by many civic leaders, I walked those creeks examining the areas the city has managed to save and those that have already fallen before the onrush of development. I challenged the people of

Anchorage to act. I told them there is something an individual can do when faced by a city problem, if he wants to do it badly enough. There *are* public funds—city, state and federal—for purchasing land valuable for recreation or just scenic beauty. There *are* funds available to build highways so that they not only provide transportation but increase the beauty of a city rather than desecrate it. So often it is up to the public and what we are ready to fight for.

It only takes people who care.

There has been an enormous and thoughtless lack of planning in the development of the United States. This thoughtlessness was something the 19th century could tolerate and the 20th century could put up with. The 21st century cannot do either. Suppose you have six industrial plants sited along the same river and polluting it. Suppose, too, that the same six plants really clean themselves up. They completely treat their discharge so that it is pure and clean, and they equip their smokestacks with filtration machinery so that only pure air comes out of the top. This is not enough. The very concentration of six plants, jammed side by side, causes intolerable "visual pollution."

So often in the past our only criterion for quality has been monetary reward. This is blatantly illustrated by the billboard blight on America, and one of the last actions I took as Secretary of the Interior was to issue an order banning all billboards from the public lands managed by the Department. (Alaska has had a law banning billboards from public rights-of-way since territorial days.)

Resources must be developed and used; homes and office buildings must be built. But it is inexcusable to do these things without considering the impact they have on the heart and soul and spirit of the American people. Industry and architects have proved that all these things can be done with proper respect for the environment. The question is: Do we care enough about our land to see that they are done in that way?

The problem of getting a clean land also involves the argument about how best to cut the timber in our forests. This is of great concern to me because much of the nation's lumber is taken from public property. I feel strongly that the emphasis should be on "selective cutting," in which a tree is cut only after it has reached proper maturity. Selectivity does not always mean the same thing; it depends on the forest and the kinds of trees you are talking about. Certain trees, the Douglas fir for instance, are subject to "blowdown" if they are left unsurrounded by other trees.

This is one of the arguments advanced by the lumber industry in favor of "clearcutting," a procedure by which, with the help of enormous machinery, a crew of men will move into a forest and level everything in a given area. But the real argument for clearcutting is that it is cheaper to do it that way and take a chance on the forest replenishing itself.

Undoubtedly there are situations in which clearcutting of trees is justified, but there are many cases in which it represents an abuse of a resource. We should take a much harder look at selective cutting, even if it does cost a bit more. Does it make sense to cut a 3-year-old tree, a 30-year-old tree and a 300-year-old tree all at the same time just because they are standing next to each other? Is the highest and best use of a tree to make it into a telephone pole? The goal should be a perpetual supply of lumber, and the protection of the forests and the land they stand on.

It is interesting that clearcutting is practiced a great deal more by private firms when they use public land than when they use their own private property.

Strip mining of coal is another example of not facing the real cost of retrieving a resource—the total cost. It is possible to strip mine without desecrating the environment. It just costs a little more. What is lacking are regulations to see that it is done correctly.

The procedure is simple. You recover the topsoil. When the dig is finished, you return the topsoil to its original contour. This should be done immediately so that your machines are never more than about 1,000 feet in advance of an area to be reclaimed.

It is important to cover the mined area quickly because when the land is open, it bleeds. Then you get erosion that silts the streams, and you also get acidity in the runoff from sulphur contact that pollutes the water as well as the vegetation around it.

The point of returning the land to its original contour is important. In a thin seam, this entire procedure costs fifteen or twenty cents a ton. There is a mandate to "return it like you found it." If you cannot do that, forget it!

7. The Widows

On February 24, 1969, one month to the day after I was sworn into office as Secretary, seven women widowed by a coal-mining disaster came to see me. Their husbands had been killed in an underground explosion at Fairmont, West Virginia, the preceding November. Seventy-eight men died in that explosion. This meeting, unscheduled and unannounced, illuminated for me one of the most pressing and oppressing problems on the agenda of the American people. I tried to deal with it as

Secretary. I did not succeed, but I have not given up the fight.

One of the gravest obligations of government regarding natural resource development is in the care for the men and women involved. The Bureau of Mines, located in the bowels of the Department of the Interior, carries such a responsibility. The history of mining, with its sorry record of mine explosions, men crippled by accident and disease, and semifeudal working conditions, is evidence enough to judge the Bureau's effectiveness.

A mine is such an inhuman thing. It is worse than a war, because in a war you can fight back. In a mine you cannot.

When I talked to these women of West Virginia, I was deeply moved. I decided that if it was humanly possible, I would change the situation. That was the beginning of frustration the like of which I have rarely experienced. Everywhere I turned for help, I ran into confusion, hesitancy or downright hostility.

As other pressing crises shouted at us in newspaper headlines, we found the coal miner's problem always pushed to the bottom of the agenda.

When I arrived at Interior, the Bureau of Mines had been under fire to make some improvement on the Coal Mine Health and Safety Act of 1952. This act was not much of a vehicle. It did not have penalties attached to it. It merely listed those things that were regarded as hazardous. It gave the Secretary no flexibility with regard to adding or taking from that list. Furthermore, he was only empowered to point out to industry hazardous situations if they came to his attention. If there was imminent danger, there was a provision under which he could close a mine. But as one long-time Bureau of Mines observer put it, "Interior just never used that."

The philosophy of the Bureau was that the way to handle health and safety was through education. I said that after fifty years of trying to educate, it was time to get a good deal firmer. Industry representatives, the United Mine Workers Union and the Bureau had completed a long series of meetings in which the industry had indicated its willingness to accept eighteen changes in the 1952 act. In the midst of these meetings, the Fairmont disaster dramatically illustrated the failure of any of the responsible parties to take the kind of action that should have been taken years earlier.

I told the Director of the Bureau of Mines, Jack O'Leary, who had been appointed the previous month by the Johnson Administration, that any new act should include authority to make industry abide by those rules. My solution was to impose penalties, both civil and criminal, on offenders.

In the midst of our fight for tough new legislation, I began receiving widely publicized pressure from the White House and Capitol Hill to remove O'Leary, a Democrat. It bothered me because I had not yet had time to evaluate the quality of his work. However, my instructions were clear: Remove O'Leary. Following my orders from the White House, I took steps to let O' Leary go. But before I could make the official announcement, I received a call from Bryce Harlow telling me to hold off for a while.

He said this would mean two more votes

on the Administration side of the ABM question. I thought to myself, "Okay, so I'll be a team player."

But I wondered: "What about the miners? How in hell do all these political games help solve *their* problems?"

In those areas of Interior where I had a handle on what was going on, I could cut right through the obstacles. I just wiped them out. But in those areas where I could not get a handle, I had to rely on someone else. They all knew if I caught them playing games, I didn't give a damn what happened. I would straighten it out. But I could never get my hands on the mining thing.

I was frankly unable to fight my way through the maze of conflicting facts and opinions to get at the clean, honest story. I never had a good "gut" feeling about it, something I consider extremely important. With Under Secretary Russ Train, I met with Arthur Burns and Richard T. Burress, the White House Deputy Counsel responsible for the mining legislation. It was apparent to me that Burress was representing the industry's viewpoint. His only concern was economics. I bluntly said, "We're talking about people's lives, not balance sheets."

8. Free Enterprise Slavery

We are supposed to be a country of great freedom. But the coal miner is not a free man. One out of six miners is going to be killed or injured this year. Someone has got to protect that man. Often today he is in slavery, like the slaves in Biblical times. But to our discredit and shame, he is a slave within a free enterprise system.

After John L. Lewis passed his peak, the United Mine Workers Union lost its militancy and cast its lot with industry during the serious depression coal experienced in the early 1950's. Possibly because he was old and tired, possibly because he felt deep coal mining could no longer compete with other sources of energy, Lewis more or less acquiesced in the scuttling of two-thirds of his own union. You can do something for the miner's children, but it is difficult to retrain a coal miner past the age of fifty to do another kind of useful work.

The remaining miners are a captive labor force. There is no place for them to go, physically and literally, except down into the mine. If they refuse to go into the mine, they cannot get unemployment compensation. But what good is it if a man earns a dollar for bread when simultaneously his mind, heart and soul are being destroyed?

Most of the mine owners do not live in New York or Washington. They live in the mountains themselves, in the "hollers" of the Bluefields and the Beckleys. This comes the closest to a plantation society that we have today in this country. The Depression of the 1930's put an end to such mastership in most of America, but mastership has persisted in the coal industry. This situation bothered me so much at the time that I pursued the problem after I was out of office. It was several months before I was able to document anything resembling the facts.

One of the travesties in the Bureau of Mines has to do with the safety records of large companies, which play games with statistics. A common gimmick is to keep a man on the payroll and not list him as injured if his layoff is a week or less. Industry has been keeping these statistics with one hand and reaching around and patting itself on the back with the other hand, telling itself what a great safety record it has. What's more, the Bureau of Mines accident report was tabulated the same way.

This is an example of the "buddy system" in which certain bureaus of the Department long ago became involved. For more than 100 years, these bureaus were actually in a silent partnership with the industries they were supposed to police. It is a shameful picture, and such an unnecessary one. What was once a great labor union and what could be a great industry are cooperating to maintain what is essentially a slavery system in the name of free enterprise. This could all be straightened out with government regulation by men who care.

9. *Filet of the Sea*

The Soviet Union's fishing fleets operating offshore in the Bering Sea look like floating cities as the big mother ships, their lights glittering, hover over the small catcher boats. To compete with mechanized fish farming, our own Eskimo fishermen have walrus-hide boats from which a few men catch a very few fish. An Eskimo at Savoonga, on St. Lawrence Island, once stood beside his little skin boat and told me, gesturing toward Siberia, "They fish all the time, and we don't even know what's there." New England fishermen are also at a technological disadvantage when they compete for fish with foreign fleets from Gloucester to Newfoundland. The seagoing American individual simply cannot hope to match the scope of nationally subsidized and often state-owned floating factories.

The nations of the world still consider the ocean something to exploit, because no one "owns" it. Each of us claims ownership just to the edge of our jurisdictional limit. But if no one owns the great expanses of ocean beyond the Continental Shelf, then who has the obligation? Who will care?

In reality, over three billion people on this planet have a share in the resources of the deep ocean. We should all care, because we all own it. Existing international fisheries treaties are clearly inadequate to deal with the confusion. Unless we can reach multinational agreement on the obligations of ocean management, we may, within the next century, despoil the sea through overharvesting and poisoning its resources, just as we despoiled a great portion of the land.

We in this country cannot wait for someone else. We must take the lead. The future of the source of life on earth is at stake.

The sea covers more than 70 percent of our earth, but less than 5 percent of this vast expanse has been charted for man's use, much less properly catalogued to show the wealth of resources. The most important part of this watery kingdom is the Continental Shelf, which comprises about 9 percent of the total area of our seas. This shelf is the relatively shallow submarine plain extending from the coasts of the continents to the steeper slopes plunging off into the deep water of the oceanic abyss. The Continental Shelf is the womb of our ocean resources.

As recently as 100 years ago, much of the world's fisheries production came from fresh water. But with the development of the steam and internal combustion engines, the commercial fishing business went to sea. Today the economy of the fishing industry is more than 90 percent dependent upon salt water. Conservation of marine resources must be a matter of economics as well as ecology. The conservationist-scientist cannot achieve balance in an ivory tower. That is why, in May 1970, I signed an order transferring the Office of Marine Resources from the Office of the Under Secretary of the Interior to the Secretary's office. I renamed it the Office of Marine Affairs.

This action was an effort on my part to bring about more direct and honest contact between the fisheries business and the science and conservation communities. We were giving top priority to development of a centralized clearinghouse for marine and coastal zone matters. The idea was to make possible the greatest use of the sea consistent with a wholesome environment.

Indiscriminate and unregulated use of the sea, even at the national level, can create conflicts unless there is proper perspective and guidance. An example of such a conflict came one day in my office during a meeting with Mike Wright, chairman of the board of the Humble Oil and Refining Company. I had asked Mike to come in for a meeting so that we could discuss my attitudes and obligations as Secretary of the Interior on oil leasing on the American Continental Shelf. More and more of the resources of the shelf are going to come from subsurface lands held in public ownership, and I wanted Mike to know I considered it imperative that the rights of the public be protected.

We were having a rather violent difference of opinion over the manner in which regulations would be used to protect this public interest, and Wright finally jumped up from his chair and stalked toward the door.

I shouted, "Mike!" He stopped in his tracks, thought a moment and finally returned to his chair. We talked for another several minutes, and I believe I finally convinced him that I was not out to "just make things tough for the oil industry." My only intent was to see that the interests of others who are involved in Continental Shelf resources development, such as the fishermen, were protected, along with the total interests of the American public.

Past experience has taught us that to have an effective program for utilizing all of our marine resources we must first catalogue them. How can we develop — or conserve — unless we know what is there?

We know that in addition to our established fisheries, there are vast potentials offered by other marine resources, and this extends to other fisheries products which we have failed to utilize.

We have become spoiled in the United States, or perhaps we just never knew any better. While the American fisheries have concentrated on what I call the "filet of the sea" — the salmon, halibut and other choice varieties — other nations, such as Japan, have learned to utilize everything. When one of their fishing fleets moves into an area, they throw away nothing. They use everything they catch, much like the meat packer who uses everything from the hog but his squeal.

An indicator of the success of foreign fishing interests in harvesting their ocean resources can be read in current import figures. Despite its own fisheries production, in 1969 the United States still had to import $692 million in fisheries products. This was a jump of $61 million in only one year. By contrast, in the mid-1960's the total value of the United States fisheries' commercial catch was roughly $390 million on a volume of slightly under six billion pounds, hardly more than half of our imports.

Historically, the United States is a maritime country. Our marine fisheries are still a major industry, but they suffer many problems. Our fishermen use a good deal of equipment that has hardly been improved upon since the time of Moses. While our annual fisheries production remains in the multimillion-dollar category, the value of *all* raw materials extracted from the sea in the United States now exceeds $2 *billion* a year — and is rising at the rate of 12 percent for those products other than seafood.

With 64 percent of all our Continental Shelf, Alaska was an ideal place for me to familiarize myself with the opportunities of the ocean. That is why I added a national fisheries policy plank to the Republican Party platform at Miami Beach in 1968. Unless there is a balance between the harvesting and reproduction of these renewable resources, they will be lost.

Jacques-Yves Cousteau, the respected oceanographer, was once asked by the United Nations to conduct a worldwide fisheries survey. He refused. He said he considered it "barbaric" that we were still "hunting in the sea" the way man hunted on the land 10,000 years ago, without consideration for future consequences. Cousteau charged that unless we underwent a basic change in philosophy toward the sea — toward a concept of "aquaculture" and farming of the renewable resources — it would take only a few decades to render practically sterile the oceans of the globe.

Our knowledge of the ocean is very limited. But the 1970's could be a decade in which America makes advances as successful in the ocean as in the conquest of space. Future generations will use the land as we know it as a place for the enjoyment and living of life. But man's needs will more and more come from the ocean, that part of the planet that is so challenging and so unexplored.

To realize its potential, we will need government that is willing to make big plans — long-range plans — for the benefit of future generations, without fear of criticism. The ocean is so close and yet so far away.

Science has accomplished such wonders but hasn't been able to duplicate a simple egg, add a little heat and make a chicken.

CHAPTER **6**

Cry of the Whale

The main source of recreation for my family and myself during my two years as Governor was to sail our boat, the *Ermalee,* from the Juneau harbor throughout the Inside Passage. The great fjords seemed endless, and we often imagined that we were the first people ever to sail along these rugged, forested banks that jutted hundreds and even thousands of feet into the sky. One of the greatest thrills we experienced was sighting whales. The sudden appearance of those great black backs, the whoosh of their blow, the echoing slap of mighty tails typified the mystery of the sea.

I will never forget the day we happened on one of the most unusual spectacles on earth. Two great whales were mating. There was such fury and apparent violence involved that my family and I stood transfixed on our boat for nearly an hour and a half watching the spectacle. The male and female whale were circling deep in the water and then rushing full speed toward each other on a collision course. They met and rose together out of the water like gigantic trout on the end of a line, thrashing and spraying mountains of water in all directions.

Over the last four decades, General Charles Lindbergh, the heroic aviator, has been one of the greatest American conservationists and one of the most avid friends of the whale. Shunning a life of publicity, he has chosen to work behind the scenes on the issues that touch him most deeply. I managed to convince him on May 18, 1968, to make a speech on conservation, the first public address he had made in ten years. He spoke to a combined session of the Alaska Legislature. That evening, in the Governor's Mansion in Juneau, Lindbergh and I talked about why mankind should be concerned about the whale.

Few creatures on this planet have awed and inspired man as much as the whale. His enormous size and power have made him a frightening symbol of forces and powers in nature—powers that are greater than man and beyond his reach. The whale has become legendary in stretching man's imagination about the intent of his Creator and ours.

Suddenly, within a generation, this great creature's survival is at the mercy of man. Our intentional slaughter of thousands of whales for profit every year and our unintentional polluting of their watery environment are rapidly diminishing their numbers. Suddenly the master of the seas is crying out to man for help.

Is the cry of the whale trying to tell man something? Is the cry of the whale really the cry of life? And if that cry falls on deaf ears, will the cry of our fellow man fall on deaf ears as well?

The person who has no heart for the value of a living creature such as the whale has no heart for his fellow human. He does not hear the depth of the cry of man, pleading for help—whether in Biblical times when it took a Moses to free the people, or in the present with the violence of some and the frustration of others who reject violence. They are crying out. The cry of the smallest child in the ghetto forgotten in the crowd, or the cry of the greatest animal forgotten in the vast open sea — these are both part of the same fabric of life.

1. When Is a Species Endangered?

After I became Secretary of the Interior, I asked my staff to research the problems involved in placing all eight species of great whales on the endangered list. The reports strengthened my fears. The whaling nations were still viewing whale resources on a short-term basis. If present trends were to continue, all large whales would be driven toward extinction within a few years. If, however, the whales' breeding stocks were allowed to build back up, a sustained annual harvest, far larger than currently being taken, would be possible. But the whaling nations and their organizing body, the International Whaling Commission (IWC) were not regarding this great resource with a long-term, wise-use outlook.

During the peak whaling year, 1930-31, whalers took almost 30,000 Blue whales, one of the mightiest creatures ever to live on the face of the earth. Today, some estimates of the number surviving are as low as 600; the highest is 3,000. They have been partially protected since 1965. But the question is: Are there enough of these animals left for males to find females across the great oceans? The numbers are so low that the death rate from natural causes and from occasional "accidental" harpooning may be much greater than the birth rate. It would be a crime beyond belief that in the same decade that we walked on the moon we also destroyed the largest animal on earth. The Humpbacked whale, a playful monster renowned for its unearthly songs and foam-splattering leaps, has also been reduced to the point of possible extinction. The Bowhead and two Right whale species almost exterminated by early hunters have never really recovered. Only the California Grey whale, after decades of complete protection, has made a partial recovery.

In 1970 the eighty-foot Finback was still being pursued down the same path. From a peak Antarctic harvest of over 30,000 in the early 1960's, these waters now yield only some 2,500 whales a year. Just a few years ago an annual harvest of 10,000 Fins could have been carried on indefinitely. But with the Fins on the way out, the whalers began concentrating on the smaller Sei and Sperm whales. They had to kill more whales and even porpoises to make the business barely pay. In 1930-31, some 43,000 whales yielded 3.5 million barrels of oil. In 1966-67, some 52,000 whales yielded a mere 1.5 million barrels.

The complexity of the problem was caused by the international character of the industry. The United States, a member and strong supporter of the IWC, could not dictate policy to this group. The IWC's rulings were based on short-term gain. For instance, the current kill quotas for Baleen whale established by the IWC for the Antarctic were 20 percent higher than those recommended by its own scientific committee. And the male Sperm whale catch in the Pacific was a shocking 2½ times the sustainable yield estimated by Japanese scientists. When the IWC agreed to reduce its Sperm quota by a meager 10 percent, the whaling nations still refused to allow international observers to supervise the regulations on quotas, size and species. On this basis, cetologists contend that these species will be commercially extinct within ten years. I have never been against using renewable resources, but to drive any animal to extinction for short-term profits is inexcusable.

For months we worked on the whale project, and the battle grew intense. Often the issue became confusing. If I were to prevent the importation of any parts or products from these animals into this country, it would cause difficulties. Although the United States has not been a major whaling nation for 100 years, it does use 25 to 30 percent of the world's whale products in making soap, margarine, beauty cream, machine oil and pet food. My friend General Lindbergh wrote me on September 26, 1970, after returning from Japan where he had studied the situation. His opinion was that if all eight species were placed on the U.S. endangered species list, including the three species still commercially hunted

(Sperm, Finback and Sei), it would not deter the great whaling nations, Japan and Russia. In fact, he feared unilateral action on our part would encourage them to exploit the situation further.

I was convinced, however, that the United States had to take the lead. Foreign whaling, which reached its height in the last decade, was launching a massive technological onslaught that no animal could endure. The lookouts of the past have been supplemented with radar and helicopters, the longboats with twenty-knot whale catchers. A factory ship can dispose of an eighty-ton carcass in thirty minutes.

On December 5, 1969, the Endangered Species Act was signed into law. This act bars the importation, except for certain educational and scientific purposes, of those species listed by the Secretary of the Interior as threatened with extinction.[1]

The question I raised was, *when* is a

---

[1] *It is a federal offense to sell or purchase any mammal, bird, fish, reptile, amphibian, mollusk or crustacean taken contrary to state or foreign laws. At the time the*

species endangered? I believe that the Endangered Species Act must be more than a last-ditch effort to save a species with its back against the wall. It must also be used to prevent other species from reaching that point.

Some Americans remember the seemingly infinite supply of passenger pigeons hunted without thought that they might be threatened. In 1898 there were perhaps a million of them. The next year there were practically none. In 1900 the last wild passenger pigeon was shot. The species came to an end at 1:00 P.M. Eastern Standard Time, September 1, 1914, in the Cincinnati Zoo. Her name was Martha. She was 29. Man was not equipped to recognize their point of no return. He wasn't listening to the cry of life.

I decided to act on the whales. The showdown came with representatives of the State Department and the Sperm oil

Endangered Species Act was signed by the President, some 275 species of mammals and 300 birds were already considered rare and in danger throughout the world.

industry. When I had disposed of the majority of their arguments, they produced an argument I had not expected.

"We have to have whale oil for the space program," the State Department official declared.

Without hesitation I demanded, "What are you going to use when the whale is extinct?"

Taken aback, the official stammered, "I suppose we'll have to find a substitute."

I announced, "You find that substitute right now, because those whales are going on the endangered species list."

My decision was responsible because special permits were allowed to market whales already caught.

The impact on the other nations involved was dramatic. General Lindbergh later explained to me the result of my action. "You touched their conscience," he said. "While others were just talking about the problem, you cared enough about the whales to take the bold action that was necessary."

2. *Creatures of God*

If all alligator eggs hatched and were to grow to full size, within 100 years the world would be four feet deep in alligators. But life is a system of complex relationships in which nature has her own ways of maintaining a balance. The young alligators fall prey to all the predators of the swamp, including their own parents. When man intervenes, however, havoc is unleashed on the entire system.

This is clearly illustrated in the Everglades in southern Florida. The mosquito larvae feed the tiny mosquito fish, which in turn are eaten by larger fish, and these are preyed upon by alligators, birds and other animals. Each creature plays an indispensable role in the total scheme. The alligator, which is at the top of the food chain, provides a life-saving service for all the others. When the dry season approaches, each adult alligator digs out a hole with its tail in the marshy bog, thus creating a small pond. These "gator holes" dot the Everglades landscape and provide great quantities of food for birds, mammals, fish and turtles. During a drought, gator holes are the only source of water, making the difference between life and death for swamp life.

Man, concerned only with his own needs, uses DDT to exterminate the mosquitos and kills the alligators for shoes, wallets and purses, oblivious of the fact that the beautiful roseate spoonbills, the flamingoes and all the other wild creatures who share the Everglades depend on mosquito larvae and alligators. While the mosquitos and other insects become resistant to the chemical poisons, the alligator faces extinction.

Today, hundreds of the earth's living animals, assaulted by pollution poisons, loss of habitat and overexploitation, face a similar fate. "When the last individual of a race of living creatures breathes no more," wrote naturalist William Beebe, "another heaven and another earth must pass before such a one can be again." Since we shall never have the capacity or technology to create another heaven or earth, we must be wary of what we destroy. As we begin to understand the fragile web of life, of which we are but a precious part, we become aware that man is the only species that willfully damages that web for reasons of greed, hatred or ignorance. Our scientists have warned us that, unless we stop now, one too many species of wildlife soon may be wiped out; one too many lakes or rivers fouled beyond redemption.

Man's ravages have already driven forty-seven species of United States wildlife over the brink of extinction. More than 120 known species have disappeared throughout the world since 1600.

In the past, wild animals have only had powerful lobbies representing their cause to the federal government if they were game birds or animals. Hunters and fishermen have contributed greatly to preserve the great flocks of waterfowl and other game species. In a sense, these groups have been some of the greatest conservation proponents in the country. However, there is an entirely new interest growing in America for wildlife of all sorts. Suddenly many people, young and old, who may never have the opportunity to hunt or fish but who may prefer instead merely to observe or photograph wildlife in its natural state, are becoming involved. This new constituency is beginning to influence government to care not only for the whooping crane and trumpeter swan, but for endangered toads, bats and even the tiny prehistoric pup fish in Death Valley. They are all part of life's cycle.

As in most of the environmental issues faced by our nation, there is a built-in conflict between provision for the needs of man and protection of the natural riches of the earth. This is especially true with regard to the wild animals we have called predators, such as wolves, coyotes, hawks and eagles. These animals have preyed on and sometimes lived off the livestock of our ranching populations. Often this need not happen. It is the direct result of natural food supplies, such as rodents, being exterminated by man.

The states have placed bounties on so-called predators, making it profitable for hunters to search them out and kill them. My own belief is that this practice should be abandoned. No potential game animals today should be labeled as predators, and no bounties should be given. The timber wolf, for instance, should be considered a game animal. It is one of the wariest animals on earth. To track and hunt a timber wolf successfully is an accomplishment of which any hunter could be justly proud. That accomplishment, not a fee paid by the government, should be a man's reward. This would be a sport, and the direct opposite of the mass extermination currently practiced through poisoning and the hateful exercise of hunting and shooting from airplanes. I'm not against hunting, but let's put the sport back in it.

3. *An Angry Rancher*

For many years the Department of the Interior has maintained a ban against killing Golden Eagles, another "predator," on the millions of acres of land under its jurisdiction, land primarily in the West, administered by the Bureau of Land Management. Unfortunately, with some regularity over the years, several of my predecessors as Secretary buckled before the demands of wool growers to waive the ban in certain areas. Many eagles were wiped out — many too many.

The sheepmen argue that they should not have to lose a single lamb to the eagles, the coyotes, or anything else. Too often they use "1080" and other poisons. In effect, they want an absolutely "sterile" range. They kill off all other life forms. They ignore the cry of life of all creatures other than the sheep.

I believe that as in so many issues we must strike a balance. Evidence available to the Department's scientists convinced me we had far from an excess of Golden Eagles. I refuse to condone practices that wipe out one species to protect another.

I had a confrontation over this issue in the spring of 1970. On May 22 I stepped aboard Arthur Godfrey's Gulf-Stream I at Dulles International Airport outside Washington. With the entertainer at the controls, we headed for Lewiston, Idaho, where we were to take a river trip through Hell's Canyon, a fantastically scenic stretch of the Snake River that provides a 200-mile boundary between Idaho and Oregon. My intention in taking the trip was to draw national interest and support to two of our programs in the Interior Department: our efforts to stop further dam construction of the Snake and our attempt to help clean up America through the Johnny Horizon Program. This was a campaign started in the Bureau of Land Management as an antilitter version of the Agriculture Department's Smokey the Bear. I had no idea, as Arthur Godfrey piloted us toward Idaho, that I was to become involved in an argument about eagles.

After we landed in Lewiston, we were joined by Burl Ives, the voice of Johnny Horizon, and Floyd Harvey, who was active in the drive to save Hell's Canyon. Harvey had lined up a fleet of special river boats equipped with powerful engines and water jet-propulsion systems, permitting them to navigate the rocky, turbulent rapids that make this stretch of the Snake one of the greatest white-water rivers in America.

It was a lively trip with Ives and Godfrey swapping yarns and trading Burl's guitar back and forth as they outdid each other with humorous back-country ballads. Burl was like a teenager when he began talking about the Johnny Horizon Program. He said it was one of the greatest thrills of his life to tour the country and sing to the young, enlisting their support to care in a practical way for the environment. He was contributing his time and effort at his own expense and loving every minute of it. Many of Hollywood's producers and personalities, including the "Laugh-In" poet Henry Gibson, were beginning to work with him. Burl proved to be a great campaigner.

At that time I was working on a proposal, which I later put into effect, to ban from the public lands all pesticides that linger in the food chain and threaten animals for countless generations. Although Burl thoroughly supported my idea, he wrote a song pulling my leg, which he called "Don't Let Them Kill the Love Bug, Wally."

We went many miles up river our first day on the water, finally camping deep in Hell's Canyon. We stepped ashore and I was met unexpectedly by a very aggressive sheep rancher. As we strode up the beach to the campsite, he blurted out, "Mr. Hickel, I lost 700 lambs to eagles last year. What do you think about that?"

I replied instantly, "I think I'd get the hell out of the sheep business." If he had said "seven" I might have been more willing to listen. But "seven hundred"? Ridiculous. I wanted to be fair, but no evidence was ever forthcoming that eagles presented any threat to the sheep business.

The Snake River and its tributaries are harnessed by more than two dozen dams. I opposed the construction of the High Mountain Sheep Dam on the Snake above its junction with the Salmon River. If built, the High Mountain Sheep Dam will wipe out Hell's Canyon — the deepest and one of the most spectacular scenic canyons on the American continent. It is also home for many forms of wildlife. I urged Congress to pass a bill introduced by Senators Len Jordan and Frank Church which would place a ten-year moratorium on such dam construction. But my thoughts went beyond that one dam. On this trip I was asked by a resident if I was in favor of such a moratorium. I replied, "Yes, and maybe we should even study which of the dams already built should be dismantled."

There are places to put dams and places not to, and this is a place not to.

During my twenty-two months in Washington, I kept hammering at the concept that one resource cannot be thoughtlessly abused for the sake of developing another, even when one of these resources might appear to carry a much higher dollar priority at least at the moment.

In Sespe Condor Sanctuary in California, we had to decide which was more important: saving a rare bird, or pumping more oil and gas from an area which is that creature's only known nesting place in North America. I decided in favor of the bird, and on March 9, 1970, I ordered a halt on all further oil and gas leasing in the sanctuary, which is part of the Los Padres National Forest. Although the forest is administered by the Department of Agriculture, the Interior Department has control over gas and oil leasing through its Bureau of Land Management. I directed the Bureau to declare an indefinite moratorium on pending leases and on any future lease applications in the sanctuary until scientists from both Interior and Agriculture could develop ways not only to protect the existing condors but to increase their numbers.

With a wingspan sometimes reaching nine feet, the California condor is America's largest bird in flight, but despite his size the condor is sensitive to man's interference. Our research clearly indicated that the birds were reproducing poorly because of the noise and blasting at the petroleum-drilling sites in the area. By 1970 the number of birds had decreased to a level lower even than in 1951 when the sanctuary was established. Today perhaps only eighty California condors are left. Only time will tell if we acted soon enough to save this creature of God.

4. He Only Looks Ferocious

The musk-ox is a heavy-set, shaggy-coated wild ox native to the Arctic. He looks like a cross between a short-legged buffalo and an old English sheepdog that never stopped growing. Unfortunately, the species in Alaska was totally obliterated by man. Whaling expeditions during the 1860's were responsible for the final extinction of the indigenous Alaska herds.

The musk-ox is a relict of the Ice Age. It represents a rare element of a great family of Ice Age goat-antelopes. In an environment where only tiny flowers and vegetation grow, most of the vegetarian animal life is small. The musk-ox is an exception. Often five feet high at the shoulder, the mature musk-ox averages 800 pounds and has been recorded as attaining as much as 1,200 pounds.

Because of its means of foraging, this animal has filled a unique niche in the ecological system of the tundra regions. The lichens that flourish in this environment are in the grazing domain of the caribou, while the musk-ox relies on willow and grasses. If the Arctic winds are insufficient to clear the vegetation of drifting snow, the musk-ox will break the crust and scrape away the snow with its hooves. Another adaptation to the rugged environment is the animal's preference for eating snow rather than drinking water.

Except in mating season when the males become feisty, the musk-ox is quite gentle. A hunter can practically walk right up to the beast and stick a gun in its ear. Their means of protection has always been the ancient maneuver of surrounding their young and facing their big, heavy-horned heads outward, thereby warding off wolves and other natural enemies. This, of course, is a futile gesture when challenged by big-game rifles.

The musk-ox's real problem is that he *looks* ferocious. To the uninitiated, a musk-ox trophy adorning the wall of a hunting lodge would be assumed proof of a hunter's prowess.

In an effort to return this relict species throughout Arctic Alaska, about thirty of the animals were purchased from Greenland in 1936. They were established on Nunivak Island eighteen miles off the Alaska mainland in the Bering Sea. The musk-ox thrived in this environment away from predators, including man, because of President Hoover's Executive Order in 1929 which established Nunivak Island as a National Wildlife Refuge. The motive of some of those who imported the first musk-ox back from Greenland was the prospect of developing another game animal, while others hoped that through careful breeding they might be domesticated.

The soft undercoat of the animal, called *qiviut,* is so delicate, warm and rare that it brings the highest price of any wool in the world, exceeding that paid for angora or cashmere. About five pounds of *qiviut* can be plucked from a musk-ox bull each year. Techniques are being developed to turn *qiviut* into premium-quality scarves and other apparel. Students from the University of Alaska are working with the Native women of Nunivak to develop the art. Exquisitely woven items of apparel are currently being produced, although production is still minute. However, the potential is there for a new industry to help sustain the Native citizens of this remote area.

The question which concerned me was how to protect the musk-ox so that the original intent of the action — to reestablish them throughout Arctic Alaska — would be realized. The musk-ox could, if treated as a domestic animal, provide great benefits to Alaska Natives. But the big game hunters and guides had a different idea.

By 1967 the musk-ox herd had prospered on Nunivak Island, reaching a population of over 700. But after more than thirty years of developing the herd, no action had been taken to relocate them in other parts of the state. In the face of this negligence, I began to receive reports which indicated that the winter range on the island was being overgrazed, and therefore it would be necessary to hunt off the extraneous bulls to make more feed available for the calves and cows.

This issue — over a rare and relatively unknown animal — became a classic example of how a government project, originally conceived with great vision, can be twisted for the pleasure and profit of a special few unless someone cares enough to see it through.

Members of the Alaska State Legislature pushed through a bill which would have authorized the state Fish and Game Department to issue big game hunting tags for the taking of musk-oxen on Nunivak. Even at $1,000 a throw, there were many hunters who were eager to bring home a trophy which would impress their friends but require virtually no skill to bag. The Governor of one southwestern state called me personally and said he had three hunters who would pay $5,000 apiece for hunting tags if the bill was passed.

But when that bill came up to me, I vetoed it.

Are seven hundred musk-oxen too many for Alaska? We have hundreds of thousands of caribou ranging in the Arctic. Even seven thousand musk-oxen would be too few.

I did not argue with those who said there were too many bulls on Nunivak. If these animals must be eliminated, it should be done by the Natives, who could put the meat and the beautiful hides to good use. But to start hunting them would be the beginning of a reversal of the original intent of establishing the herd in Alaska. This would be private exploitation of a public resource.

I wanted to know why none of the animals had yet been relocated. To get that accomplished, I had to put the full power of the Governor's Office behind it. We had to fight almost every official down the line. And we did it because we shared the vision of those in the 1930's who realized that the Arctic needs more wildlife and *can* sustain it.

We flew small herds to half a dozen sites including Barter Island, in the Arctic National Wildlife Range, and Feather River near Nome. A total of more than 150 musk-oxen were freed to roam the vast, windswept plains in the far north, their natural and original home.

The hunters and guides complained about my veto, and their friends in the Alaska Legislature did not give up. A year later, when I had moved to Washington, another state bill, similar to the first one, was passed. This time we acted at Interior. By federal edict, as Nunivak is a National Wildlife Refuge, we prohibited any musk-ox hunting.

I'll always wonder why others in positions of responsibility failed to have the imagination to think beyond the revenue of a few hunting tags.

The battle still goes on. The Nunivak herd is back up to 700. "Overgrazing" is again the issue being used to renew the effort to hunt the musk-ox. Nonsense. The problem is, no relocations have taken place since I left the government.

5. *A Time to Harvest*

One of the most controversial issues in the media that has concerned the public during recent years is the taking of fur seals in Canada and on the Pribilof Islands in Alaska. Certain practices in this trade are inhumane and must be stopped, especially clubbing baby seals, which have a coat in their earliest weeks prized by furriers worldwide. The killing of baby seals is forbidden in the United States.

A sizable portion of fur sealing had traditionally been conducted on the high seas. The animals were shot and speared from boats. Using this method, it was impossible to predetermine the sex or age of the animals. Many were only wounded, or sank before they could be retrieved. When a mother seal that was nursing a pup was killed, the pup would face starvation as mothers nurse only their own young.

Almost one million fur seals were taken in this way at sea during the last quarter of the 19th century and during the first decade of the 20th century. No one can calculate how many seals were lost in the process.

By 1911 only about 200,000 fur seals remained on the Pribilof Islands. During the century of Russian control of the islands, they reportedly took 2.5 million pelts. Indiscriminate fur seal slaughter on the high seas was halted in 1911. Under a four-nation treaty, the North Pacific fur seal herds prospered and have now been completely reestablished. The Pribilof herd is now close to 1.5 million. If the size of the herd grows beyond the point the environment can support, the rookeries would become overcrowded. This would result in higher mortality among the seal pups, increased disease and starvation.

For this reason also, 50,000 three- and four-year-old "bachelor" male seals are harvested every summer. This is responsible management on the part of man, and it provides a livelihood for the Aleut population of the area.

The seal population not only *can* be harvested responsibly but it *must* be. This is a reality that the informed public must understand. The question goes back to a rule of thumb especially relevant to renewable resources. Regulations must be established so that there is *wise use without abuse*. When this is applied to the fur seal question, the Aleuts will have a continuing source of livelihood and the fur seals will thrive.

Protecting the polar bear is another difficult situation because the bears roam in an area of international jurisdiction. The top of the world cannot be policed by America alone. All the Arctic regions, especially that belonging to the Soviet Union, are involved.

The Russians do not cause the problem. Rather, it is *our* people illegally taking polar bears in international waters. Today, polar bear hides are stashed offshore beyond the twelve-mile territorial limit;

then they are flown from their iceberg hideaways to Seattle to be sold. One action our government could and should take unilaterally would be not only to limit further the number of polar bears that can be hunted in American territory, but to seize as contraband any illegal hides that come into the American market — from anywhere.

Within the last few decades, the polar bear, the whale and the tiniest living creatures have all become dependent on man. It is entirely up to us whether they survive, not just as zoo exhibits but as free and wild as part of the wonder of this earth. We are the animals of reason and the managers of this planet. The future of our own race may well be determined by hundreds of wild species that play a vital role in the chain of life on which man depends. And there are other considerations. Within the whale, the porpoise and other species of marine life exist mysteries of guidance and communication man is working to unlock — mysteries that one day may help us crack open the secrets of the sea.

But most important, as man evolves to the realization that other creatures and other values may be as important as he is, we suddenly feel the need for our companions on this planet. The inescapable challenge we face at this moment is whether we will hear the cry of the whale and the other animals in time for future generations to be able to enjoy and appreciate all the creatures of our animal world — and whether heeding that cry will teach us to listen also to the cry of man in all corners of the earth.

Love of land and nature is more deeply embedded in the heart and soul of the American Indian than in any other people in our country. While some say the Indian has a lot to learn, I think he has much to teach.

CHAPTER **7**

The American Man

The non-Indian is only beginning to comprehend the nature of the first American man. Although curious about his origin, culture and tradition, we have failed to grasp and appreciate his values. Land, to the Indian, is interwoven with his religion, as is the air and water. For this reason he has sometimes been called, with real truth, the greatest of all conservationists. He learned to live off the land without harming it.

When the white man first arrived in North America, the Indians did not generally object to his settling here. They negotiated treaties determining land boundaries, as there appeared to be room enough for all. Belligerence and war began principally when the white man's government broke or altered treaties without mutual consent. The Indian wars of the 19th century were fought by the Indian for those things he regarded as "his" under agreements he had made with successive generations of white men whose word and signature he had taken in good faith.

Understanding the fact that land has a deep spiritual importance to the Indian, one can begin to gauge the devastation to the Indian culture caused by the crimes of broken treaties and stolen properties.

When the Interior Department was founded in 1849, the Bureau of Indian Affairs (B.I.A.) was transferred from the War Department and placed under the jurisdiction of the Secretary of the Interior. The main reason it was given to Interior was the federal government's approach of looking at Indian problems as problems of reservations and public lands; Interior's primary mandate was to be trustee of those lands. The same philosophy put under

Interior the external territories later acquired by the United States, along with responsibility for governing their peoples.

The B.I.A. is responsible by statute for those Indians who live on the public lands or reservations. They number 462,000. At least another quarter million Indians have left their ancestral homes and moved into urban communities, where they do not come under federal jurisdiction. There are 257 tribes under the B.I.A. and 268 reservations in the lower forty-eight states. There are fewer than half a dozen reservations in Alaska, although there are about 200 Native villages located on federal property.

1. Comradeship in the North

The word "Native" is used in Alaska to identify any descendant of the first Alaskans, which include not only Indians but also the Eskimos and the Aleuts, a distinct ethnic group descended from the original habitants of the Aleutian Island chain.

In contrast to what took place in the "lower forty-eight," the "Native wars" in

Alaska were limited in scope. In the summer of 1741, a Danish sea captain named Vitus Bering, in the pay of the Russian navy, dropped anchor in a ship named *St. Peter* off Kayak Island near the mouth of the Copper River. Many of the seventy-eight men aboard were scholars, not seamen, and it appears they were all appalled by the hostile look of the environment. After taking on fresh water, they could hardly wait to get away. Battling North Pacific gales, they put into what is now Ostrova Bering in the Komadoski group of islands. About half of the *St. Peter*'s complement, including Vitus Bering himself, died of scurvy, but those who survived the vicious winter of 1741-42 eventually sailed their eighty-foot ship into the Siberian port of Kamchatka, carrying with them a fortune in furs.

This very nearly resulted in the end of the native Aleuts as a race. A stampede of unprincipled Siberian freebooters to the island chain led to the systematic elimination of the Aleuts, whose population dwindled in fifty years from 25,000 to 2,000. This was too much even for Catherine the

Great, who proceeded to charter a Russian-American Company to set up a civil government. A talented Irkutsk merchant named Alexander Baranof was put in charge.

In 1791 he arrived in Sitka, in southeastern Alaska, and established a Russian capital there. He restored some order to the situation, but he ruled with a hard hand and incurred the hostility of the Tlingit Indians. In 1802 the Tlingits attacked Sitka, then a community of 452 Russians and friendly Indians; only 42 survived. Baranof took Sitka back two years later. But Baranof had other problems, including personal enemies in St. Petersburg. Driven from power in 1818, he died at sea on the way home, and Russian influence in Alaska deteriorated so badly that the Russian Minister in Washington was only too glad to sell Alaska to the United States for $7.2 million in 1867.

After that, and particularly after the gold-seekers had come and gone in the first decade of this century, a close relationship developed between most Alaska Natives and non-Natives. The harsh climate was partly responsible. It was so difficult to eke out a living and survive the challenges of the environment that a sense of comradeship naturally developed. The community approach to bare survival, common to all lands that lie in the far North, soon erased most of the differences between peoples in Alaska. And the distances and resources of Alaska appeared at that time to be endless. Except for some of the more recent arrivals who live in the comfort of such cities as Anchorage and Fairbanks, Alaskans still consider themselves Alaskans first before they think of themselves as Natives, whites, blacks or Orientals.

However, in the 20th century those newcomers with technologically oriented backgrounds and education brought to Alaska skills that quickly surpassed those of the Natives. In many instances today the Natives, from an economic point of view, live in conditions of extreme poverty and need.

Having known and worked with Alaska Natives for more than twenty-five years, when I became Alaska's Governor I began to reach out and try to do something about these inequities. The great fact I discovered was that members of the Native community were also eager and ready to participate. Their ability and enthusiasm were immediately obvious, and I was determined to appoint Native Alaskans to important positions in various areas of the State government.

One of my first acts was to create the Rural Affairs Commission, an agency designated to deal directly with Native needs. I approached the Alaska Federation of Natives (A.F.N.) and asked its leaders for a list of individuals they felt should be appointed to this commission, which consisted of more than thirty members. In almost every instance we accepted those nominated by the A.F.N. The commission became an active and innovative organization. Up to this time one major problem in Alaska had been that the Native communities were so far away from the seat of State government that they could not afford to send their spokesmen to Juneau. The Rural Affairs Commission provided a structure to fund transportation so that the Native's authentic voice could be heard where it counted.

Our emphasis was on those things that really *meant* something to rural citizens. For example, we created a Remote Housing program. Native leaders could use this to get together and develop their own housing ideas. Natives planned the programs and appointed their own representatives to implement them. They traveled to Washington to apply for federal funds, and they approved the villages that would be eligible for housing as well as the designs of the housing — and the grant-loan ratios.

The key to the success of these programs was active participation rather than passive acceptance. In the spring of 1967 I was informed that there was a need for a school at Pitkas Point, a small Eskimo village on the lower Yukon River. This village had never had a school, and I demanded an explanation for this failure. Officials claimed they would need about two years to design and construct such a school. Further, they claimed that it would cost in the neighborhood of $200,000 — and the appropriated funds had been impounded and frozen by the B.I.A.

We refused to be stopped. I suggested that the villagers build the school on their own time, using their own materials, and we would provide direct assistance from the State. I said, "We can do it on our own."

The school was completed in less than four months, and it opened the following fall. It was built entirely by local citizens with the materials at hand, and cost only $24,000. I made a special trip to Pitkas Point to visit the school, flying in a small float plane. When we landed, the children swarmed down to the river bank to welcome me. It was one of the highlights of my many trips into rural Alaska. The children were proud of their school. The teacher was delighted, and the parents felt a new kinship to government and to the school itself. It was *theirs*. It was not something prefabricated and flown in from somewhere else at great government expense.

I will never forget walking by the school building with the children. They did not say much. They just reached out with their hands and gently stroked the logs in the walls.

Our attitude was that we should look at a situation and humanize the problem. I have always tried to make sure that as we develop natural resources, we also develop our human resources.

We found a similar situation in Tanana, practically in the geographical center of Alaska, where the Indian community needed a sawmill. We provided the saw assembly, and the Indians hewed their own logs and built the mill. It was not a grandiose program involving thousands of people and a mountain of paperwork. It was simply putting tools in the hands of individuals so that they could implement their own ideas. When I visited Tanana, the satisfaction the people felt in their accomplishment was obvious. You could see the dignity of the men working that mill. They asked me, "Governor, how long can we keep it?" I replied, "As long as you keep it busy." Before long they had built a Community Hall and had begun several other projects.

The key to our success was that we did

not pay lip service to the theory that the Native peoples can become involved, contribute positive thoughts and resolve their own problems. We accepted the theory as fact and provided the means and encouragement for the Natives to seize opportunities and prove themselves.

2. And in Washington, Too

I took the same approach when I became Secretary of the Interior, responsible for the Bureau of Indian Affairs. One of my practices in government has always been to surround myself with people, generally young people, who want to do things a little differently than they have been done in the past, and who—most importantly—are men and women of action. Having achieved some successes in this area in Alaska, I decided in Washington to try to find out why the B.I.A. had been so overwhelmed by problems and why it has traditionally been so unresponsive and top-heavy. Determined to make the Indian question one of my priorities, I wrote letters to the leaders of the National Congress of American Indians

(N.C.A.I.) throughout the country, informing them that I was going to reorganize the B.I.A. at the top, placing Indians as leaders in executive positions.[1] I stressed that I was looking for people who had a desire to solve a problem, because it has always been my belief that if you have the desire you are halfway home.

We scoured the country for the new personnel. In several instances I personally went out and recruited. When you have a large organization and you bring in one guy to try and give it a new direction, it's tough.[2] The others close in around him. We wanted a whole new team to run the B.I.A. Collectively they could do a lot of new and original things.

I brought with me to Washington one of my aides from my days as Governor, Morris Thompson, an Athabascan Indian from Tanana in his late twenties. I created a

[1] *The N.C.A.I. represents 350,000 Indians who live on reservations in America. The one major tribe that has not chosen to join the group is the largest Indian nation, the Navajos, who number over 100,000.*

new position for him — Special Assistant to the Secretary for Indian Affairs. I wanted someone working closely with me so I would have direct access to an Indian thought or an Indian idea. In the earlier system, such thoughts moved from the Indian tribal council to the reservation agency, then to the B.I.A. Superintendent, to the Area Director, to the Commissioner in Washington, to the Assistant Secretary for Public Land Management — all before they got to the Secretary. This was impossible for dealing with the human needs to which I wanted to be responsive. I sent Thompson to travel throughout the country, visit the Indian communities and then report back to me and to the B.I.A. Commissioner the problems and opportunities he saw.

"If you liked Custer, you'll love Hickel." This was the slogan with which a group of militants greeted me in Albuquerque, New

[2] *The B.I.A. had 15,000 employees. Most Indians were employed in lower echelons.*

291

Mexico, on October 8, 1969. I had arrived to address the National Congress of American Indians at their annual convention. The militants swarmed into the hall when I began speaking, protesting loudly. At the root of the hostility was fear that the Republican Administration, which I represented, would reactivate the policy of the Eisenhower years known as "termination." This policy was initiated to thrust the Indian population into the mainstream of American life by terminating the trustee relationship between the federal government and the reservation Indian.

Five tribes were "terminated," and the results were disastrous. Unprincipled land developers moved in on the Indians, and their properties and holdings melted away. Having been systematically excluded from the white man's government, the Indian could easily be bilked by civil processes of which he had no knowledge. The whole concept of private ownership was alien to the Indian, who had always based his life on community concepts.

In the past I had been critical of the

Bureau of Indian Affairs, and my previous criticism was interpreted by some as evidence that I favored termination. The relationship between the reservation Indian and the B.I.A. is a complex one. The Indians bitterly criticize the inefficiency and oppressiveness of the Bureau. Yet, if others attack it, they will be the first to come to its defense. They recognize that the Bureau, for all its mistakes, has served as a buffer between the Indian people and Congress. It really is "theirs." Time after time, when Congressional leaders talked of termination or attempted further land and mineral grabs from Indian reservations, the Bureau fended them off. And for this the Bureau is to be commended.

In my speech at Albuquerque I set the record straight:

Neither I nor this Administration have a pro-termination policy. Such a policy can only be established by the Indian community itself, through a clear mandate on the part of your people. Another way of putting it is that I personally, as Secretary of the Interior, and the Bureau of Indian Affairs which is under my jurisdiction, do not intend to tell you what to do. Rather, we will listen to you, work with you and implement the policies which through mutual understanding, will be designed to further improve your state in life.

When I had first entered the hall in Albuquerque, I was greeted by boos, hisses and shouts of "Hickel is a termination honky." Halfway through my speech, N.C.A.I. President Wendell Chinon had to take the microphone to plead with the militants to "offer the Secretary due courtesy as an official of this great country of ours. The Secretary really has the concern of the Indian at heart." I turned a corner with the delegates, and when I finished my address I received a standing ovation.

3. *The Hunt for a New Team*

Soon after taking office, my Assistant Secretary for Public Land Management, Harrison Loesch, helped me assemble a team of five excellent Indian leaders who agreed to take over the B.I.A. This was not a simple task. Many able Indians do not wish to be branded "B.I.A." Furthermore, each appointee must be approved by a Civil Service Board whose standards inherently stack the cards against some Indians. For instance: each top job in government commands a certain level of pay. To qualify, an applicant must already have an income of not less than 10 percent of that attached to the job, and the top executive positions of the Bureau command around $30,000 a year in salary. Secondly, the Civil Service puts a great deal of weight on educational achievement and the absence of a police record. Many of the most capable Indian leaders in America do not have college degrees, and reservation life being what it is, most young men of ability and spunk have been in and out of jail once or twice.

There is enormous pressure that each applicant be of the political party currently in power. It was next to impossible to find a Republican Indian in the United States, especially after the Eisenhower "termination" years. My staff, however, succeeded in convincing Peter Flanigan at the White House that these five Indians, although Democrats or independents, were the men who could do the job.

Our high hopes were soon dashed. When Senator Gordon Allott of Colorado, the ranking Republican on the Senate Interior Committee, heard of our plan, he called members of my staff to his office. He said our nominees would never be confirmed by his committee. He wanted Republicans for these positions. I could understand his position, but in this situation it was impractical and unacceptable if the problem at hand was to be solved.

Ironically, one of the first names we had submitted earlier was a Republican Indian, Peter MacDonald of the Navajos. He was well qualified and available, and I pushed hard for his appointment as a member of the top team. We were not allowed to hire him. The reason given was that he had an illegitimate child. Peter never tried to hide this situation. He was open, aboveboard and honest about it, and was conscientiously supporting the child. He returned to the Navajo reservation to run against the powerful tribal chairman Raymond Nakai for the top position in the biggest Indian tribe in America. He was rejected by the people in Washington, but his people elected him and I congratulated him.

It was one of my most disappointing times when I was told that we had to break up this dynamic young team that had the desire to solve a problem, but even then we had no idea of the further delay this was to cause in finding the right B.I.A. leadership. Refusing to be thwarted in our efforts, we set out to remove from office seventeen of the top executives running the Bureau, all of whom were non-Indians. It was a tough and lengthy struggle that went on for months.

We finally found an acceptable Republican Indian—in Greenwich Village, New York—for the position of B.I.A. Commissioner. His name was Louis Rooks Bruce. He was a Mohawk and Oglala Sioux. Bruce was a founding member and a secretary of the National Congress of

American Indians. For more than a year, however, we did not succeed in filling the top positions under him with qualified Indians. In the meantime, the Bureau was forced to limp along with stopgap leadership.

In spite of resistance from all sides, I was not about to be frustrated. I called in Morris Thompson and other aides and said, "Find me a way to clean this mess up. If we go the legislative route it will take years. I want action now!".

They found a way, but they had to go back to a law written 136 years ago.

4. *The Zunis Take Over*

In early 1970 we sent representatives throughout the country to make it known to the Indian leadership that the B.I.A. was shifting from a management organization to a service one. From now on its role was not to run things but to provide those services that the tribes needed and wanted. It was no longer to be the dominant presence, the all-powerful provider that often usurped the Indians' most valuable assets — their confidence, their manhood and their unique life styles.

Tribes throughout the country were given the option of taking control of any or all of the B.I.A. program functions. In order to allay fears that this was termination in disguise, we guaranteed that the Bureau would provide assistance or reassume control of the functions if requested to do so. We also guaranteed that funding for the programs would not be cut once they were turned over to Indian hands.

The first people to take us up on this offer were the Zuni Indians in New Mexico. On May 23, 1970, the Zuni Governor, Robert Lewis, signed two sets of documents, one in English and the other in Zuni, giving him the responsibility for directing Bureau activities. We had found the legal authority for this action in the original Act of Congress of 1834 that created the B.I.A. It states: "Where any of the tribes are in the opinion of the Secretary . . . competent to direct the employment of their blacksmiths, mechanics, teachers, farmers or other persons engaged with them, the direction of such persons may be given to the proper authority of the tribe." This was yet another example of our whole approach to the way we made government work throughout the Department of the Interior: *Dust off—and use—the laws you've already got on the books, rather than wasting your time trying to ballyhoo unnecessary new laws through Congress.*

We gave total responsibility to the Zunis for directing Bureau programs and employees on its 405,000-acre reservation with its population of 5,000. Our purpose was not to force initiative on any tribe, but to be ready when the tribe was.

Federal employees were given the opportunity to stay with the Zunis and work for the tribe, but with the understanding that at the same time each one would be training a Zuni replacement.

The idea began to catch on. In Ramah, New Mexico, the Navajos signed a $368,000, three-year contract with the B.I.A. to run their own high school. The money was equivalent to what the B.I.A. had been spending to educate the 167 children from the Ramah area. The change meant the school would be Indian controlled, and the children would not be scattered over three states at B.I.A. boarding schools. The latter practice has been particularly hateful to the Indians since family loyalty and cultural awareness were directly undermined when their children were sent away to school.

5. 'Like an Indian Said It'

On July 8, 1970, President Nixon delivered a message on Indian affairs to Congress. It was an historic document and the culmination of months of labor. This statement was so revolutionary that I wondered if the Justice Department fully understood its ramifications. I became involved in its preparation when I received a visit from a twenty-six-year-old woman on the staff of White House Counselor John Ehrlichman. This was Bobbie Green Kilberg, a lawyer from New York who won a White House fellowship and was assigned to work for Ehrlichman on domestic affairs. She especially committed herself to champion the Indian cause in the White House.

I was impressed by Bobbie's commitment and her willingness to stick her neck out. I told her that I would back her all the way, for I immediately had confidence in this girl. Morris Thompson and the top Indians on the B.I.A. staff were instructed to work with her. I said, "When the President addresses the Indian question, it has to sound like an Indian said it."

The greatness of the President's statement was not only that it pooled Indian thought and philosophy, but spelled out concrete steps to rectify injustices and facilitate Indian aims. Rather than just stating the Indian's plight, the message was positive. It articulated eloquently the capacities of the American Indian and the contribution he has made to our national life. The introduction read in part:

The story of the Indian in America is something more than the record of the white man's frequent aggression, broken agreements, intermittent remorse and prolonged failure. It is a record also of endurance, of survival, adaptation and creativity in the face of overwhelming obstacles. It is a record of enormous contributions to the country—to its art and culture, to its strength and spirit, to its sense of history and its sense of purpose.

It is long past time that the Indian policies of the Federal Government began to recognize and build upon the capacities and insights of the Indian people. Both as a matter of justice and as a matter of enlightened social policy, we must begin to act on the basis of what the Indians themselves have long been telling us. The time has come to break decisively with the past and to create the conditions for a new era in which the Indian future is determined by Indian acts and Indian decisions.

The reaction to the President's message from Indian leaders across the nation, even militant groups in the urban areas, was overwhelmingly enthusiastic. At the next Cabinet meeting, I told the President that the finest compliment I had heard came from an Indian who told me, "It sounded like an Indian said it." I had known then that the message was a success.

I committed myself fully to persuade Congress to take action on the specific proposals in the message which could not be handled by executive order. Most important in my opinion was the restoration of the Sacred Lands near Blue Lake, New Mexico, to the Taos Indian Pueblo; the establishment of an Indian Trust Council Authority to assure the independent legal representation for the Indian's natural resource rights; the creation of an Assistant Secretary of the Interior for Indian Affairs, elevating the Indian's voice to a sub-Cabinet position; and a proposed Amendment by Congress to the Johnson-O'Malley Act, authorizing the Secretary of the Interior to channel funds for Indian education directly to Indian tribes and communities instead of to local school districts that are not Indian controlled. This provision would give financial leverage to Indians to shape the school their children attend, and in some instances to set up new school systems of their own.

When I testified before the Senate

subcommittee on an Indian Trust Council Authority, I stated that the white man, on issues relating to Indian rights, had indeed spoken "with a forked tongue." The Authority would bring this to an end. In the present system, the Secretary of the Interior and Attorney General must at the same time advance both the national interest in the use of land and water rights, and the private interest of Indians in land that the government holds as trustee. The evidence is that the Indians are the losers when such a situation arises. If the Indian Trust Council Authority were to be set up by Congress, it would be entirely independent. It would be governed by a three-man board of directors, at least two of whom would be Indians. In its trustee capacity it would be expressly empowered to bring suit in the name of the United States.

Legislation to establish the Trust Council Authority did not get through this particular session of Congress. But in the four and one-half months I had remaining in the federal government, I was able to help win several other battles — including the one involving return of the Blue Lake lands.

6. *Victory at Blue Lake*

The Blue Lake battle—and it was a real battle—had been going on for over sixty years. It was a deep and significant issue because it had to do with the principal religious symbol of an Indian people.

The Taos Pueblo is home for one of the most traditional tribes, traditional because the people have maintained a day-to-day way of life handed down from their ancestors. Their religious leaders, for example, appoint their political leaders. Their religion, a sacred and secret one, is practiced daily. Since the 12th century, Blue Lake has been the site of their annual religious ceremonies, which are closed to non-Indian visitors. But in 1906 Blue Lake was taken over by the Department of Agriculture and made into a National Forest. Since then the tribal leaders had been struggling without success to get it returned.

I will never forget when the Taos Pueblo leaders came to see me for the first time. They were led by the most revered religious leader Taos had, ninety-year-old Jesus

Romero. He was an extraordinary godlike figure. His bearing and carriage symbolized the greatness of the man and his race. Refusing to sit down, he stood with his shawl wrapped tightly around him. Speaking through an interpreter, he said to me: "I am an old man with few years left to live. I heard of this man Hickel in this Washington, D.C., working on our behalf. For the first time in my life I rode in an airplane to come to thank him for his support."

The Blue Lake lands were considered the Taos church, and it angered me that instead of returning it, some Senators wanted to compensate the Indians monetarily for the loss. I asked: "How do you buy a church? How do you buy a culture? How do you buy a way of life?"

I testified before the Senate Subcommittee on Indian Affairs, chaired by Senator George McGovern. Immediately after my testimony he turned the questioning over to Senator Clinton Anderson of New Mexico, who for years had opposed the Taos request. I suspect Anderson's position stemmed in part from the demands of the timber interests in his State and those of downriver water users. We did not have political weight behind our position. There would be no great benefits for large numbers of American people if we won. We were fighting great legislative powers, and our argument was based on the need of a people small in number. We were fighting the issue on its pure, clean merit.

Some of the exchange between Senator Anderson and myself went as follows:

SENATOR ANDERSON: "You say restoration of the Blue Lake land to the Taos Pueblo is a symbolic issue. Where does that restoration begin? What title did it have?"

SECRETARY HICKEL: "What I was thinking, Senator, was giving them back their 48,000 acres as a restoration of the Blue Lake."

SENATOR ANDERSON: "If the Indians never had title how can they restore title?"

SECRETARY HICKEL: "As I recall, Senator, the Indian Claims Commission said they had title."

SENATOR ANDERSON: "No, aboriginal title but not actual title. So, the aboriginal issue has long been decided because 89 percent of all land in North America was involved in this aboriginal title. Do you believe in transferring all of the lands to the Taos Indians?"

SECRETARY HICKEL: "No, Senator, we think . . . that this is a unique situation because of the religious significance of that land."

SENATOR ANDERSON: "It has been a long story of their use of it, but who had title to it?"

SECRETARY HICKEL: "If you mean many years ago, I would say the Indians."

SENATOR ANDERSON: "Does that agree with the courts?"

SECRETARY HICKEL: "According to the Indian Claims Commission. We are just trying to restore, give this land to the Indians as an historical right."

SENATOR ANDERSON: "You mean give and not restore?"

SECRETARY HICKEL: "Okay, yes, I would agree, as long as they got it."

SENATOR ANDERSON: "I am merely trying to say we don't know for sure that this land is restored. Theodore Roosevelt said it was public domain and put it under the Forest Service. Was he a thief?"

SECRETARY HICKEL: "I would not think so."

After a half hour of questioning, Senator Anderson and his staff had implied that I was trying to have the lands moved to the jurisdiction of the Interior Department for personal reasons, that I would let the land and lake be polluted by allegedly unwise grazing practices used by the Indians, and even that I was undoing the conservation work of Theodore Roosevelt. I held my ground.

The Taos leaders themselves testified, as did others who began to rally to our support. To my great delight, the Indians won their case and the Blue Lake lands — their church — were returned, evidence that a new day can come for the American Indian if the people will care.

The signing of the bill took place in the White House after my firing. The Taos elders came in, looked around at the President and all the dignitaries. One of them said, "Where's the Secretary?"

7. *A Moral Claim*

One of the items of unfinished business before Congress that most concerned me was the question of what Alaska lands and benefits should accrue to the Native population. The State's right to select 103 million acres was held up until this could be resolved. Although this caused difficulties for the young State, I maintained as Governor and later as Secretary that this was a priority issue and should be honored by Congress.

Before any attempt was made by the federal government to try to settle the Native claims, I put in a bill to the State legislature that said that if the land freeze was lifted by the Secretary of the Interior by a certain date in October 1968, the State of Alaska would award the Natives the sum of $50 million. This was not an attempt to settle the claims but to show our concern and demonstrate we were dedicated to getting a settlement. Fifty million dollars was a lot of money for our State; this was before the value of the oil on the North Slope was fully appreciated. Our bill passed both Houses in Juneau and I signed it.

Later, Secretary Udall, under the Johnson Administration, proposed a settlement for $185 million. In October 1968 I accompanied him when he went to Fairbanks to make this announcement to the Alaska Federation of Natives. I spoke off the cuff for fifteen or twenty minutes about my deep concern for the Native people of Alaska. Afterward, Udall was introduced. He threw away his prepared speech and also spoke extemporaneously. I always wondered what was in that speech and why he had not made a serious attempt to settle the issue during his eight years as Secretary.

A few months after I became Secretary, we introduced a bill to settle the claims for $500 million plus 8 to 12 million acres of land. This was a great breakthrough. I personally battled to convince the Administration that this was a priority item. It was President Nixon's decision to make the Bureau of the Budget support our testimony on the $500 million. At first the Bureau of the Budget objected and wanted more time to study the idea. I had to testify, so I told the Bureau, "I'll give you until 5 P.M. tomorrow to decide, because I'm going to testify for it anyway." At 4:55 P.M. the phone rang, and Sam Hughes of the Bureau of the Budget said, "Go ahead."

On July 15, 1970, this bill passed the Senate only to get lost in the House Committee on Interior and Insular Affairs. This was a great disappointment. The battle had to continue.

From the very first, my position was clear. Regardless of whether the Natives had a legal claim, they had a moral claim. And this is what Congress will eventually realize and accept.

8. *Pipe Carrier*

In early July 1970 I accepted the invitation of the leaders of the Crow Indian Nation to visit their rugged and beautiful ancestral land near Billings, Montana. Nine months after I had been heralded as Custer reincarnate, the Indian people demonstrated to me their gratitude for the direction we were beginning to take on federal Indian policy.[3]

After welcoming me to the reservation, the Crow leaders took me to a secluded spot isolated from human habitation. Unfolding blankets, we sat together on the ground in

---

[3] *An ironic touch was that this same reservation is the site of Custer's Last Stand. The annual reenactment of the event came one week after my visit.*

314

reverence and solitude as Crow Indian prayers were recited. They offered the pipe of peace, first to "the One Above, the First Person, and the First Maker"; then to "Mother Earth so that our moccasins may follow the trail of beauty forever"; followed by "the East from whence Grandfather Sun brings us daylight; the South, where eternal summer lives; the West where the Sun wraps his scarlet robes around him"; and finally to "the North, where eternal winter lives."

Barney Old Coyote spoke: "This ground is sacred ground. It is here that we return our blessings to nature. We did not attempt to control it. We lived in harmony with our surroundings."

I was adopted into the tribe and given the name of Pipe Carrier. This I considered a great honor, as the bearer of the peace pipe was a position of high trust in the tribe. Carrying the pipe, the bearer could approach an enemy without harm in order to negotiate peace.

"We depended on our pipe carriers," Barney Old Coyote explained. "They were above petty things. They provided advice and guidance. They dealt with our enemies, but more importantly, they determined how we dealt with nature."

As the pipe of peace was passed, the Indians grouped around me and watched carefully. I had been told that the mouthpiece must always face the next person in the line as the pipe is passed. What I did not know was that the pipe must not be turned too far. By instinct or by luck, I received and passed the pipe in perfect Indian style, and a report that reached me later stated, "Everyone was pleased, for this was a good omen."

When asked to say a few words, I spoke from my heart: "We can learn a great deal from the Indian people about nature, for you know how to use her, not abuse her. The spot where we stand today shows wise utilization of land, and we are grateful to you for showing us the way. I hope that I can live my life so as to show in some small way I understand you."

I concluded by recalling that we had been told to think serious thoughts as we smoked the pipe. I told them what had gone through my mind at that moment: "The White Man has worn a war bonnet since time began. Wouldn't it be great if we could all sit down and smoke the pipe of peace?"

9. 'Go Ahead and Make Mistakes!'

On October 21, 1970, the National Congress of American Indians invited me back to speak to their annual convention. This time it was in my home town of Anchorage, Alaska. I was proud that three days earlier we had been able to announce to the nation the creation of the new team to run the B.I.A. In the seventeen top posts under the Commissioner, fifteen were Indian men and women.

Aware of the ways of government, I knew that even though the career non-Indian men and women had been removed from the top slots, there would be others hovering over the new team, waiting for it to slip. The audience in Anchorage gave me a standing ovation in the middle of my address when I stated, "There will be those who will wait for the new leadership to make mistakes so they can say, 'I told you so. He's not qualified for a job that size.' Well I say to the new team: 'Have the courage of your convictions. *Go ahead and make mistakes!* As long as your aim is to better conditions for *all* Indians, I will back you 100 percent.' "

I stressed that it is not only the Indian and Native peoples who are facing a dramatic reexamination of values. A metallic society has lost its attractiveness to millions of Americans, especially among the young. Money is not the answer to all problems. It does not satisfy the spirit of man. As modern man realizes more and more that materialism is not the ultimate goal in life, he will turn to those such as the American Indian, who has a deeper relationship with the essence of living. The original American man not only understands that relationship, he lives it.

One of my few regrets in leaving Washington was that I would no longer be in an official position to help advance the vision we had of launching and sustaining a united effort to bring the American Indian to his full stature in American life. Still ahead of us is the task of fashioning the kind of quality education in which every young Indian not only is prepared to meet the challenges of modern society, but understands and is proud of his identity. We must develop health and support services so that the young can grow up with full access to one of the greatest freedoms of all, the freedom from malnutrition and illness. And we must move forward in our programs to develop the talents of leadership and management so that every tribe in America can be rid of the fear of losing its properties, and begin to take full advantage of the opportunities available.

Above all, and I concluded my remarks to the Indians with these words, "Let's provide the vision for our young people, of all races of America, so that they can look forward to the future with eager expectancy and can demonstrate a promise for the rest of the world of how men are meant to live."

Confine the automobile and free the person. Don't confine the person to free the automobile.

CHAPTER **8**

A New Way Out

What Henry Ford conceived when he built the first Model T was a great idea; a dream of much-needed personal transportation for rural Americans. But this concept has become a nightmare for urban Americans, where the automobile has become our number-one environmental problem. I have often said, and not altogether facetiously, that what we need in the United States is a pill for the automobile.

There are now about 105 million cars, buses and trucks on American roads — more than one wheeled vehicle for every two people in the United States. The automobile has simply had too high a priority in this country. It overwhelms the parks, the cities and the highways. It may soon overwhelm

America. It is also responsible—though by no means entirely so—for polluting the air, attacking man's health, fouling his nest and undermining his morale.

This is not just a matter of "air pollution." Even if pure oxygen came out of all the exhaust pipes of America's automobiles, the same automobiles would still pollute. They crowd and bump each other on the freeways and on the streets of the central cities; they take up too much space by jamming millions of square miles of asphalt and concrete. When an automobile wears out and "dies," its corpse is dumped to lie exposed in one of the great open-air graveyards that curse our metropolitan environs and our countryside. Each such piece of junk has burned up enormous amounts of fossil fuels. Like the farms that blew away in Kansas when I was a boy, this involves a wanton waste of our natural resources.

The automobile is a basic necessity, but it also has created a social problem in urban America that is nearly insurmountable. What we are dealing with in this world, as I see it, is the environment of the mind, tied into the environment of the soul. The problem is not just money. It is not just education; it is not just security; it is not even the problem of a job. It is the combination of these problems that causes a man to become depressed. And a large part of this stems from the problems of transportation in a society now overly dependent upon the automobile. How do we deal with the frustration of a person who, when he gets up in the morning, is tormented by questions like: *Is the weather bad? When will I get to work? What's the traffic going to be? Where am I going to park? When will I get home?*

Although not yet a problem in rural America, it is devastating our great metropolitan areas. This does not mean that the automobile is not necessary. It is, and we could not live without it. But our dependence on it without choice has begun to enslave us.

1. A Roadbed in the Sky

How do we free Americans from their enslavement to road transport? What kind of transport is in the best interests of this country for moving people? The answer lies in high-speed mass rapid transit, elevated and electrified over long and short distances.

The technology is there. It has been there for at least twenty years, but it has been almost totally ignored by this country. The fast Metroliner rail service belatedly put into operation between New York and Washington is a partial solution at the surface level to a special problem, and the Metroliner's high-density passenger load indicates that people will still ride fast trains if there are fast trains to ride. But long before the Metroliner came into service, I had several rides on Japan's elevated Tokyo-Osaka express which, with one stop at Nagoya, averages more than 100 mph on a 350-mile run—a little more than three hours of travel time, downtown to downtown. Northern Europe has its splendid Trans-European Express; the Italians have their Rapidos.

These trains are all ground-level trains, with the exception of the Tokyo-Osaka express, and we need the elevated concept if we are to be able to move people around in speed, safety and comfort. We should be thinking about American needs in the year 2000, and the time to turn this thing around is now.

Suppose we took a high-speed train and, using existing right-of-way facilities, put the track on stilts? This is an engineering and economic feasibility. The train can and should be the most dependable form of all-weather transport, and elevated trackage would eliminate many of the old railroad problems like grade crossings and wooden tie maintenance. Electrically powered, such a train could use the Water Level Route of the old New York Central to cut the running time between New York and Chicago to eight hours. It could take aboard trucks and transport them, safely and pollution-free, up to 900 miles overnight in half the time required to drive the same distance over existing freeways that simply cannot be rebuilt to make truck transport move much faster than it does now. In the long run, the cost of moving foodstuffs and manufactured goods from one place to another would come down if we did the job on elevated rails—and the reduction would show in the housewife's budget. Additionally, the thousands of people who genuinely prefer a more leisurely mode of travel to the frustrations of airport traffic jams, both on the ground and in the air, would have a transportation alternative that most other industrialized countries provide their citizens as a matter of course. We also would be creating transportation corridors to achieve the highest and best use of our space without polluting it.

We have only ourselves to blame for the fact that in most of our cities today the only option available for personal transportation is an automobile or a crowded bus. We once had a good mass rapid transit system in this country, and we once had a good long-distance surface transport system on rails. But the Highway Trust Fund, established during the Eisenhower Administration at a cost to date of about $62 *billion*, has created an environmental abomination.

Now we even plan cities around the automobile without any thought for the spiritual environment. A highway engineer comes along and complains that the city is in the way of his road. This is crazy. The new approach to the city should start with closing off some of its streets to the automobile, as Mayor John Lindsay of New York has begun to do during certain hours and on weekends in selected areas such as Fifth and Madison avenues and Central Park. We ought to be establishing a freeway for the people of this country, not just the automobiles. To make a point, if we confined the automobile to the space given the American pedestrian and gave the pedestrian the space used by the automobile, we would be better off.

We ought to be merging the various modes of transport — air, necessary short-haul trucking, long-distance elevated rail — in a balanced and coherent system regulated at the federal level. Such mergers should not only be permitted but encouraged. It is ridiculous that we should have forbidden a railroad to acquire an interstate trucking company, or vice versa.

It was not government regulation that caused the financial troubles of the railroads following World War II, but the *lack* of regulation. We do not need less government, but more effective government. When American government reacts, it usually overreacts. What we did in the 1950's is a classic example of overreacting. Looking upon the railroads as corporate villains, we created the Highway Trust Fund, which has now become so powerful that a community is penalized if it does not take advantage of the financing it provides. San Francisco is one city that refused the bait and declined to have more freeways ripping through its middle, loaded with cars and trucks giving out noxious fumes. With considerable courage, San Francisco turned down federal funds and at great cost put together the financing of a rail system known as **BART** (Bay Area Rapid Transit). This is a difficult decision for any communtiy to make. But San Francisco looked at the problem on a long-term basis, not for short-term gain.

Elsewhere, the Highway Trust Fund grew more powerful year by year, and while wheeled vehicles multiplied on the new roads, the number of daily passenger trains dwindled in 1971 to less than 200 as compared with 20,000 forty years ago. As trains were dropped, the American people were the losers. Most of the various rights-of-way came from grants of public land originally owned by all Americans. Now these weedy rights-of-way, along with boarded-up depots and rusty rails, mock our memories of a once great passenger transportation system, conceived and built for the public good.

2. An Iron Wheel and a Rail

Old-fashioned surface rail transportation, whether powered by steam or by diesel fuel, accounted for less pollution of the atmosphere than cars and trucks do today, riding the freeways that have destroyed the look of some of the most beautiful areas in this country and wasting an enormous amount of resources. Yet the old steam locomotive did pollute, and so does the diesel. It is unthinkable to rebuild the railway system as it was; but it is also unthinkable to lie down and let the automobile and the truck continue to run over us. We must build a new system, with electrical power and elevated tracks to take care of the environmental problems — and give us "a new way out."

Can we afford this?

The disappearance of the passenger train from the wide reaches of America is a public disgrace, but there is no point in minimizing the financial troubles of American railroads. Because of a poor competitive position, these troubles are very considerable. This was brought home when the management of the Penn Central, an amalgam of the New York Central and the Pennsylvania Railroad, called it quits and went into bankruptcy overnight. This was a perfect example of *bad* private management and *poor* government regulation.

Yet the trains that remained kept running — or some of them did. Why? As a mode of transporting people and goods, the iron wheel and a rail still make a combination hard to beat. I felt this way when I was Governor of Alaska. In my first State of the State message, delivered in January 1967, I asked the State House of Representatives and the Senate, sitting in joint session, to fund a commission to explore the future of transportation in Alaska. I had in mind primarily the iron wheel and a rail—that is, the expansion of the federally owned Alaska Railroad to points such as Prudhoe Bay, where the oil strike was beginning to come in, and to Nome on the Bering Sea.

I had in mind the coordination of *all* overland transport inside "corridors" that could make manageable the delivery of goods and people to their destination. It would also provide a practical system for millions of Americans to see and enjoy the scenic grandeur of this vast area—the finest kind of development and conservation.

The legislature appropriated $750,000, and I appointed ten members of what came to be known as the NORTH Commission, "NORTH" being an acronym for "Northern Operations of Rail Transportation and Highways." I appointed five Alaskans[1] and five men from

---

[1] *The five Alaskans: Chairman Al Swalling, Anchorage contractor and civic leader; Jack White, Anchorage realtor long interested in*

outside Alaska. Among the five "outsiders" were Reginald Whitman, former vice-president of the Great Northern Railroad, later President Nixon's Railroad Administrator in the Department of Transportation; Sam Pryor, vice-president of Pan American World Airways; and Everett Hutchinson, Under Secretary of Transportation in the Johnson Administration. Ex-officio members were Brigadier General Charles A. Lindbergh and Sargent Shriver, former Peace Corps director.

The State of Alaska was funding research work the federal government should have done long ago. Washington showed its usual lack of interest in Alaska, and oil companies who could have used the railroad to carry their produce in and out showed no interest at all. Had the railroad been extended, an enormous area of northern

Arctic development; John Manley, general manager of the Alaska Railroad; William Snedden, publisher of the Fairbanks Daily News-Miner; *Jack Coghill, Mayor of Nenana, near Fairbanks.*

Alaska would have been opened up wisely for its highest and best use, and many of the environmental dangers mentioned in the argument about the building of an Alaska pipeline from Prudhoe Bay to Valdez would have been avoided.

There was considerable public benefit to be gained by improving the condition of the railroad industry—and there still is. Industries have declined and become extinct. Of course, it should not be government policy to preserve each and every declining industry. But the railroads are unique. They are *essential.* They can move goods and people overland in quantity and at a speed no other transportation mode can match. With all their financial troubles, railroads still carry twice as many ton miles of manufactured goods inside the United States as does the trucking industry.

Railroads are not technologically obsolete; if they were, we might as well forget the argument. They have the permanent advantages of exclusive rights-of-way, simple guidance systems and narrow route requirements per unit of carrying capacity. These technological advantages readily translate into lower costs of delivering anything. For bulk commodities, rail cost is a tiny fraction of what it costs to ship by truck, and although the margin is much closer for high-value manufactured goods, the iron wheel still has the edge.

The solution is to electrify, elevate where possible and make the iron wheel turn faster. As for financing, we built a magnificent railroad system once before. At the end of the Civil War in 1865, the United States had 35,000 miles of rail trackage, more than existed in all of Europe; by 1900 we had more than five times that amount. If we performed this miracle with an industrial capacity much less than what we possess now, we can surely build a modern rail transport system for 300 million Americans by the year 2000. But we can do it only if we "turn it around" *now*.

To begin with, the Highway Trust Fund should be renamed the Transportation Trust Fund, and the bulk of the money should be rechanneled into the building of high-speed elevated conveyances. The same financing, and the same research, would contribute to the creation of new mass rapid transit for local purposes.

3. Too Many Automobiles

Transportation as such was not my department in Washington, so it was not immediately possible for me to get a handle on a problem that had concerned me for years. However, I did find the occasional opportunity to move on it. In early 1970 the officials of Yosemite National Park in California communicated to me the seriousness of the crowding problem they were facing in the beautiful Yosemite Valley. After evaluating the situation, I told the officials, "You don't have too many people in your park; you have too damned many automobiles." As I had suspected, the Yosemite people were trying to cope with the same logjam that Yellowstone National Park encounters every summer when visitors are funneled along one road bumper to bumper, barely able to move and unable to enjoy what they came a long distance to see. I have never been pleased by the automobile industry's boast that 95 percent of the 40 million people who visit our national parks every year arrive by car. The trouble with that statistic is that it is probably accurate, and any attempt to commune with or commute to nature is frustrated by the kind of surface traffic that one associates with the downtown rush hour of a large city.

The upshot was that we banned automobiles from key areas of Yosemite and substituted a simple and unobtrusive means of public conveyance. We gave visitors parking space outside the park and then transported them on land-tour buses that they could hop on and off at will. What some people might have thought was a restriction on their freedom in fact was a device to provide more freedom for all.

I put my staff to work developing similar types of conveyances to operate in great parks such as Yellowstone. I visited Yellowstone personally and toured it by horseback. It seemed to me that visitors ought to be able to leave more freely the tiny ribbon of asphalt to which they are now restricted and move out into the wild and the wilderness to enjoy the refreshing character of nature in its raw state.

This was unfinished business when President Nixon fired me as Secretary of the Interior. I still believe that public conveyances can be built and operated in parks such as Yellowstone. People who are limited in time could then get in and out of remote areas of beauty in a single day.

But at the time I was not thinking just about parks — I was trying to demonstrate a possible answer to some of the environmental problems of urban America.

4. Street Scene

In early 1969, Mayor John Lindsay of New York came to see me. I have always liked the imagination of this man. Lindsay and I have the same concern for what the automobile is doing to the quality of American life; in fact, the Mayor once remarked, while riding in a helicopter over New York City, "If I had a laser gun, I'd destroy all those cars down there."

Lindsay and I discussed the problems of the urban environment and my ideas for taking parks to the people, especially with regard to the Gateway recreational area on the outskirts of New York City. Our conversation laid the groundwork for a program that came to be called "Street Scene." It was the first step in our effort to reclaim the cities from the automobile and give them back to the people. It was about time that a Secretary of the Interior, through the Bureau of Outdoor Recreation, addressed himself to the pressing needs of urban dwellers.

The idea was simple. We offered federal money to any municipality that would dedicate a street or series of streets to be totally free of automobiles. We would rip up the asphalt and substitute trees, park benches and playgrounds—whatever the city and its people desired. We wanted to start making the cities of America come alive again.

We began in Washington, D.C., itself. On August 10, 1970, Mayor Walter Washington and I jointly announced an $800,000 project, the cost shared equally by Interior and the District of Columbia, to close off five city blocks and make them into accessible recreation areas for all age groups. Mayor Washington hailed the program as a "great step in improving the quality of life for Washington residents." When I left Interior, we were programmed to handle at least 100 similar applications.

I shall never forget that autumn night in New York, in November 1970, when I walked the streets of midtown Manhattan with Mayor Lindsay. These were streets that had been blocked off from traffic. Every two or three blocks as we walked, followed by a festive and happy crowd of New Yorkers, we encountered a musical group, a guitarist or a band, playing to amuse people of many races and backgrounds, playing for the enjoyment of making people happy. Shop owners had kept their stores open for the evening and would invite people to come in for a cup of coffee just because—for one night at least—it was fun to live in a city that cared more for its people than for its automobiles.

The whole issue of the urban environment fascinates me because it is in the urban areas that 85 percent of America lives.

Some people have wrongly imagined that the battle to improve our environment involves simply ocean front and forest, or mountain range and meadow. In reality, the environment means the surroundings in which a person may live. It could be a junkyard across the street. For this reason, the urban environment is a top priority in America.

The urban problem has as its central core the fact that people need to live with reasonable access to their work but still crave the open spaces of country living. The inner-city problem is created when we force a man to come into a metropolitan area for his economic survival—and live there unhappily. He may be able to afford the price of commuting, and be willing to pay it. But what a price! In the one and three-quarter hours that it takes some commuters to get to their jobs in New York, three men in a spacecraft can orbit the earth. The same American technology that made it possible to land men on the moon can make it possible to take other men to and from their work efficiently. The answer to part of our urban crisis lies in a transit system that will move the worker from his home, fifty or even seventy-five miles away, to his city job in far less time than it takes him to get there now. The central city would then become what it ought to be — a harmonious workshop — and people working there would be able to live about as far away as they pleased. Those who genuinely preferred to live in urban apartments could continue to do so, but they would no longer be trapped there.

It is not true to say that thousands and millions of people cannot live together; they can, but not if they are jammed together in the wrong way, even for pleasure. I remember going aboard a pleasure boat in Balboa Bay, California, in the summer of 1969. The boats were so thick that they could hardly move around; in fact, you could barely see the water. I said at the time, "This is a perfect example of pleasure pollution." I meant what I said. It is insane for people to be irritating one another for "pleasure" when a better system of transportation can be built to move them around the open spaces owned by all Americans for the enjoyment of all.

The freedom to move, the freedom to find "a new way out," is a desperate need shared by millions of people living in our cities, and practically all those who live in slums. I made that point at a meeting in Washington I attended with Transportation Secretary John Volpe and Secretary George Romney of Housing and Urban Development. I stated that if we were going to plan new cities around old ideas, they could count me out.

5. Moving People

I was never one of those who raised their voices against the development of an American supersonic transport airplane (the SST) *just* on environmental grounds during the great controversy that raged in the United States until Congress finally voted to shut off the money in the spring of 1971. The federal government had, and still has, the power and the ability to lay down regulations that would force the SST to be environmentally "clean."

I always felt that the issue was how best to move people from one place to another.

Undoubtedly the SST, if built correctly, could cut a couple of hours off the flying time between New York and London. But we could use the Boeing 707's and 747's and Douglas DC-8's and DC-10's to cut the same two hours off the *total* travel time by building a high-speed monorail from midtown New York to Kennedy International Airport and another one from Heathrow to the West End of London. We could do that at a fraction of the cost of building, flying and servicing the SST.

I never had any objection to an SST being completed by private industry through its own financing, after the initial investment of nearly $800 million of federal funds. But I thought that a higher priority on the spending of public money in the 1970's should be on mass rapid transit to benefit tens of millions of people rather than a few thousand.

I was unimpressed by the "prestige" argument, which was advanced because the Russian and Franco-British SST's were already being flight-tested. In the summer of 1970 it was becoming widely known that the French and the British were having second thoughts about whether their Concorde would ever be a profitable aircraft. In relation to the American prototype, the figure of 300 SST's started to be mentioned as an economic break-even point; and who in the world needed 300 SST's to haul people? Especially if they did not fly overland? Could the airlines commit themselves to buying that many SST's without going bankrupt?

That was my frame of mind when the President wrote me a letter soliciting my opinion:

July 23, 1970

Dear Mr. Secretary:

As you will recall, the Administration conducted a searching review last year of the Supersonic Transport development program, and of the consequences of either continuing it or abandoning it. As a result of that review, I concluded in September that the national interest required us to go forward with the program.

As you are also of course aware, debate over the SST has continued in Congress

343

and elsewhere around the country. I should greatly appreciate, at this time, an expression of your current opinion of the SST program and its effects on such matters as the balance of payments, the environment, employment, or the economy and commerce of the nation as a whole. I shall especially welcome your views on these questions as they relate to the responsibilities of your own Department.

Sincerely,
Richard Nixon

I replied eight days later as follows:

July 31, 1970
Dear Mr. President:

I have given great personal consideration to your July 23 letter requesting views on the SST. The magnitude of the project requires that each member of the Cabinet respond with the highest sense of public responsibility.

Of most immediate concern to my

344

mandate at Interior is the effect of the SST on the environment, specifically in the areas of 1) sonic boom, 2) airport noise, and 3) the addition of water vapor in the stratosphere and related changes in ozone concentrations. I am pleased by the strong efforts being undertaken by Secretary Volpe in environmental research on these issues. I agree with the Council on Environmental Quality that the two prototype aircraft in themselves represent no threat to the environment. Equally, I believe it is important that the horse be kept in front of the cart and that we insure that satisfactory solutions to these environmental problems actually exist before a major commitment is made for commercial production.

In turn, it is of concern to me that foreign developments of supersonic transports might significantly impair the favorable trade posture of our aircraft industry. In considering all factors, however, I cannot say that I have complete confidence in the economic justification for the SST.

Enough doubt exists to persuade me that SST production could have a negative rather than a beneficial effect on our balance of payments.

Another concern bears upon the wisdom of the Federal Government in assuming the full risk of this venture without sharing the benefits if development is successful. The risks are compounded by the uncertainty as to the ability of private enterprise to finance development following the prototype stage, and especially when one considers the current fiscal condition of the airline industry. In accepting this risk, I have long thought that the Administration might consider the COMSAT model as a way to allow the Government to share substantially in both the uncertainties and the revenues.

We must maintain our technological superiority in air transportation; however this superiority must be carefully related to the environmental and sociological costs. I am convinced that with proper balance and effective planning, we can achieve both goals.

Respectfully yours,

Walter J. Hickel
Secretary of the Interior

I have added the italics to point out the two paragraphs in this letter, here published for the first time, that caused a sonic boom in the White House. John Whitaker of the President's staff telephoned to say this was not the reply that "we had in mind." I told John emphatically that the President had asked for my opinion, and this was my honest answer.

The letter was sent back to the Department of the Interior with the two offending paragraphs marked for deletion, and we began studying the problem of drafting a substitute letter that would convey the sense of *their* views. The final version went like this:

August 3, 1970

Dear Mr. President:

I have given great personal consideration to your July 23 letter requesting views on the SST. The magnitude of the project requires that each member of the Cabinet respond with the highest sense of public responsibility.

Of most immediate concern to my mandate at Interior is the effect of the SST on the environment, specifically in the areas of 1) sonic boom, 2) airport noise, and 3) the addition of water vapor in the stratosphere and related changes in ozone concentrations. I am pleased by the strong efforts being undertaken by Secretary Volpe in environmental research on these issues. I agree with the Council on Environmental Quality that the two prototype aircraft in themselves represent no threat to the environment. Equally, I believe it is important that the horse be kept in front of the cart and that we insure that satisfactory solutions to these environmental problems actually

348

exist before a major commitment is made for commercial production.

We must maintain our technological superiority in air transportation; however, this superiority must be carefully related to environmental and sociological costs.

Respectfully yours,

Walter J. Hickel
Secretary of the Interior

We probably have not yet heard the last of the SST argument, but until we solve the "people problem" of the airport, we really cannot get anyone from here to there much quicker. Like so many things in our society, the airport now gets built around the automobile. One of my favorite airports is Seattle-Tacoma International. But they are now building a garage there for 8,000 automobiles. With efficient mass rapid transit, possibly using Seattle's existing monorail as a model, large airports would cease to be parking lots and would become what they should be—places where you step off a comfortable surface conveyance, get on the airplane and go.

The proper place for an airport servicing a large city is fifty miles or more outside the center of that city. Dulles International Airport in Virginia, thirty-five miles outside Washington, D.C., is probably closer to what I have in mind than any other large American airport. The trip to and from the airport is efficient within the limits of rubber-wheeled bus transport, which is subject to rush-hour traffic jams. We could make it much more efficient by putting the conveyance on elevated steel rails. The federal government owns plenty of land between the City of Washington and Dulles, including the median space on the divided highway. Who owns that right-of-way? You and I do. All Americans own it, and we share the obligation for its wisest use.

To turn your mind off from your heart when you make a decision affecting human lives is to isolate yourself from reality and morality.

CHAPTER **9**

An Isolation of Thought

The adversary principle is deeply rooted in American government. It is the basis of frank and open political debate. It is the reason the press conference evolved as it did in American public life. Unlike their British opposite numbers, the President and the members of his Cabinet do not appear on the floors of Congress in full session for questioning. So the press performs the questioning (or "adversary") function on behalf of the public. Someone has to do it, because even aggressive questioning by newsmen beats tame acceptance of an executive decision that otherwise would go unquestioned.

A strong Cabinet system is essential for

American government, because people have more faith in decisions they know have been debated and thoroughly thrashed out at that level. There have been many "adversaries" in American Cabinets, starting with Thomas Jefferson, our first Secretary of State. His concept of government was so different from that of Secretary of the Treasury Alexander Hamilton that it still seems a wonder that George Washington, as President, was able to keep them in the same room. When I raised my adversary's voice in the Nixon Administration, urging action, I was following guidelines set by the President-elect himself when he introduced the members of his Cabinet: "I haven't found any one of them who agrees with me completely on everything that I believe. . . but that's all to the good. I don't want a Cabinet of yes-men."

I was also following the natural instincts of Walter Joseph Hickel to fight positively for the programs I believed in, to find ways to do things rather than reasons not to do them. I encouraged my own assistants at Interior to be adversaries, to challenge my reasoning and my positions. If none of them did so, I would proceed to rip one of my own programs to shreds. I wanted my people to tell me if they thought I was wrong and had an alternate position to advocate and defend. In government you meet with those who are with you and those who are against you. If you start locking out people who are against you, pretty soon you are standing alone in a closet and afraid to look in a mirror.

It is not my nature to fit old solutions to new problems, so in the Cabinet I was always looking ahead, not back. I won some of my battles and lost some. As an adversary, I thought of myself as one of the President's truest and most loyal friends. The adversary nearly always is a friend, because within the house he usually has a greater love for the structure than anyone else. He cares enough to communicate, and he wants to preserve the house that others merely want to use as long as it stands.

1. A Deafening Silence

I think in retrospect that my first strong disagreement with the Administration took place at an April 1969 Cabinet meeting at the White House. The subject was money. Largely because of the Vietnam war, we had inherited a serious inflationary situation from the preceding Administration, and I was convinced that the medicine we were prescribing for the American people was the wrong kind.

When the discussion turned to fiscal matters on that spring day, I determined to try to hammer home the point that high interest rates *cause* inflation. I was sitting beside Secretary of the Treasury David Kennedy when I spoke up.

Kennedy was shocked. He was absolutely astonished that I should question the orthodox view that higher interest rates would automatically dry up buying power, choke the inflationary process and make everybody better off. This may have been true in the days of a *cash* economy, but definitely not in 1969. We were now living in a *credit* economy. I felt strongly that raising the prime interest rate charged by the Federal Reserve would make a bad matter worse. In fact, I felt that we would end up with the worst of both worlds—inflation and unemployment—and I said so.

There was a deafening silence around the Cabinet table. The President knew the point I was trying to make. We had talked previously about the fiscal situation in the United States, and I had aired to him my views on the subject of high interest rates when we met at his New York apartment in 1967, before he announced his candidacy for President.

President Nixon looked across the table at me and finally said: "I understand Wally's situation. I understand his thought, and I respect his opinion." The thrust of his response was clear. The President realized how I felt about this subject, but he did not expect me to dwell at length about fiscal matters and high interest rates.

This was the first signal I had that there were those in the Administration who were experiencing what I called "an isolation of thought." Little consideration was being given to unorthodox proposals or to ideas not already "accepted." As the weeks and months went by, I would meet often on various budgetary and fiscal matters with other members of the Cabinet: Secretary Kennedy of the Treasury, Secretary Maurice Stans of Commerce, Secretary Romney of HUD and Secretary George Shultz of Labor. When we worked on the budget, I strongly expressed my thoughts to Robert Mayo, director of the Bureau of the Budget.

I never got to first base. At one meeting, Postmaster General Winton ("Red") Blount said: "Wally, if we're going to talk about that interest thing again, you've got to understand that we can't save the world. Let's not waste any more time on that."

I turned to Paul McCracken, chairman of the President's Council of Economic Advisors. "Paul, sometime I'd really like to talk to you about this problem. We're going to increase inflation, not ease it, if we keep raising interest."

He nodded, but that was that. We never did have that talk.

2. Mission for the President

The morning of May 1, 1969, was a spring morning at its best in Washington. The

356

grass sparkled with dew and the world looked fresh and clean. As I walked out of the home I had recently bought in the Maryland suburb of Kenwood, I felt good. We had moved into the house less than a week earlier after living for nearly four months in an apartment at the Sheraton-Park Hotel, two floors below Vice President Spiro Agnew's apartment.

I stepped into my limousine and my driver, Hilton Coleman, began the thirty-minute run to Andrews Air Force Base, where I boarded an Air Force jet. By 8:15 A.M. we were rolling down the runway headed west to the Pacific—bound on a special mission for the President.

I had received President Nixon's approval for a trip I considered of considerable importance to the nation: a 14,000-mile fact-finding mission to Micronesia, the Trust Territory of the Western Pacific, for which the Department of the Interior has administrative responsibility.

Ermalee went with me. Our party also included Mrs. Elizabeth R. Farrington, director of Interior's Office of Territories;

Edward E. Johnston, whom the President had nominated the previous month to be the new High Commissioner of the Trust Territory; and members of my staff and the press.

The purpose of my trip was to assess for the Administration the needs and desires of the native peoples of Micronesia regarding their future political and economic development. What form of government did the Micronesians want? Who *owned* these 2,100 islands, anyway? The Trust Territory, wrested from the Japanese during World War II, had been administered by the United States since 1947 under an agreement that required our government to report at least once a year to the United Nations Security Council.

The direct, nonmilitary administration of the Trust was carried out by a civilian High Commissioner under the Office of Territories, but the agreement with the United Nations resembled in one important detail the League of Nations mandate given the Japanese over the same islands following World War I. The Japanese had full authority over the islands, and they used that authority between World Wars to build military installations like the huge naval base at Truk, which cost America much blood in the 1940's. Now the United States had the same full authority, including the right to establish military bases. What would we do with that authority?

The story behind my trip started in the middle of February, less than a month after I became Secretary of the Interior. My staff brought to my attention a report that the United States was likely to be seriously criticized during the next session of the United Nations General Assembly for mishandling its responsibilities in the Trust Territory. I directed that all available information be summarized for a presentation to me. The information on the Trust Territory indicated that we *had* been lax in caring for the needs of the people of the Territory. The report showed desperate needs for better education and health facilities and—most important—for some mechanism allowing the voice of the Micronesians themselves to be heard in the decision-making that affected them.

I assigned a number of my staff members

the responsibility of preparing recommendations we might make to Congress for improving conditions for the Micronesians. I also dispatched members of my staff to Saipan and throughout the Territory to meet with its leaders to get their assessments of some of their more basic problems.

As the matter developed, I became more and more convinced that there was a need for me to visit Micronesia personally and determine first-hand what could be done to help these people.

The President agreed.

Twelve hours after we lifted off from Andrews, our aircraft began letting down over Honolulu's Hickam Field, where we were to spend the first night of our tour.[1] I told Dick Prouty of the Denver *Post* and

---

[1] *This was Aircraft 24129, nicknamed by the Air Force "the McNamara tube." A C-135 — the military version of the Boeing 707 — the plane had been converted from a freighter into a long-range executive*

Reginald Bragonier of *Life:* "There are 90,000 people who've been ignored too damned long. I have lived in a Territory much of my life under the heavy hand of federal government. I know its strengths and I know its weaknesses, and I think I can be of help in Micronesia."

Mine was the first trip to the Trust Territory taken by a Secretary of the Interior in seven years. As we visited some of the major islands—Saipan, Truk, Tinian—I was impressed by the cordial personal welcome extended to us by these warm and outgoing people.[2] I was particularly taken by their beautiful and friendly children, and I loved every minute I spent with them. Harking back to my earlier experiences in Alaska, I tried, throughout my trip, to stress that Micronesians needed and deserved a much louder voice in their own affairs. And I

aircraft at the direction of President Kennedy's Defense Secretary Robert McNamara. The passenger compartment of "the Tube" had no windows, which proved disconcerting at first.

exhorted them to "dream big dreams."

On Monday, May 5, I stood on the outdoor stage of a mission school and spoke to the people of Saipan who had gathered before me, plus thousands of others throughout the islands who were listening to the Micronesian Broadcasting System: "You will help develop the legislation which will end the trusteeship and build a lasting political partnership with us." I pledged immediate steps to improve the Micronesian judicial system, ease tariff barriers and travel restrictions, gear up for major educational and health programs and invite new investment capital to the islands: "For years you have had little voice in your government. This is wrong. Only when the people lead their government can that government be great and people prosper. And while that work goes forward, land will not be taken from Micronesians for any

[2] *Hardly anything remains today on Tinian—site of the flights of the B-29 bombers* Enola Gay *and* Bock's Car, *which in 1945 dropped the atomic bombs on Hiroshima and Nagasaki—other than*

government purpose without full consultation with all parties involved and full and adequate compensation to land owners."

"Full compensation" was an extremely important point, one that would put me in conflict with some of the White House people later, especially Dr. Henry Kissinger, assistant to the President on national security affairs. But we left Saipan that night and headed for home with a feeling of pride and accomplishment. We had made *contact*. We had established rapport. The people of the Trust Territory and I understood each other. It was a human thing. I tried to symbolize this rapport by swearing in High Commissioner Ed Johnston in Saipan, the seat of the territorial government, rather than in Washington, D.C., 6,778 miles away, where the ceremony had always taken place before.

hundreds of thousands of square yards of concrete runways. On Saipan, the other major island in the Trust Territory, one need push only a few feet into the jungle to find rusting Japanese artillery.

I believed then, and I believe now, that the people of the Trust Territory had the right to own and dispose of their own land with full agreement and compensation. If I now ask "Who Owns America?" then the Micronesians have every right to ask "Who Owns Micronesia?"[3]

3. 'Hickel's Disease'

We must understand that we have the greatest political system ever put together on this earth. That system fits attitudes in the United States which have been imported from Europe. Our ethnic roots extend primarily back to Europe, and this has influenced the entire fabric of our social, political, academic and judicial thinking. Our Founding Fathers were naturally oriented to the way of life they had brought from Europe. They started the American Revolution as freemen claiming only the natural rights of Englishmen. But this does

[3] *As this book is written, the political situation in Micronesia remains unresolved and deteriorating.*

not mean that our systems, and all our attitudes, will work when applied to our other doorstep: the Pacific Ocean, gateway to two-thirds of the population of this earth.

In Micronesia, the overriding desire and need of the people is to own their own land. That is all they have. But Henry Kissinger argued that the United States had to have the right of eminent domain—the right to condemn what Micronesian land we wished; to build what bases and other facilities we wished, with little regard for the moral (if not legal) rights of the people who inhabited this land.

We had this argument out at a meeting that took place in Secretary of State William Roger's office. Along with Rogers, Kissinger and myself, Harrison Loesch and Mitch Melich were there. I might have gone along with almost anything less than the argument for eminent domain—such as negotiated purchase or lease of land. We had established military bases in Turkey and Spain without right of eminent domain. What right did we have to invoke eminent domain on the Micronesians? They had little enough land for their own needs, and their very livelihood depended on that land and the surrounding ocean. They wanted to work with us. They told me in Saipan that all they wanted was a voice in our decisions.

But Kissinger's answer in Roger's office was: "There are only 90,000 people out there. Who gives a damn?"

I did. In fact, I was totally shocked by this remark. This seemed to me an inhuman approach to a situation involving human beings, and therefore totally wrong. If we think of 90,000 people only as statistics to be juggled around and resettled for reasons unacceptable to them, then an American mission of trusteeship—in Micronesia or anywhere else—is doomed to failure.

It was about this time that the expression "Hickel's Disease" turned up on the news tickers. The Associated Press, in a file from Washington dated June 25, 1969, observed that "frustrated Democratic leaders have come up with the term 'Hickel's Disease' to describe President Nixon's agility at turning issues to his own advantage."

The story continued, "Around

Democratic National Committee headquarters, 'Hickel's Disease' means preempting the other fellow's thing before he gets a chance to do it himself. The allusion is to the transformation of the image of Secretary of [the] Interior Walter J. Hickel from hard-nosed businessman into that of a conservationist of the first water after he took office.

"National Chairman Fred Harris [the Senator from Oklahoma] complains to colleagues that every time the Democrats set up a good issue, Mr. Nixon comes along and carts it away—say, by personally visiting a ghetto or checking Washington traffic jams from a helicopter. It's not so much what Mr. Nixon says that Harris is complaining about; it's the image the President is creating for himself. . . ."

This article did not sit well at all with some of the White House people, who thought it would have been just fine to have it reported that a Cabinet officer had caught "Nixon's Disease," but not the other way around.[4]

4. Henry

Even before I went to Micronesia, Kissinger had become annoyed by my keen desire to go to the Soviet Union. I was serious about wanting to make the trip, because the issues were serious. The Arctic areas of the world within the United States, the Soviet Union, the Scandinavian countries, Greenland and Canada comprise 2.35 million square miles of land. While the Russians have developed cities as large as Murmansk, with a population of 262,000, residing above the Arctic Circle, we are still in the board-shack era in the American portion of the Arctic. Approximately one-half of all the public land America owns is in the Arctic and sub-Arctic of Alaska, along with two-thirds of all our Continental Shelf.

I knew the Soviets, along with the Canadians and Scandinavians, could teach the United States much in terms of their

[4] *It probably had wider repercussions than I realized at the time. Seventeen months later, when six of my top Interior assistants were purged the day after the President*

northern experience. I had no desire to do the tourist routine and go to Moscow and Leningrad, then come home. I wanted to go to Siberia—the 4,000-mile-wide land that has as its eastern border the cliffs staring at mainland Alaska across fifty-four miles of the Bering Sea. This was obviously one of the world's greatest storehouses of resources and would affect America's position in the Pacific during the foreseeable future.

The State Department had advised me it would take at least a year to arrange such a trip. I doubted that. Then, on April 28, 1969, I met in my office with Boris F. Bratchenko, the Soviet Minister of Coal Industry, who was accompanied by Ambassador Anatoli Dobrynin. Bratchenko was the nearest thing to an opposite number that I had in the Soviet Union.

Bratchenko and I got along well from the

fired me, one White House staff member was to ask: "Are they Nixon men or Hickel men? There's no damned way they can be both." Perhaps this was true.

moment he walked in. We started to talk through interpreters, but soon, in our excitement, we were communicating without their help. I was reading him and he was reading me. It was a great exchange. I told him I was not interested in going to a cocktail party in Moscow. I wanted to see the Siberian Arctic. I was thinking quickly, and the State Department caution about a year being required to make "arrangements" was in my mind when I asked through an interpreter, "Mr. Bratchenko, how long would it take to set up such a trip?"

He raised one finger and said in Russian, "Give me one week!" I exclaimed, "Great!" The two State Department representatives were visibly amazed, but joined the laughter that swept the room. Bratchenko added that he would be my personal host and guide to Siberia, but that I must promise to stay in the Soviet Union for at least fourteen days, the last two days being set aside for a holiday with him on the Black Sea.

I wanted to present Bratchenko with a gift as we closed the meeting. I took from the wall of my office a fine lithograph of the old Russian Orthodox Church in Sitka, done by Mrs. Dale De Armond of Juneau. It was a spur-of-the-moment choice on my part, but if we had looked for weeks we could not have done better. Bratchenko had made a hobby of studying Russian church architecture; he was intimately familiar with the Sitka church, and he was charmed.

A year later, when a nine-man delegation from the American coal industry visited Bratchenko in his office in June 1970, the Soviet minister instructed an aide to take down from his office wall a lithograph of the Kremlin cathedrals. It was about twice the size of the lithograph I had given Bratchenko. He said to the Americans, "Tell Secretary Hickel that I remember his gift to me, and I ask you to give this personally to him." Upon their return, E. B. Leisenring Jr. of the Westmoreland Coal Company, Thomas C. Mullins of Peabody Coal and W. L. Crentz of the Bureau of Mines visited me in my office to make the presentation on Bratchenko's behalf.

The fact that Bratchenko had not been able

to hand me the lithograph personally was not his fault or mine. Three days after our 1969 meeting in Washington, I left for Micronesia. When I got back, I received a call from Henry Kissinger making it clear that my Siberian trip was going to be postponed — but not by the Soviets. And about the time I received Bratchenko's present, the argument about my trip erupted again.

Despite Kissinger's misgivings, I finally made a visit to the Arctic areas of Finland, and also Sweden and Norway, in September 1970. [5] Then, on July 28, 1970, Daniel Schorr of CBS in Washington did a broadcast in which he said: "Hickel, as an Alaskan, has a long-standing interest in neighboring Siberia, and the Russians invited him for a trip. . . . Twice Hickel planned such a trip. Twice it was knocked down at the White House, reportedly by presidential assistant Henry Kissinger, who jealously guards Exterior affairs from

[5] *Kissinger felt that my visit might be a distraction during the Strategic Arms Limitation Talks (SALT) in Helsinki.*

Interior people. . . .Hickel has now been permitted to schedule a trip, for early September, to Sweden and Finland, which borders on the Soviet Union. There seems to be a tacit understanding that unless something comes up by then to prevent it. .. Hickel will add Russia to his itinerary, and who knows, maybe he'll even get to Siberia."

I first heard about the Schorr broadcast when the White House telephone rang in my home. It was Kissinger calling from the Western White House at San Clemente. He had clearly lost his cool: "I've been seeing it on TV and hearing it on the radio, it seems like, every hour; they must be repeating it. I'm not standing in the way of your going to Russia, but you have to understand the decision-making that must take place at the White House. You know how we make our decisions at the White House, Mr. Secretary."

I said, "Henry. . ."—I repeated it slowly—"Henry, I really have no idea how you make your decisions over in the White House."

5. A Little Fat Girl

Nor do I know how a White House decision was finally taken on a departmental matter that engaged me in the summer of 1969. This was the problem of financing new and upgraded secondary sewage treatment facilities for about 4,000 American communities. When we took office we had inherited a $214 million budget item for this purpose from the Johnson Administration. The Bureau of the Budget wanted to stick with that figure, which seemed to me palpably inadequate. When I was invited to testify on February 28, 1969, before Senator Muskie's Public Works Subcommittee, it was directed that I defend the $214 million figure. Obviously Muskie thought I would try to do that when he asked me if an annual appropriation of that sum would be enough.

I replied: "I don't think it is possible, Senator. We need a minimum of $600 million or perhaps $800 million a year."

Actually, both Republicans and Democrats on Capitol Hill had been mentioning those figures informally as possible minimum bases, but the White

House was upset with me for mentioning them, and let me know about it.

No matter. A whole new approach to this problem of financing was taking shape in the back of my mind, although we still had a lot of work to do before I could mention it outside the Department.

The problem was that cities throughout America that did not have secondary sewage treatment depended on the federal government for grants if they were to plan for years ahead. They were reduced to gambling on whether Congress would appropriate the money year after year. Consequently, they were falling further and further behind in both planning and construction.

We were about to propose an ongoing program that would eliminate the guesswork. When a city — any city — needed a secondary sewage treatment plant, it could automatically go ahead and design it, knowing full well that when the community went to sell its bonds, the federal government would be responsible for capital repayment. And this repayment, scheduled over a period of twenty years, would be guaranteed right on the face of the bonds. All the local taxpayers had to do was pay interest to the bondholders during the same span of time. For example, a million-dollar city sewage treatment plant would cost the federal government only $50,000 a year for twenty years. I called this the FHA of pollution financing. This was virtually a fifty-fifty proposition—the finest kind of "revenue sharing." We could start cleaning up the nation's dirty rivers immediately, avoid escalating construction costs and have the use of the facility while we were paying for it.

I first surfaced the idea on August 6 when I was at Camp David, the President's Catoctin Mountains retreat, during an informal discussion with Secretary Kennedy, Economic Counselor Arthur Burns and John Ehrlichman. Ehrlichman liked the idea and said, "Wally, let's discuss this at greater length soon."

One week later I wrote the President a memorandum indicating the principle of what we were working on, but without going into much detail. Then, on September 1, during a flight to San Clemente aboard Air

Force One, I outlined the plan informally to John Mitchell. He seemed highly impressed and encouraged me to pursue the idea with the President personally.

I waited until after Nixon had returned to Washington before moving further. A meeting was finally arranged at the White House on the morning of September 17. Ehrlichman was there, along with Budget Director Mayo.

When I explained the plan, I never saw the President more immediately fired up about an idea than he was about that one. The beauty of what we were offering was its simplicity. Visibly delighted, he told Ehrlichman: "Get Pat Moynihan, get the financial people. This is a great program and we've got to see it through."

I was highly pleased by the outcome of the meeting. I flew to Chicago the same day, and I felt sufficiently encouraged to put a piece of the idea into a speech I made to the Chicago Executives Club two days later: "In the future we cannot afford to go the conventional appropriations route. . . .We have got to provide municipal waste treatment construction to bring the nation abreast of the problem — and that includes at a rate sufficient to provide for population growth." I mentioned "a long-term contractual financing plan on top of any federal appropriations that will be forthcoming."

I never heard from the President directly, but the White House staff was annoyed. John Whitaker called and advised me to say no more about my program in public. I wondered, at a time when the White House was making a great public push on selected issues such as the ABM, why they did not want me to speak out on a proposal that had tremendous possibilities for millions of Americans. This worried me because I feared the program might leak out in bits and pieces and not be presented correctly.

I pushed it anyway, but as weeks went by I became more and more concerned. I felt that John Ehrlichman was on my side, but I suspected I had problems with "the money men."

I took the idea to Hugh Scott and Gerald Ford, the Senate and House minority leaders, and they both loved it. "Wally," Scott said, "introduce the legislation. This is the kind of program—the kind of legislation—we can win with." Their enthusiasm was genuine. This program would solve a problem for American cities on a long-term basis.

The Washington *Post* published a fairly good description of our program, but the story lacked depth. As a result the Municipal League came out in opposition because it sounded like just another bond program. No one had explained that right on the face of the bonds the federal government would guarantee to repay 100 percent of the capital costs. John Whitaker telephoned again to say, "Well, Wally, the idea is out in the open." I said, "Yes, but not in good form."

I was again having a difficult time with the Bureau of the Budget. On the day I made my speech to the Chicago Executives Club, Robert Mayo wrote me a formal letter requesting me not to present my program, in talks with Congressmen, as the only alternative being considered. I met many times with Mayo, Whitaker and Ehrlichman. And I got one commitment out of Whitaker: If the program did not go, I would have the last opportunity to talk to the President. I felt sure that if I explained the proposal in detail to Nixon, he would override any Bureau of the Budget objections.

Dave Kennedy did not like the idea. He called it "deficit financing," and he said the bond houses would fight it bitterly. I called it the finest kind of government participation, paying for something as you were using it, and lowering the cost of money to the cities. Unless we used private financing with the government's support, there was no way we could find enough money to solve the pollution problem.

I went to Anchorage for the Christmas holidays. On December 23, John Ehrlichman called me at home "Wally, Merry Christmas. Your package is complete, and I see no problem with it at all. The President likes it." That was the finest Christmas present I could have received.

Later, during the holidays, the economic advisors met in San Clemente. Something happened. After I returned to Washington I was asked to schedule a January 29, 1970, meeting in my office with Ehrlichman, Mayo, Peter Flanigan and John Whitaker. I knew something was up, but I did not know what.

They all walked in, and I soon learned that my program was in trouble. Mayo led the attack. He had a proposal of his own that he argued was much better than mine. His approach involved conventional appropriations. I explained again the problem of straight appropriations: Cities could not plan far enough ahead.

I looked at Ehrlichman and said: "John, is this the President's decision? Is the decision over? If the decision's over, there's no use talking. If it's not over, I'll see the President."

The meeting went on for an hour. I was not winning, and I finally asked, "Is the decision made not to go our way?" Ehrlichman said, "Yes, for all practical purposes it is."

"If that's the President's decision, I'll go along. But I don't like it. We've lost a great program."

"Wally," said Mayo, "the programs are really quite a bit alike. Your program and mine aren't really different."

"Bob," I said, "the only similarity between your program and mine is that they're both little girls. I've got Shirley Temple, and all you've got is a little fat girl who can't dance or sing."

The problem remains unsolved.

I talked to Hugh Scott and Jerry Ford a couple of times after that, and they asked what had happened. I never did find out. And I never had a chance to put my case directly to the President; John Whitaker's commitment to me was not honored. Once, at a Cabinet meeting when the President was trying to figure out how to save some money, John Mitchell slipped me a note: "Wally, what happened to your sewage treatment financing program?" He knew the long-term financing plan I had developed would have saved several hundred million dollars on our current budget and gotten the job done better.

I tried one last time at that meeting to bring it up. The President waved his hand and said, "We've gone all through that."

I realized immediately that the money men had sold the President a program, convincing him it was just like mine. It was not, and I knew they were wrong.

At the time I was furious about the attitude that we could not afford to clean up our environment "for economic reasons." My plan would have done the job and saved money.

6. 'Who's Your Ad Agency?'

We did somewhat better with "Parks to the People," but not without rubbing some people the wrong way. I went to San Clemente to make a presentation to the President during the last week of August 1969. I directed the Bureau of Outdoor Recreation to assemble a collection of slide photographs to illustrate our proposal. At the Newporter Inn, Douglas Hofe, the Director of BOR, and I, along with my assistant Tom Holley and two of Hofe's associates, Lawrence N. Stevens and Robert Eastman, worked late into the night of August 24, sharpening and refining the presentation.

The next morning we boarded a White House helicopter for the short flight to the Western White House. Vice President Agnew was there, along with most of the Cabinet and the White House staff. We were meeting as an informal environmental committee, a forerunner of the Council on Environmental Quality set up later.

The President walked in, and we got down to business. Secretary Romney spoke on solid waste problems. Bob Finch then took the podium and turned it over to one of his Health, Education and Welfare people for a presentation that went on for about twenty minutes. The President tried to make appropriate comments, but he had not been exactly "turned on."

Now it was my turn. I made a brief opening statement explaining what "Parks to the People" was all about; then the lights were turned out and the slide presentation began. It ran exactly nine and one-half minutes. Holley, Hofe and our other people had done a hell of a job. When the lights came back on I was supposed to make another brief statement, then present another nine minutes of slides. But the

President was obviously excited. He started jumping around in his chair, and he poked Secretary of Agriculture Cliff Hardin with his elbow. "That's the best presentation I've seen yet," he said. "Cliff, all of you — when you're going to present something, why don't you present it like this?" He kept saying, "What a wonderful program. . . .This is really getting to the people."

Ehrlichman nudged Tom Holley in the ribs and asked, "What ad agency did you have prepare this?"

Holley did not even know who Ehrlichman was when he replied, "The Department of the Interior."

"You didn't do that in Interior," Ehrlichman said.

"The hell we didn't!" Holley retorted.

We never did get around to finishing the presentation. Despite Nixon's enthusiastic reaction, there was a feeling in the room that we did not show proper respect for the economics of the situation. As we walked out of the building, Arthur Burns came to me and said, rather sourly: "Young man, I don't want you to be so cocky about getting your money. You've got a long way to go."

7. Lunch for the Senators

I was practically the only one who thought it a good idea to invite the members of the Senate Interior Committee, which had given me such a going-over the preceding January, to a pre-Christmas lunch on December 11, 1969—one year to the day after Nixon announced my appointment as Secretary. Tom Holley thought the gesture would look arrogant, "even if you don't mean it that way." Dave Parker, who handled my scheduling, questioned "the propriety of it," and from the department press office Joe Holbert feared reporters would "play it up the wrong way." Solicitor Mitch Melich thought the Senators might take it the wrong way: "They don't like to be kidded."

Speaking for the White House, Herb Klein went even further. He told me not to give the lunch. "You'd be slapping the Committee in the face," he said.

I gave the luncheon anyway. On December 11, I dispatched Dave Parker and my limousine to pick up Senator Jackson, the chairman of the Interior

Committee, the same man who had presided over my confirmation hearings. Dave told me later that as they drove to the Interior building, Jackson seemed nervous. He seemed to think I had invited him down to my office on committee business. As Scoop walked into the executive dining room, he started to hand me a memorandum.

"Oh, Senator," I said, "that's not what I invited you down here for. I wanted you to come down so I could give you a little gift of appreciation." Only a few members of my staff knew I had personally purchased from the Government Printing Office copies of the "Green Bible," the 459-page record of my January confirmation hearings. I had arranged the rest with a private printer. The book even had a new title. Emblazoned across the top, above the photograph of Walter Joseph Hickel chewing on the frame of his eyeglasses, the title read: *How to Get a Job in Government Without Really Trying or: How to Write a 450-page Book in Just Five Days.*

Scoop Jackson and the ten other Senators who had been able to accept the luncheon invitation opened the books and cracked up to a man. The whole room collapsed in laughter. Scoop Jackson thought that this made me the first member of the Nixon Administration to be "published," although we could not make up our minds whether my "book" was to be considered fact or fiction.

Senators, like Interior Secretaries, are human beings, and that December 11 lunch ended with a new warmth and cordiality. I remain convinced that a sense of humor and the desire to communicate human warmth are critically necessary ingredients in good government. Although Herb Klein had told me not to give the lunch, and most of the staff was against it, I autographed a copy of the book and sent it to the President. He thought it was great, and he mentioned it at a Cabinet Meeting.

Exactly one year later, in the issue of *Life* dated December 11, 1970, Hugh Sidey observed in his weekly column ("The Presidency"): "For the most part, the men around Nixon, even in the administrative and political branches, are individually pleasant and alert. But something seems to happen when they come together. They form an engine of great efficiency and precision but no heart. . . ."

There was an "isolation of thought" developing. In early 1970 I was conscious of a deepening malaise inside the Administration—and a sense of vague uneasiness. Others in the Cabinet shared my feeling that some of the White House staff were stepping up their efforts to filter contacts between the Cabinet and the President. It appeared that an effort was being made to centralize control of all executive branch activities of the government immediately within the White House, utilizing the various departments—represented by Secretaries at the Cabinet level—merely as clearing houses for White House policy, rather than as action agencies.

Should a department—for example, Interior—develop policy for those activities under its control, submit those ideas to the White House for approval or disapproval, then follow through at the administrative level? Or, as some of the White House personnel seemed to want it, should a department wait only for marching orders to be issued by the Executive Mansion?

I favored the first option, and I was not alone. George Romney at one time told a newsman, "The key question that the President is going to have to decide is whether he is to have the White House staff people basically responsible in policy areas and playing leadership roles, or whether the Cabinet officers are going to do it."

8. 'Screaming Inside'

I was aware of these springtime rumblings in Washington, and I was conscious that some of them concerned the complicated problem of Vietnam. That sorry conflict had lasted a decade. The cost in American lives was approaching that of World War I. This is not the place to go into the rights and wrongs of the Vietnam argument. But there must have been a time when we could have adopted Senator George Aiken's suggestion that we announce we had "won" and then go home. Instead, the war went on, and half a million American combat troops were committed to a conflict that had large elements of a purely civil war. The physical destruction of a small country by the armed might of the world's greatest power became repugnant to more and more Americans. This was particularly true among American youth, as the 1968 Democratic Party convention in Chicago and subsequent events during the presidential campaign should have made clear.

I thought this was as clear to President Nixon as it was to me. But it may be that no President since Herbert Hoover, an honorable and humane man under whose desk the Depression of the 1930's exploded like a land mine, was ever so isolated in thought as Richard Nixon was by the spring of 1970.

I really had no worries about Vietnam on the afternoon of April 30. The Nixon Administration had taken office pledged to wind down the Vietnam war, and I thought the President was doing an excellent job — in an admittedly difficult situation — to fulfill this pledge. I genuinely thought we had turned the corner in Vietnam.

Almost everyone can remember precisely where he was, whom he was with, and what he was doing on certain dates.

Such a date, for me, was April 30, 1970.

It had been a fairly busy but generally rewarding day, devoted to a series of in-house Interior briefings. Dr. Donald Dunlop, my science advisor, came to see me about our efforts to eliminate leaded gasoline. Bill Pecora, Director of the Geological Survey, had an appointment to talk about personnel, and Under Secretary Fred Russell another to review our public information activities. Solicitor Mitch Melich and Assistant Secretary Hollis Dole reviewed legislation dealing with petroleum leasing, and Tom Holley came with Frank Bracken, our legislative counsel, to brief me on coastal zone legislation.

I broke out of the staff functions three times during the day, starting with a brief hand-shaking ceremony with a group of Indian students from Alaska. I had lunch with Ron Walker, earlier my assistant at Interior and now one of the President's chief advance men. I kidded Ron about his name getting in a Washington *Evening Star* story that told how the advance men—who are supposed to be "invisible" from the press—move mountains to make the President's road tours a success. Later in the day I saw John Stacks of *Time* for an interview on the Alaska pipeline project.

After lunch and before the Stacks appointment, Pat Ryan, my new executive assistant, came in and said: "Alex Butterfield [deputy assistant to the President] just called. You're supposed to be at the White House tonight for a special Cabinet meeting, promptly at seven forty-five."

Butterfield did not say what the meeting would be about, although I knew that the President had scheduled a special television broadcast for nine o'clock that same Thursday evening. I was neither particularly excited nor uneasy, although I was somewhat puzzled by the suddenness and the timing of the meeting. Normally the President's Cabinet meetings were announced at least a few days in advance to permit the shuffling of other appointments, and almost always we were advised of the general topics to be discussed so that we could be suitably prepared.

I left my office earlier than usual, and my driver was able to beat the rush-hour traffic on Rock Creek Parkway. I walked into the house about four-thirty in the afternoon. I told Ermalee that the President wanted the entire Cabinet at the White House an hour and a quarter before he was due to go on television. We wondered what might be going on as we ate a light and quiet dinner by ourselves. I cancelled an appearance at a seven-thirty reception being given by the White House News Photographers Association.

A minute or two before seven-thirty I arrived and sat down.

We did not have long to wait. The President walked in. Then he announced the decision to use American troops in South Vietnam to invade Cambodia.

I listened with horror. I had knots inside my stomach. Over and over — but only in my own mind — I kept saying: *No, Mr. President. No, no, no! I thought we had turned that corner. Don't say it. Please don't say it!*

He said it. When I walked out of that room, I was screaming inside.

BOOK **3**

Age of Voices

Lack of communication with the public causes frustration and fear. Fear leads to hate, and hate leads to violence.

CHAPTER **10**

'Faithfully Yours, Wally'

After I left the Cambodia briefing and watched the President on national television at the White House, I went home. There have been few times in my life when I was so upset. Convinced as I was, until that evening, that we had turned the corner with the American people on South Vietnam, I did not think this invasion was acceptable. I mentioned to Ermalee how terribly disturbed I was. I knew that something had to be done. But what?

The night passed as all nights pass when you are disturbed. You are restless. You wonder. You know not what to do, but your mind turns over and over. I went to the office the next day and there was no doubt that those on my staff close to me knew something was wrong.

My concern was eventually to force me to write a letter to the President, a letter that would touch a mood in the country.

I really think that in my mind I began writing that letter to the President six months earlier, in November 1969. Hundreds of thousands of Americans, young and old, had made their way to Washington to tell the nation's leaders that they felt the time to end the Vietnam war was now. They called for a moratorium. These were various statements to the press coming out of the White House that the President was not about to be pushed into doing anything by a minority group, and that rather than paying heed to the demonstration he was enjoying football on television.

Now, there is nothing wrong with watching football. It is a great American sport, and watching it is one of my favorite pastimes. But when a group of people in America wants to express an opinion, and is asking to be heard, I think it is the duty and obligation of those who are the leaders, whether in business or in city, state or federal government, to hear these people out. Therefore, when the President showed what appeared to me a lack of concern, it bothered me greatly. After all, the Administration, led by the President, had done such an outstanding job in its first nine months of scaling down the war and rallying the public behind our policies. That fall the Gallup Poll recorded 65 percent of the American people supporting the President's approaches to foreign and domestic affairs. So I began to formulate my thoughts about how I could help him understand the mood of America, especially among the young.

Early that month, on November 13, Vice President Agnew, speaking in Des Moines, Iowa, launched his celebrated attack upon the news media. Joe Holbert called me to tell me the Vice President was on TV. I immediately switched on my set, watched it for a moment—and turned away. I told Ermalee, "He is making a point, but it is so negative it could hurt." Joe drafted a letter of congratulations to the Vice President for my signature. I had the letter on my desk for many days and finally took it home. I had a funny feeling about that speech. Yes, Agnew had touched a very sensitive issue in America. But there seemed to be a tone or an attitude that I sensed would go too far. I never mailed the letter.

It was the Des Moines speech that made everyone sit up and take notice. It also made a lot of people, including myself, take a second look at some of the language the Vice President had used earlier. He had been saying quite a lot, although his reference to "effete snobs" on American campuses had either been ignored or taken as a joke. But one week before he spoke in Des Moines, he addressed a Republican dinner in Harrisburg, Pennsylvania, in these terms: "In the case of the Vietnam moratorium, the objective announced by the [demonstration] leaders — immediate unilateral withdrawal of all our forces from Vietnam — was not only unsound but idiotic. The tragedy was that thousands . . . were used by the political hustlers who ran the event. . . .

"Think about it. Small bands of students are allowed to shut down great universities. . . . It is time to question the credentials of their leaders. And if, in questioning, we disturb a few people, I say it is time for them to be disturbed. If, in challenging, we polarize the American people, I say it is time for a positive polarization."

For the life of me I could not see how "polarization" could be "positive."

Then, three days before he took on the media in Des Moines, the Vice President told the National Municipal League in Philadelphia: "I would guess that many in sophisticated America consider love of country gauche or irrelevant." This was a slander on the millions of concerned Americans who may disagree with the policies of their government but love their country, just as I love my country, enough *not* to leave it—no matter what the bumper stickers say.

There did seem to be a general feeling among those at the top Administration level at the White House that "the youth thing" was to be put on the back burner and sort of brushed aside. This concerned me, because I knew that young America wanted to participate in solving the problems faced by the country. Of course, the young were loud in their criticisms, and like any group they had elements who only wanted to tear things down. But the vast majority eagerly wanted to be included in positive programs. This was certainly true in one of my principal areas of concern — the environment.

In December 1969 the first Earth Day was being organized for the following April. I called John Whitaker at the White House and suggested that Earth Day be declared a national holiday by the President. John thought it might be a good idea, so I said, "Does it merit writing a letter to the President?" He did not have a comment one way or the other, so on December 16 I wrote:

Dear Mr. President:
To demonstrate your commitment to the fight to preserve and protect our Nation's environment, and to acknowledge youth's role in that fight, I strongly recommend that you declare April 22 — the date of the Environmental Teach-In — a National Holiday. This need not be a Holiday in the sense of releasing employees, closing

banks, etc., but rather one that clearly demonstrates your understanding of the problems of the environment and your appreciation for the commitment and concern shown by young people. In addition, an executive order might direct all pertinent government agencies to aid the Teach-In, something most offices are already doing as part of their information function.

This action would be beneficial not only to our fight for the environment, but also to our continued efforts to involve young people in national concerns.

Respectfully yours,

Walter J. Hickel
Secretary of the Interior

I received no reply from the President, and unhappily let the suggestion drop. A year later, after I had left the Administration, the President designated April 18-24 as Earth Week.

1. The Birth of 'SCOPE'

Earlier that same December, working with my Assistant Secretary for Water Resources, Carl Klein, we developed an idea to form a student group on campuses called SCOPE (Student Councils on Pollution and the Environment). We did this without new appropriations or legislation. During Christmas week, representatives of the Interior Department were sent to speak in nine regions of the country to get out to the campuses the idea of what we were doing. We wanted to create a sort of Paul Revere alert system on pollution, which would make it possible for some of these problems to be spotted early enough and reported to us so that they might be solved. I stated publicly that the meetings we had held were just modestly successful, but the success was that both undergraduate and graduate college youths found the idea attractive. All we had to do was give it a new approach, broadening it to all areas of the environment. The nine regions each elected a governing board of students which in turn picked one representative each to fly to Washington to see me so that I could explain the depth of how SCOPE would operate.

When the SCOPE leaders came to my office on February 20 they were so hostile some of my aides wondered if they were going to "occupy" it. Instead of the invited nine, fifteen arrived and they all demanded to get in. It was obvious that although they liked the SCOPE concept in general, they were afraid that the federal government was going to "use" them, instead of work with them. Steeped in the typical student suspicion of government, they fired belligerent questions and demands. I knew they were testing me to see if I truly shared their urgency about the environmental crisis or whether I was just using the issue for political benefit.

These students were mostly working for their doctorates in biology, architecture and environmental sciences. Their questions were penetrating, technical and sometimes biting. After hearing them out, in an atmosphere charged with feeling, I began to speak. I encouraged their impatience and their commitment. "You may not realize,"

I said, "that only a few years ago I was sitting on the other side of this desk where you are now, pounding on it, fighting for Alaska statehood. I want your ideas, and SCOPE will be the vehicle to open up a channel from the youth who care about the environment to those agencies in government who can do something about it on a national scale." The tension left the room.

The excitement was there; and there was more work to do than we could complete that day. Someone in the group wondered out loud if it would be possible to carry on the following day, a Saturday. I jumped at the idea and told my staff to cancel my meetings. On Saturday we met together for another three hours.

SCOPE became the channel for a unique relationship between the federal government and the student community. Never before, to our knowledge, had there been a program in which students still enrolled in college worked on a volunteer basis with the federal government to tackle problems of concern to both parties. We set up what we called a "hot line" directly into the Secretary's office. This was manned by a Task Force on Youth and the Environment headed by Mike Levett, a 25-year-old UCLA graduate, assisted by Linda Pettey, a 24-year-old Vanderbilt graduate who was on Carl Klein's staff at Interior. They put together an outstanding staff detailed from other bureaus, thereby not costing the taxpayers an extra cent. They had direct access to me. When there was a pollution problem, whether it was inadequate sewage treatment in a city, threatened desecration of land by an irresponsible government or private project, or whatever, the SCOPE representatives called directly to my office and it was brought immediately to my attention. SCOPE worked because it was not just words; we made things happen.

My interest in direct youth involvement has been a continuing pattern in life both in business and government. I have always believed that if you want to discover the truth you should ask the very young or the very old. The very young are completely uninhibited in saying what they think. They are the most punishing of people because they will say it exactly like it is. Old people have nothing to lose. They no longer have to worry about who cares. So the truth of the world comes from the very young; the wisdom of the world comes from the very old.

In business in Alaska I always hired the young person who was looking for a break to prove himself. In 1954 I hired Dick Kukowski to manage the Anchorage Travelers Inn. I did not realize it at the time, but he was only nineteen, so Johnny Woods, the bartender, would not let him into the cocktail lounge. When he finally turned twenty-one he walked into the lounge and announced to Johnny, "Give me a drink, and I'm *still* the boss."

Surrounding yourself with young-thinking people is essential in government if you are to make the right decisions in a world changing at the pace it is today. Your mind has to be open to all alternatives. If you or your staff are locked in to the ways of the past, you are likely to suppress the vitality of the new and the original, which have been the lifeblood of the American experiment. Both in Juneau and Washington I hired young talent. But I made sure they were competent as well as creative. My theory is always to hire "up," to find those staff members who in their areas are more able than I.

One time I was presented with an impressive resume of a potential staff member with a doctorate in political science and other academic disciplines. I asked, "How old is he?" When told he was around forty, I replied, "Well, I guess our staff could use some old men."

As we charged ahead with SCOPE, a debate built up in the press and on the campuses about the growing alienation of the young from the Administration. This debate became a raging thing as Vice President Agnew continued to move away from our campaign of "Forward Together" with his verbal attacks on any and all voices of dissent, especially the new voices of the young. I could not understand these statements coming from a person of his rank and from our Administration. Agnew told a Lincoln Day dinner in Atlanta: "To penetrate the cacophony of seditious drivel emanating from the best publicized clowns in our society and their fans in the fourth estate, yes, my friends, to penetrate that drivel we need a cry of alarm, not a whisper. And if the hippies and the yippees and the disrupters of the system in Washington . . . will shut up and work within the framework of our free-system government, I will lower my voice. . . ."

In effect the Vice President was letting the extremists call the tune. Picking up their tactics, he was using raw, ugly words that were fanning hatred on both sides.

All this was going in a direction exactly opposite to that taken by the President in his Inaugural Address, a truly visionary statement that succeeded in uniting the country at a time of great disunity. I always kept a copy of it in my office desk.

The President said in part:

We see the hope of tomorrow in the youth of today. I know America's youth. I believe in them. We can be proud that they are better educated, more committed, more passionately driven by conscience than any generation in our history. . . .

We find ourselves rich in goods but ragged in spirit; reaching with magnificent precision for the moon, but falling into raucous discord on earth.

We are caught in war, wanting peace. We are torn by division, wanting unity. We see around us empty lives, wanting fulfillment. We see tasks that need doing, waiting for hands to do them.

To a crisis of the spirit, we need an answer of the spirit. . . .

In these difficult years, America has suffered from a fever of words; from inflated rhetoric that promises more than it can deliver; from angry rhetoric that fans discontent into hatred; from bombastic rhetoric that postures instead of persuading.

We cannot learn from one another until we stop shouting at one another — until we speak quietly enough so that our words can be heard as well as our voices.

These were the thoughts that had kindled my imagination as we set out to give new leadership to our country in January 1969. Now the Vice President was indulging in exactly what the President had said he condemned.

2. *The Eye of the Storm*

On February 28, 1970, just a week after I met with SCOPE representatives, I was asked to answer questions at the annual Conference of College Editors in Washington. I was advised that the group would be hostile, but I was eager to reach out and try to show the direction we were beginning to take in government. No one else in the Administration would go. I walked into a large banquet hall at the Twin Bridges Marriott Hotel. The room was full, with close to 800 students sitting on the floor and packed to the walls. The atmosphere seethed with anti-Establishment hatred. The conference chairman introduced me and sat down, letting the delegates fire their questions at will. It was chaos. A member of my staff, Joe O'Hara, stood nearby eyeing the exit to the kitchen in case a rapid departure was required. Questions, laden with profanity, were shouted one on top of the other.

I tried to confront the questions directly and answer them as honestly and candidly as I knew how, but each time I began to answer I was interrupted by more profanity. At one point a girl climbed on the podium, thrust at me a glass of water taken from the Potomac River and challenged me to drink it. I responded, "I've never had Potomac fever yet, and I'm not about to get it now."[1] I was attacked on issues outside my purview, such as foreign policy, but when backed into a corner, I said, "I'll stand by my President!"

After twenty minutes of taking the abuse and responding forcefully and sincerely, I

[1] *I fared better than Atlantic-Richfield Chairman Robert O. Anderson, who later that day, at the same conference, had a quart of oil poured over him.*

began to feel the mood in the hall change. The majority of students started to listen. Then a student jumped up and shouted down those who were launching the barrage of angry questions and taunts. He said: "Shut up and listen! The Secretary is being honest! Hear him out!" The crowd applauded, and the corner was turned.

As I made my way out of the hall, dozens of students crowded up to me to thank me and apologize for the others. When I got into my limousine, two of my assistants who were working on developing rapport between government and campus youth, Mike Levett and Malcolm Roberts, expressed concern that the open hostility demonstrated toward me would sour my approach to young people. I said: "That wasn't bad. The Senate confirmation hearings were tougher!"

This was not to be my last experience with student animosity. The following month I was invited to address an environmental conference at Princeton University. Before I left Washington the afternoon of March 5, we had received word that Princeton's Students for a Democratic

Society (SDS) were organizing a demonstration against me. President Robert Goheen was concerned that I be afforded the courtesy normally extended to a Cabinet officer, and he took elaborate precautions. While we were driving to the campus from Mercer Airport, the campus police were radioing reports to our driver and the situation appeared in hand. As we waited in an office at Jadwin Gymnasium before going into the hall to speak, the Dean of Students, Neil Rudenstine, came in and reported that seventy-five or eighty students dressed and painted up as Indians had just entered the hall. "We checked and I don't think they are carrying garbage to throw at you as we had feared," he said.

I laughed, "If they do, I'll catch a grapefruit, peel it and hand out sections to the front row."

President Goheen gave the word and we walked into the hall. As we approached the platform, the "Indians" began to heckle. The shouting took me on personally but mostly attacked the government's Vietnam policy. They considered me a member of the "war cabinet." After President Goheen's introduction, I began my speech. I proposed the creation of a domestic Environmental Peace Corps, an idea I had developed with eager help from SCOPE members. But my proposal was lost to the audience. Most of the 1,500 students, alumni and guests were unable to hear anything but the shouting, but I continued with my remarks, ignoring the chanting and profanity. Finally, President Goheen got up and said to me, "Mr. Secretary, for the record, I must say something." Taking the microphone, he warned the students who were making it impossible for the others to hear that if they continued they would face disciplinary action.

The hecklers still refused to let me be heard. I doggedly continued with my speech and read it to the end. I stressed that to approach the total environmental issue we needed the emergence of an entirely new profession. "Men and women are wanted," I said, "who can literally redesign the country so that it is *people-oriented.*"

I concluded, "At stake is man's very habitat, and also man's mind and soul. We are awakening to an entirely new set of values. . . . The values of a consumer society which have been sacred for generations ring hollow to many. Let's welcome this reevaluation going on in the soul and the spirit of the nation. Let's participate in it, and let's learn from it."

When I ended my speech, President Goheen thanked me for my "eloquent and important address" and apologized to the audience, to my wife and to me for the actions of a few of his students. He announced that the scheduled question-and-answer session would be impossible to hold and was therefore cancelled.

I left, boarded my plane and flew to Washington.

A few days later, on March 13, Bradley Olsen and Jeffrey Stahl, both seniors at Princeton, came to see me. They brought with them a petition signed by 1,400 Princeton students and faculty members. It read in part: "We wish to extend to Secretary Hickel our sincerest apologies for the disgraceful and disruptive behavior which he faced during his address. We believe that such behavior has no place in a university and must be met with appropriate disciplinary action."

This confirmed what I already knew: The great majority of college students, at Princeton and elsewhere, support a mature and free exchange of ideas in an orderly atmosphere. The disciplinary action called for in the petition was meted out by a Judicial Committee composed of students and faculty members. Twelve students were disciplined, including three who were suspended for a year.

In the flood of letters of apology I received from individuals at Princeton, many indicated their desire to work with us in the environmental area. This convinced me that every government official who was invited should participate in Earth Day the following month.

Others in the Administration disagreed. Rumors were being spread that the entire event was anti-American. Ridiculous telegrams arrived at my office warning that April 22 was Lenin's birthday and had been chosen for that reason. Those who researched this information ignored the fact that it was also the traditional American date for Arbor Day, the day to plant trees.

In a meeting with some of the Cabinet present, Earth Day was brought up, and the Vice President warned against anyone getting involved. As quietly and calmly as I could, I spoke my mind. I stated that none of the others had faced the student heckling to the extent that I had, and that if we had nothing to hide and stood on our record, we could communicate with the young.

I proceeded with my own plans. The only other Cabinet officer to speak at an Earth Day event was Secretary of Transportation John Volpe. John subbed for me at Johns Hopkins University. Swamped by dozens of invitations from campuses throughout the country, I decided I would speak in my own State of Alaska, the battleground for many crucial environmental issues. Secretary Volpe did a magnificent job, receiving a standing ovation from what at the outset had appeared to be a hostile crowd.[2]

[2] *Of all the others in the Cabinet, Volpe did the most with the youth of America, helping*

The Interior Department had marching orders from me to be on the campuses on April 22. Twelve hundred Interior employees participated, speaking, answering questions and helping with exhibits and films. The reports they brought back were outstanding. In many instances they learned as much from the students as the students learned from them.

I knew then for certain that the gulf between government and the youth did not have to exist.

A week later Agnew, in Hollywood Beach, Florida, attacked University Presidents Kingman Brewster of Yale and Robben Fleming of the University of Michigan in a law-and-order-on-campus speech. Using language such as colleges becoming "circus tents or psychiatric centers for over-privileged, under-disciplined, irresponsible children of the well-to-do blase permissivists," he torpedoed the delicate trust we were beginning to establish.

with the SCOPE program and encouraging his staff to become involved.

One of my special assistants, Malcolm Roberts, wrote me a memo the following day:

I feel the Vice President is going to radicalize the large, middle group of the student community if he continues to use name-calling as a means to deal with student violence.

Most of today's youth reject violence. But when their fellow students are labeled as "the criminal left" and "kid extortionists" they are going to rally to the cause of their peers and go further than they normally would.

I totally agreed.

It was the following night, April 30, that I went to the White House for the Cambodia briefing and the President delivered his television address.

3. State of Shock

At 11:30 the next morning, May 1, I met with my assistant secretaries and principal

423

staff members to brief them on the President's Cambodian decision. My distress showed clearly; indeed, I made no effort to conceal it. One of those who sat in on the meeting was my assistant for scheduling and appointments, David Parker. Dave recalled the meeting later: "Secretary Hickel came to work in a mustard-colored sweater. Distraught, and almost with disbelief, he explained the decision that the President had made. He didn't say anything adverse regarding the President's decision. At the same time, if you knew Wally Hickel, you could read it all over his face that he was dejected and dismayed."

Even as I conducted the briefing, my worst fears had begun to materialize. Already students on campuses, reacting furiously to an apparent widening of the Vietnam war, had begun to rally behind the most anti-government spokesmen in their midst. We did not have to wait long for the culmination — the tragic climax.

It came on Monday, May 4, when the Ohio National Guard and the students at Kent State University confronted each other on the Kent State campus. Shortly past noon, four young people were shot dead, and the nation went into a state of shock.

The following morning, Tuesday, our usual weekly staff meeting at Interior began promptly at 8:30 A.M. All five of my assistant secretaries were there, plus my solicitor and ten of my closest staff members. The agenda was full of questions concerning natural resources, but my mind was simply not on such things. I was too wrapped up in the events going on in the country, and my mood was obvious to everyone in the room. America was as close to getting out of hand as I have ever known it to be. We plowed on through our work anyway, but nobody had his heart in it.

When the agenda was covered, we still had a few minutes left. Sensing my deep concern, Mitch Melich asked to say a word. "I had a phone call from my daughter at the University of Utah last night," he declared. "She said the students out there are desperate. They're lost and angry. She's afraid that her campus will explode like Kent State. Could we ask Mike Levett how he assesses the situation?"

I turned to Mike. He angrily recounted that reports he was receiving from campuses throughout America indicated the Administration's credibility was being irretrievably lost and that the Interior Department's efforts were going down the drain.

I agreed. I said I was sick at heart. Someone had to help the President. Something had to be done to help the country. I then asked everyone in the room to comment. Malcolm Roberts emphasized that all American youth were being polarized needlessly. Their views were receiving no hearing, and their legitimate concern was being interpreted as being antipatriotic.

Mitch Melich wondered why we as an administration had failed the young, and expressed hope that we could turn our policies around. I was convinced that we could. Assistant Secretary Harrison Loesch hammered away at the need to emphasize the positive, not the negative.

The Assistant Secretary for Administration, Lawrence Dunn, sat like a stone statue, saying nothing but taking it all in. Dunn had come to his position in Interior from the White House staff.

Increasingly disturbed, I brought the staff meeting to a close and went up to my office. I told Dave Parker to cancel my meetings for the morning. I called in my Executive Assistant, Pat Ryan, along with Malcolm Roberts and Mike Levett. "I have to get my thoughts to the President to help him," I said.

When they left, my concern shifted. I had been aware that the President was planning to leave Washington that weekend. I felt it imperative that he remain in town. The news media were full of reports that up to 500,000 youths were going to march on Washington to protest the Kent State killings and the Cambodian invasion.

My preliminary inquiry to the White House brought the response that a decision on whether the President would leave town had not been reached. It was unbelievable to me that the White House could even be contemplating such a thing. I called John Whitaker and said, "I must see the President today." He said, "I'll try to set up an appointment, but it's going to be very difficult." I said, "I know the difficulty of it, but John, I haven't asked many times, and I *must* see the President. The situation is getting out of hand."

About noon John Whitaker called back and said, "It's going to be very difficult to see the President." I replied, "Well, John, if I can't get through to the President, get me Ehrlichman." He said he would see what he could do and let me know, but his tone implied that the White House "wasn't interested." I finally demanded, "John, what in the hell do I have to do? Call a press conference? Is that the only way I can reach the President?"

During the next hour, I called Secretary of State Bill Rogers and asked to see him. I went over to the State Department, just three blocks away, about three o'clock. I said, "Bill, you've got to help me convince those in the White House that the President must stay in town at this time."

Rogers agreed. He understood the situation.

4. The Decision

I went back to my office. There was a message from Whitaker: It would be impossible to see the President that day. There was no indication that I could see him the next day, and I could not see Ehrlichman because he was out of town.

I called in some of my staff along with my private secretary, Yvonne Esbensen, and said, "I'm going to write a letter to the President." I asked Malcolm Roberts, Mike Levett and Linda Pettey to write up some input, but I knew at that point that no one could write that letter but myself.

I dictated the letter in parts. There were many subjects that I was covering. Some of the letter I dictated to Yvonne, some to Joe Holbert. I had so many things on my mind that I even got into the Administration's fiscal policy, which had always bothered me. I tore that up in anger, because I knew that was not part of the problem I was trying to relate. I tried to tie the American Revolution to what was happening in the country, but I could not figure out how to say it. The letter was coming together, however. It had to be a letter of hope, not of criticism.

We worked for many hours. It was about eight o'clock that night when I talked to Joe and said, "We can't finish this letter, because it's not yet clear in my mind." I was concerned about how I was describing the American Revolution. I didn't want to discuss Vietnam as such, but to emphasize that youth must be heard. The thought that was most important in my mind, the thought that was really crying to come out, was that this country of ours was created by a revolution led by the young against the oppression of the British. And it was really the young today who were hollering and pushing. We should listen. Not that they would always be right; but we should *listen* before making up our minds.

As various parts of the letter were drafted, I passed them out to members of my staff—Dave Parker, Pat Ryan, Joe Holbert, Malcolm Roberts, Mike Levett and Yvonne, plus Mitch Melich. Normally I would have dictated only to Yvonne and the letter would have been routinely processed. But this was not a normal situation. When we went home that evening, we left our desks just as they were, because I said I wanted to finish the letter first thing in the morning.

Upon arriving home that night, I told Ermalee that I was writing a letter to the President. I had various drafts with me, but it was not quite right. I just didn't have it the way I wanted to.

Finally, late in the night, I woke up Ermalee and said, "I have it!" It was the age of the men who led the American Revolution that had to be emphasized — *young* men who were protesting, men like Thomas Jefferson and James Madison, men worth listening to. Then I went back to sleep.

I got up early the next morning. Although I was definite about how the letter should read, I began to fight with myself about whether I should go through with it. My conscience was telling me it had to be done, but I am not politically naive, and I knew the risks involved. I mentioned my struggle to Ermalee. "Wally," she said, "you didn't come to Washington to play it safe."

I went to my office and finished dictating

the letter in its entirety. I called in Mitch Melich, along with Pat Ryan and Joe Holbert, to read the finished version. The letter then was typed. Photostats were given to several members of the staff for their comments. No further changes were made.

Dave Parker came in and I asked him to read the letter. He said he felt it captured the mood of America, but he advised me to delete the reference to the Vice President in the second from the last paragraph.

I said, "No way."

Then I reached for my pen and signed the letter. Dave folded the letter and put it in an envelope, and I dispatched him to the White House. He delivered it to John Whitaker. The total elapsed time from when the letter was signed to when it was in Whitaker's hands was probably no more than twenty minutes. Meanwhile, I telephoned Bob Haldeman, the President's Chief of Staff, and said that a letter was on the way.

Haldeman called back about eleven-thirty or twelve and said, "I have the letter, but it's already on the AP wire." Within moments Pat Ryan brought in a couple of paragraphs of the letter that were on the Associated Press news ticker. Mitch Melich and Mike Halbouty of Houston were sitting with me in my office. I read the dispatch. Halbouty said later that I literally turned white. I said to Pat, "This is disastrous."

After Haldeman's call, I checked the staff. The security of the letter was something that had not been thought of. The important thing in our minds was to get the right message to the President.

The two paragraphs that appeared in the AP story were in the original draft of the letter that I did Tuesday night as well as in the final version. These two paragraphs first appeared in an early edition of the Washington *Evening Star*. We tried to find all the photocopies that had gone around the staff for comment. In our effort to present our thinking in the most balanced manner possible, we had distributed copies to almost everyone's desk. The press had called our PIO office and asked if it had any comment on the Secretary's letter to the President. A few days earlier, Fred Russell, my new Under Secretary, had removed Alex Troffey as Interior's PIO director, and that position was not yet filled. Not having a director, PIO called down to my stenographic pool asking for a copy of the Secretary's letter to the President, thinking it was public. The secretarial pool gave copies to PIO as requested. Within a matter of minutes everyone had a copy of the letter, and no matter how hard I tried, and no matter what I did, it was too late. The letter was out, and later that afternoon it appeared in full on the front page of a late edition of the *Evening Star*.

The text of the letter read:

Dear Mr. President:

I believe this Administration finds itself, today, embracing a philosophy which appears to lack appropriate concern for the attitude of a great mass of Americans — our young people.

Addressed either politically or philosophically, I believe we are in error if we set out consciously to alienate those who could be our friends.

Today, our young people, or least a vast segment of them, believe they have no opportunity to communicate with Government, regardless of Administration, other than through violent confrontation. But I am convinced we — and they — have the capacity, if we will but have the willingness, to learn from history.

During the great depression, our youth lost their ability to communicate with the Republican Party. And we saw the young people of the 1930's become the predominant leaders of the 1940's and 1950's — associated not with our party, but rather with those with whom they felt they could communicate. What is happening today is not unrelated to what happened in the 1930's. Now being unable to communicate with either party, they are apparently heading down the road to anarchy. And regardless of how I, or any American, might feel individually, we have an obligation as leaders to communicate with our youth and listen to their ideas and problems.

About 200 years ago there was emerging a great nation in the British Empire, and it found itself with a colony in violent protest by its youth — men such as Patrick Henry, Thomas Jefferson, Madison and Monroe, to name a few. Their protests fell on deaf ears, and finally led to war. The outcome is history. My point is, if we read history, it clearly shows that youth in its protest must be heard.

Let us give America an optimistic outlook and optimistic leadership. Let us show them we can solve our problems in an enlightened and positive manner.

As an example, last December 16, I wrote to you suggesting that April 22, Earth Day, be declared a national holiday. Believing this would have been a good decision, we were active on university campuses over the Christmas holidays with a program called SCOPE (Student Councils on Pollution and the Environment). It was moderately successful, and it showed that it was possible to communicate with youth. I am gratified that on April 22, I, and approximately 1,000 Interior employees, participated in Earth Day commemorative activities all over the United States.

I felt, after these meetings, that we had crossed a bridge; that communication was possible and acceptable. Likewise, I suggest in this same vein that you meet with college presidents, to talk about the very situation that is erupting, because before we can face and conquer our enemies, we must identify them, whether those enemies take physical or philosophical form. And we must win over our philosophical enemies by convincing them of the wisdom of the path we have chosen, rather than ignoring the path they propose.

In this regard, I believe the Vice President initially has answered a deep-seated mood of America in his public statements. However, a continued attack on the young—not on their attitudes so much as their motives, can serve little purpose other than to further cement those attitudes to a solidity impossible to penetrate with reason.

Finally, Mr. President, permit me to suggest that you consider meeting, on an individual and conversational basis, with members of your Cabinet. Perhaps through such conversations, we can gain greater insight into the problems confronting us all, and most important, into the solutions of these problems.

Faithfully yours,

/s/Wally

Walter J. Hickel
Secretary of the Interior

As I look back on the situation, there were some deep moments of depression for the next few hours. But I remember the feeling I had Wednesday evening when I got home. I said, "Ermalee, it was a disastrous thing. But I have a feeling of relief. I think that it will help the total mood in America and that we will have a quiet weekend, where once it appeared that there would be bloodshed.

"It will be a quiet weekend and the young will go away, but the mood will not."

Washington believes that everyone has a price.
Washington didn't understand Wally Hickel.

CHAPTER **11**

To Limbo and Back

John Ehrlichman called the day after I wrote my letter to the President. He said that although there was some "distress" over the fact that the letter had reached the press, "The President understands. Don't worry, Wally."

However, I quickly learned that privately both the President and his chief advisors were very angry. I was puzzled at the time why they did not understand the spirit in which the letter was written and benefit from the tremendously positive response it had brought from the American people. My office was bombarded with telegrams and letters—about 17,000 in all. I saw this as a great plus for our credibility as an "open" Administration.

440

The White House staff did not take this in the same spirit. John Whitaker called Pat Ryan and demanded: "You find the son-of-a-bitch who leaked that letter and fire him."

Pat replied angrily, "You find the son-of-a-bitch who wouldn't let Hickel see the President and fire him!"

In the Department of the Interior's seventh floor press office, orders were circulated — at Herb Klein's direction — that any queries about the letter, or even Hickel, were to be ignored or referred to Ron Ziegler's presidential press office.

In my own office Dave Parker was at a point of almost total frustration in trying to schedule meetings or maintain any sort of regularity, because of all the public and private pressures either to elaborate upon or deny authorship of my letter. And throughout the Department, anyone who had any sort of pipeline to the White House was getting the word: "Hickel's in trouble."

That Friday afternoon, hundreds of thousands of students from throughout the country swarmed into Washington for Saturday's massive anti-war rally. In the evening, as Ermalee and I picked at our dinner at our home in Kenwood, I determined that I had to talk to these young people. I wanted to communicate, and I wanted them to know that the Administration was willing to listen. I decided that I would go unannounced to the rally the next day to circulate and talk with as many young people as I could.

Saturday morning I went to the Executive Office Building to make arrangements to visit the demonstration.

As Hilton Coleman wheeled my limousine through the police lines surrounding the White House and the EOB Saturday morning, the swarms of demonstrators reacted with distaste at the sight of a government Cadillac. They waved and shouted, and one young man was shoved back by a District of Columbia police officer as the youth shook his fist at the car.

Ermalee and Joe Holbert went with me to the EOB. I talked to Herb Klein and explained my plan to meet with the young people. Klein was convinced that my visit to the rally would be a mistake. I was not convinced, and as I left his office I was still planning to head for the Lincoln Memorial, a main gathering area for the demonstrators in addition to the Ellipse behind the White House.

As I walked out of the Executive Office Building to my limousine, Joe came up with an inspector from the National Park Police. "Mr. Secretary," the inspector said, "we can't guarantee your safety." We talked about the situation for several minutes, but after shortwave radio calls to his headquarters and various checkpoints on the police lines, the inspector remained adamant that I should not go to the demonstration.

I told Hilton to drive us home to Kenwood. But I was frustrated. I *knew* I could have communicated with those young people. It was a scorching day, with the temperature hovering close to 100 degrees. One of the first calls I made when I returned home was to the National Park Service, to make certain someone had followed through on my earlier order to set up portable drinking fountains and toilets throughout the demonstration areas.

The White House had determined that the Department of Health, Education and Welfare would serve as the lead agency in communicating with the demonstrating students, setting up meeting facilities at HEW and at other sites scattered around the inner city. I called Bill Pecora, Mitch Melich and David Dominick, my 32-year-old director of the Federal Water Quality Administration, and told them to get over to HEW and see how things were going.

Bill called me at home as soon as he arrived at the HEW auditorium: "Mr. Secretary, this looks like a small revolution. There is no rapport. You ought to be here. The kids are demanding dynamic leadership, but there's nothing here."

Pecora called me back again several minutes later. With Melich and Dominick, he had been circulating around the auditorium, talking with various groups of students. He said that at the moment he was with a group of about forty young people: "They want to talk to somebody high up in government—they want contact with someone in a policy position."

"They don't want to talk to me," Bill added. "They want to talk to the President or at least to a Cabinet officer."

Pecora asked if he could put some of the students on the telephone. "Absolutely—put them right on," I replied.

I spoke first with a young woman who started out by saying, "The only way to fix the system is to burn it down."

We talked for several minutes. I told her I felt that the critical element we needed was communication: "If we can communicate we can solve problems. But if we're afraid even to talk to each other, we'll only have anarchy."

Calming down, she said over and over: "Yes, sir. Yes indeed, sir. I'm glad to hear that. I'm all for you."

I asked her to give the telephone back to "Doc."

She said, "Who's Doc?" I replied, "That's Bill Pecora, the man you're meeting with as my personal representative."

Bill put on the line a young man who was a student at Ohio State University. He went through the same aggressive preamble, but finally ended up turning 180 degrees. We agreed that if we worked together we could bridge the gap between young people and government.

The same thing happened as I talked to other students Bill Pecora brought to the telephone. The last young man I talked to said: "This is great. We can't even see our Dean, and we thought the government was unavailable to us. We thought this was a put-up job, Mr. Secretary, but we were wrong. Thank you."

1. 'Is It the President's Wish?'

That Saturday night I was at home in Kenwood, having dinner with the Ryans and Mitch Melich and his wife, Dori. Joe Holbert joined us after dinner, and we watched a short pre-taped interview I had done earlier with Dan Schorr of CBS.

Shortly after nine o'clock the White House telephone in our bedroom rang. It was Bob Haldeman, the President's Chief of Staff: "Mr. Secretary, it's thought best that you not come to services in the morning."

I was thunderstruck. The next day, Sunday, was Mother's Day, and we had been planning to go to the church services scheduled in the East Room of the White House. We had invited Tom Holley and his wife to go with Ermalee and me, and three of our sons, Karl, Joe and Jack. Jack had flown in from the University of San Francisco.

When we had attended the White House services previously, we had found them inspiring. I particularly recalled the service we attended at the Executive Mansion on the morning of July 20, 1969, only five hours before Apollo 11 touched down on the moon. Colonel Frank Borman, commander of the earlier Apollo 8 mission, had read a passage from Genesis ("In the beginning God created the heaven and the earth."), the same passage he had read from deep space the preceding Christmas Eve as he circled the moon with his fellow astronauts Jim Lovell and Bill Anders.

To me, the White House church services were not political or social functions. To me, they were opportunities to consider man and his future in a more thoughtful and spiritual manner.

I simply could not imagine what Haldeman was talking about. Over and over I said: "It's incredible. This has got to be incredible." I was practically shouting, and Ermalee walked in from the living room looking alarmed. I told Haldeman: "This can't be true. Is this the President's wish?"

He said that a meeting had been held that day and it had been decided that I should not be present at the church service. Again I asked, "Is this the President's wish?"

Haldeman said, "The President was in the room when the decision was made."

I said, "I'll accept the decision if it's the President's wish, but this has got to be totally incredible."

I hung up, then lifted the receiver again. A White House Signal Corps operator came on the line. I asked that he connect me with Herb Klein.

The corpsman found Klein in Williamsburg, Virginia. I asked if he knew about the decision that I was not to attend church at the White House the next day. "It's true," Klein said. "You might be a distraction. There will be press there." He also confirmed that the President had been present when the decision was made.

I was stunned. As I put the receiver down, Ermalee said, "We will not play games with our faith."

2. A Simple Story of Reason

From the moment that my letter to the President became public, I was inundated with requests from the press for interviews. One of the most persistent newsmen was CBS correspondent Mike Wallace, anchorman for the network's news magazine program, "60 Minutes."

I had misgivings about appearing on television. Yet I also felt that perhaps there was a story that needed to be told: a simple story of reason, a story that could help America. I thought Wallace would give me a fair hearing, but it was a difficult decision.

I told Joe Holbert to advise Wallace that we would think about it and get back to him. Joe called Alvin Snyder, one of Herb Klein's assistants, and then Klein directly, telling them of the Wallace request. Klein was curt and said that he did not want me to do the program.

At one point I talked to Klein. He was completely callous about the mood in the country that had me so disturbed. He said, "Cool it, Wally, this will blow over in twenty-four hours."

Yet it also appeared that the President's Director of Communications was reluctant to have it known that he had veto power over television appearances by Cabinet officers. After a direct call from Wallace to Klein, in which Wallace pointedly asked if Cabinet officers were being told which television programs they could do, Klein withdrew his objection.

I spent nearly five hours in front of the CBS cameras at our home on Sunday, May 10. Wallace fired the questions and I responded. As we filmed take after take, Producer Don Hewitt took notes for the editors in New York who would condense the film down to the final twenty minutes, which would be shown on "60 Minutes" the following Tuesday.

When the filming was over and the hot lights were finally extinguished, I was tired and really could not judge how the program had come out. My only goal had been to be open and honest. I felt that the most important question Wallace had asked was: "The President is generally acknowledged to be an introverted man and a solitary man, even a lonely man. What kind of staff, then, if you agree with that analysis, should he have?"

I replied that an introspective man should have an extroverted and outgoing staff—one which would "make as many inputs as possible." I agreed with Wallace that the White House staff was not like that. The men around Richard Nixon tended to play it "very close to the vest."

Although I did not lay much significance to it that Sunday, my nineteen-year-old son, Jack, made a comment during the filming that probably further aggravated my relations with the White House. During the latter part of the program, when he and Ermalee joined me in front of the cameras, Jack commented that he was pretty sure that I had disagreed with the President's order sending troops into Cambodia.

The President's first public comment on

my letter came the next evening—Monday, May 11, during a presidential press conference. He was asked by Charles W. Bailey II, Washington bureau chief for the Minneapolis *Tribune:* "Sir, without asking you to censure the Secretary of the Interior, could you comment on the substantive points that he made in his letter?"

I was intently watching that press conference on television, hoping that the question would be asked and the President would use the opportunity to call once again for the nation, young and old, to move forward together. When he answered, however, I detected a tone of bitterness in his voice.

"I think the Secretary of the Interior is a man who has very strong views," the President responded. "He is outspoken. He is courageous. That is one of the reasons that I selected him for the Cabinet, and one of the reasons that I defended him very vigorously before this press corps when he was under attack. As far as his views are concerned, I will of course be interested in his advice. I might say, too, that I hope he gives some advice to the Postmaster

General. That is the fastest mail delivery I have had since I have been in the White House."

On Tuesday, May 12, I flew to San Francisco to keep a long-standing commitment to address the American Society of Newspaper Editors the following day. But before I left Tuesday evening, I had a two o'clock afternoon appointment with John Ehrlichman.

We discussed the problems that seemed to be accumulating between the White House and me. He said that I had some problems I had not had before the letter, and if I wanted a meeting with the President, that could be arranged. He indicated that the President was upset. I could understand that — although I did not realize just how upset he was. Basically, Ehrlichman and I agreed that a meeting between the President and myself would be arranged in the near future.

In San Francisco I was introduced to the ASNE by John B. Oakes, editorial-page editor of *The New York Times,* who called me "the man who was once known as the bad guy but who is now the good guy of the

Administration." I treated lightly the matter of the now famous letter, at least in my opening remarks, referring to the editors as "fellow readers of letters." But I tried to stress a serious note: "A few thought the letter might have been merely fast footwork to avoid violence last week; but most, I trust, recognize it resulted from a deep moral conviction."

I was followed as a speaker by the environmental scientist Dr. Barry Commoner, who described my letter as "a document that has done more to restore the confidence of the American student in government than anything that has happened in the last ten years."

When I got back to Washington I called Ehrlichman again to pursue the matter of meeting with the President privately. I did see the President at a routine Cabinet meeting on May 19. The matter of the letter was not mentioned. I sensed a certain chill in the air, but the White House seemed to be making an effort to maintain an appearance of tranquility. Newsmen were told afterward, "There was full discussion by every member of the Cabinet."

The following weekend was taken up by my four-day flying trip to the Snake River with Arthur Godfrey. My appointments on Tuesday, May 26, were routine, and so were all but one the following day. At 3:30 that Wednesday afternoon, John Ehrlichman came to see me in my office. My private appointment with the President was now set for 3 P.M. Thursday.

I wanted to talk first with Maryland Congressman Rogers C. B. Morton, chairman of the Republican National Committee, who was destined to succeed me at Interior. I had always considered Morton a good friend. I started trying to reach him on Thursday morning as soon as I arrived in my office—about eight o'clock. The Signal Corps found him in Chicago. He was flying back to Washington, and he asked me to meet him at National Airport three hours later—2:30 P.M. Washington time.

That was cutting the timing of my appointment with the President pretty fine, so Hilton Coleman drove fast and Morton and I talked fast on the way from the airport to the White House. Morton said, "Wally, you're one of the great effective things we've got going in the Republican Party. Hang in there." As I stepped out of my limousine at the White House, Morton agreed to meet with me again after I had seen the President.

3. 'Do You Want Me to Leave?'

I went straight to the Oval Office. During our forty-five-minute session, the President did most of the talking. He mentioned the good job that I had done during the 1968 campaign as one of his ten surrogates, and what we were doing at Interior to help the environment and eliminate pollution.

But he repeatedly referred to me as an "adversary."

Initially I considered that a compliment because, to me, an adversary within an organization is a valuable asset. It was only after the President had used the term many times and with a disapproving inflection that I realized he considered an adversary an enemy. I could not understand why he would consider me an enemy.

As I sensed that the conversation was about to end, I asked, "Mr. President, do you want me to leave the Administration?"

He jumped up from his chair, very hurried and agitated. He said, "That's one option we hadn't considered." He called in Ehrlichman and said: "John, I want you to handle this. Wally asked whether he should leave. That's one option we hadn't considered."

The President left the Oval Office, telling Ehrlichman to "stay with it and discuss it." But John had to leave to catch a plane, and I was joined by Bryce Harlow, who said, "The President wants me to follow up on this."

Bryce and I had been friends for years, and we talked at great length. He said he would be back in touch with me later. "But for the lack of any other decision now, keep on going like you are, Wally. Just keep doing the job you're doing and we'll look at the situation later."

I went back to my office, called Rogers Morton and he came right over. We talked for a very long time.

I told Rogers that I had asked the President whether I should quit. He exclaimed: "Don't quit! You've got to stay on the job. Tell them to forget all this crap about the letter. I've been in fourteen states in the last few weeks. You're an asset to the Administration and you've got to keep going. You've got to keep doing what you're doing. Let's get on down the road."

I had a feeling later that if I had met with Morton a day or two before seeing Nixon, instead of a matter of minutes before, things might have turned out differently.

As the month of May 1970 continued to run its course, I was determined to maintain my positive attitude and not to go on the defensive. I felt that I had done nothing that needed defending. There was no question in my mind that, given hope and determination, I could turn around the negative attitude that seemed to be permeating the Administration, although one suggestion that I had made in my May 6 letter to the President—that Vice President Agnew would do well to temper

458

his remarks about young people — appeared to have fallen on deaf ears. On May 17 the Vice President, in a television interview, said that if there was to be any cooling of rhetoric, "The first place it should begin is on the editorial pages of some of the eastern newspapers." As for himself, he would "continue to speak out," and he would not lower his voice until campus radicals lowered theirs.

The first of June came and went quietly. That was the deadline for filing for public office in Alaska, and many Washington political observers had speculated that I would go home and make a bid for another term as Governor, rather than stay on at Interior. In fact, many of my friends and political acquaintances had been urging me to do exactly that for some time. But I never gave the idea serious consideration, and Ermalee agreed. She told me one night: "Wally, I have mixed feelings about what is going on. But you must never turn back. You would never be happy with yourself if you did."

Those who wanted me to go home and run for Governor again argued that if I stayed in the Cabinet I was only running the risk of being isolated, ignored and frustrated by the White House; in effect, I would be "sent to Coventry," an old English expression that describes a man who is given the cold shoulder.

I might as well have been in Coventry on June 5, 1970. James Doyle of the Washington *Evening Star* wrote in his column the next day: "Minor White House annoyance with Hickel's public dissent has been no secret, but yesterday the signals seemed so clear. . . . Hickel was 'disinvited' from a trip to the White House to brief reporters on something he considers one of his crowning achievements—the canceling of oil and gas leases in the Santa Barbara channel."

Ever since the terrible Santa Barbara oil spill in January 1969, I had been fighting—and this included fighting with other departments—to buy back the leases and create a marine sanctuary. I felt this would eliminate the risk of further pollution in that California resort area, while still meeting our resource needs through an arrangement to get these resources from the

Elk Hills Petroleum Reserve farther north in California.

We had worked on the project for months. Finally the Department's Office of Information prepared a news release spelling out the details of our plan. But the news release was never issued, and Bill Pecora, then head of the Geological Survey, was told to substitute for me at the White House briefing.

John Whitaker called me at home the night before the briefing. "It would be better if you didn't come out of the room with the President," he said. "Senator Murphy, fine. But not you." He said they wanted Pecora "just to answer any technical questions. The President wants to emphasize the local angle by letting Murphy and Teague get the play."

Senator George Murphy and Representative Charles M. Teague were both Republican incumbents up for reelection in California. The White House felt that the exposure they would get in the briefing would enhance their chances. (Teague made it in the November election, but Murphy did not.)

I thought the whole thing was a bit odd. I didn't give a damn about the "public exposure" the briefing might provide. My concern was that the story of the Administration's program to buy back the Santa Barbara leases needed to be told effectively and forcefully if we were to sell the idea to Congress. As far as the technical points were concerned, I had *lived* with the project for months and knew its details intimately.

Ron Ziegler, explaining my absence from the briefing, announced: "There's no real reason why Hickel wasn't here. Pecora was here. It was pretty technical stuff and so Pecora briefed on it."

Of course, Ziegler did not mention my call from Whitaker, or the fact that I had briefed a large group of reporters on the whole program—including its technical points—at a breakfast meeting that same morning. Peter Braestrup wrote in the Washington *Post:* ". . . Moreover, Ziegler said, Hickel had chosen to stay away from a Thursday White House meeting with the President and the press on a pet Hickel bill. . . . (Interior sources said that Hickel had been 'invited and disinvited' by the White House.) Did all this mean that the White House would be happy if Hickel stayed on as Secretary of the Interior? 'That is not relevant,' Ziegler said. 'How could I answer that without getting into trouble?' "

4. Forward Alone

Above all, I had decided that I was not going to quit. There was so much to be done, and as far as I was concerned, we were just getting started. The job at Interior was full of challenges. In early 1969, a bureau chief asked me, "How can I help you?" I told him: "Bring me your problems. I'm a problem solver."

On June 8, I sought a fifteen-month moratorium on the Cross-Florida Barge Canal, a construction project that was not only environmentally harmful but had lost its original economic justification. I immediately ran into disapproval at the level of the White House political professionals, who were afraid of the implications such an action would have for the forthcoming congressional and gubernatorial elections.[1]

On June 18, fed up with the waffling of the various agencies responsible for pesticide control, I banned sixteen "hard" pesticides on all federal properties administered by the Department of the Interior. Late that month I began a long-scheduled inspection tour of crowded national park systems. The following month I continued to concentrate on an Alaska Native land claims settlement, a problem the federal government refused to recognize for years and one that remains unsolved as I write this book. We also initiated the first public hearings on offshore oil lease sales[2] and took on the problem of mercury pollution.

On July 14, I telegraphed the Governors of the seventeen states where the threat of mercury pollution was most serious and warned the industries involved. Eight days

[1] *Shortly after I left Washington, and after the elections had wiped out most of the Florida Republican candidates, President Nixon announced that he was stopping the Barge Canal project.*

later we submitted the names of thirteen firms to the Justice Department for possible prosecution for "discharging into the nation's waterways sufficient quantities of mercury to constitute a serious hazard to public health." By September 16, industrial mercury discharges were reduced by 86 percent.

During the months of the summer and into the fall, we began a National Urban Recreation Study Plan. We fought for and won legislation making the Chesapeake and Ohio Canal, which borders the Potomac River, into a National Historical Park. We launched the "Street Scene"; developed with Burl Ives the Johnny Horizon anti-litter campaign on federal properties; banned all billboards from Interior lands, and put whales on the endangered species list.

However, there was one major battle we did not win. President Nixon had

[2] *These hearings took place in Louisiana and were a real triumph for a balanced approach to resource development. When the public was presented with all the facts,*

commissioned Roy L. Ash, president of Litton Industries, to head a group to study the reorganization of the executive branch of government. When I was asked for my opinion, I strongly urged, and repeatedly fought for the transforming of Interior into a Department of Natural Resources and the Environment. I reasoned that it was self-defeating to separate resource development from environmental protection. If you alter a resource in any way, if you cut a tree or plant a tree, you change the environment for better or for worse. I stated flatly, "I don't care who heads it, but set it up so that environmental desecration is stopped before it takes place."

The President chose another course. By executive order he set up the Environmental Protection Agency, which served as an umbrella for all anti-pollution bureaus. This decision of the President removed from Interior the Federal Water Quality Administration as well as several other

from the points of view of both development and conservation, responsible decisions were agreed to and made.

offices dealing with pollution control. I still believe that the environment suffers when the policing function is isolated, and I believe that as we come to grips with these problems with more knowledge and realism in the next decades, a Department of Natural Resources and the Environment will inevitably be created.

One of my greatest hopes, as a private citizen, as Governor of Alaska and as Secretary of the Interior, has been to alert the United States to the potential of its Arctic areas. The Soviet Union, the Scandinavian countries and the Canadians have far greater knowledge of their Arctic areas than we do. They could teach us much.

During two trips in 1970 I explored the potential of the Arctic. In August I took a 4,000-mile trip through the North American Arctic with my Canadian counterpart, Jean Chretien, Ottawa's Minister for Indian Affairs and Northern Development. In September I visited the Arctic regions of Finland and also traveled in Sweden and Norway—10,000 miles in all.

In Finland I felt that the door was being opened to much closer understanding and cooperation between our two nations. I met with President Urho K. Kekkonen, Premier Ahti Karjalainen and Foreign Minister Vaino Leskinen. With Leskinen in particular I discussed at great length Arctic development and other mutual interests. I thought that President Nixon had considerable interest in my mission since the White House had asked me to hand-carry to Helsinki a personal letter to President Kekkonen from Nixon upon the occasion of the Finnish chief of state's seventieth birthday.

In consultations with United States Ambassador Val Peterson, I was told that the Finns would be eager to increase the exchange of Arctic knowledge on such matters as ice-breaking and the construction of ships for Arctic conditions, at which the Finns excel. Later, in Stockholm and Oslo, I met with various officials of Sweden and Norway to discuss Arctic development and international efforts to eliminate pollution. In Oslo Ambassador Phillip Crowe and I were taken on an inspection voyage in the Oslo Fjord and were shown techniques the Norwegians are using to trace and eliminate water pollution caused by industrial discharges and low oxygenation. This is a problem in the Baltic Sea because of its generally shallow depth and because of a sill between Norway and Denmark that tends to limit the intake of new water into the Baltic from the North Sea.

When I returned to Washington on September 7, 1970, I felt that I had an important report to make to the President. On September 11, I wrote a letter to the President requesting an appointment.

For three weeks I heard nothing. Then I received a letter from Hugh W. Sloan Jr., staff assistant to the President. Sloan advised me that an appointment with the President would be "impossible." There was no qualification—not impossible until next week; not impossible until next month or next year. Just "impossible."

5. Not 'If' but 'When'

In retrospect, there is no question that even though we were fighting to maintain our momentum on the issues of the environment and on our other Interior responsibilities, I was getting no support or encouragement from the White House. I began to wonder why the President had not asked for my resignation after the letter incident. Financing for our programs became harder and harder to get out of the Office of Management and Budget (the new name of the Budget Bureau). My new Under Secretary, Fred Russell, a close personal friend of the President and a heavy campaign contributor, was constantly working at cross-purposes with me, especially on conservation questions.

My job was getting to be like walking in space with the knowledge that your oxygen supply was slowly being cut off. Never one to fear a fight, I was not at all intimidated; but this time I did not know who all my opponents were.

I did not doubt for a minute that the public was counting on me to represent its best interests. I believed that the credit would accrue to the Administration as a whole and that President Nixon would comprehend the value of my actions. For this reason the continuous flow of rumors about me, emanating from the White House, made me more and more upset. These rumors usually seemed to be a result of the journalistic "backgrounder."

Under the rules of a "backgrounder," a government official calls in certain trusted reporters and tells them something with the understanding that the material is authoritative but the official is not to be quoted or identified. The newsman is enjoined to write his story in such a way that it appears the judgment he is rendering is strictly his own.

During the summer of 1970 the White House "backgrounder" concerning me flourished. Ron Ziegler told press intimates at Key Biscayne, Florida, where the President was vacationing, that "it's only a matter of time until Hickel leaves," while officially he was saying, "I know of no intention for Secretary Hickel to leave his post." Back in Washington, James Keogh, a chief White House speech writer about to move on himself, told reporters at a breakfast meeting that Hickel was through a few hours after Herb Klein had denied any such thing in a press conference on the West Coast. For better or worse, the backgrounder is part of Washington politics. But the significant point at the time, to me, was that it was easy to tell when it was "backgrounder time" by the flurry of almost identical stories that would appear simultaneously. For example, within days of each other in the summer of 1970, we had such items as these:

The Washington *Evening Star,* in an editorial: "The major decision still to be reached is the manner of [Hickel's] going... An ice curtain [has] descended between the White House and the Interior Department."

E. W. Kenworthy, in *The New York Times:* "The relationship between President Nixon and Secretary . . . Hickel has deteriorated to the point where there is widespread speculation here that Mr. Hickel will soon resign or be dismissed. ... [In] several ways . . . informants said, the White House has . . . gone out of its way to humiliate him publicly."

Of course, as a natural-born "positive thinker," I have always tried to find something lighthearted or humorous even in dark hours. While most of the press was engaged in a solemn analysis of my future—or lack of it—I could still laugh at myself when this scenario by the syndicated columnist Arthur Hoppe appeared in the June 23, 1970, Baltimore *Evening Sun:**

Scene: The offices of Walter J. Hickel, Secretary of the Interior. The room is bare of furniture, the window is boarded over and Mr. Hickel is perspiring profusely as he speaks to his secretary, Miss Pangloss.

Mr. Hickel: About the air conditioner, Miss Pangloss . . .

Miss Pangloss: They said maybe they could have it fixed by a week from next Tuesday, sir. Maybe.

Mr. Hickel: They promised to have the

furniture back last week. Are you sure those fellows who carted it out were upholsterers? The tall one looked just like Bob Haldeman with a black mustache. (Hopefully). Wasn't that the phone, Miss Pangloss?

Miss Pangloss: No, sir. Just your imagination again.

Mr. Hickel: All right. To business. What's on my appointment schedule today?

Miss Pangloss (reading): 8:45 A.M., arrive at office, 6:15 P.M., leave for day.

Mr. Hickel: I think I'll leave a little early. With my limousine called back to the factory, it's a long bus ride home. I don't suppose there's any mail?

Miss Pangloss: Yes, sir. You received a reply to your letter to the President, asking him to lay to rest these false rumors that he wants you to resign.

Mr. Hickel (eagerly): I knew he'd stand behind me! Read the letter, Miss Pangloss.

Miss Pangloss: "Dear Fellow American: The President has asked me to inform you that he shares your concern over ending the war in Vietnam as quickly as . . ."

Mr. Hickel (frowning): Do you think they're trying to tell me something, Miss Pangloss?

Miss Pangloss: They often get their form letters mixed up at the White House, sir. And after all, Ron Ziegler . . . said publicly that they definitely wouldn't ask for your resignation.

Mr. Hickel: Yes, that was reassuring. Still . . . there's one thing to do. I'll call up the President and have this out once and for all. Do you have a dime, Miss Pangloss?[3]

6. 'An Unfortunate Remark'

On September 25, 1970, eighteen days after I had returned from Scandinavia, I went to

[3] *We may assume that "Miss Pangloss" is a reference to Voltaire's classic satire* Candide, *in which the philosopher Dr. Pangloss insists, from disaster to disaster, that this is still the best of all possible worlds.*

the Sheraton-Park Hotel for an evening dinner speech before the national conference of the Association of Student Governments. Secretary of Defense Melvin Laird and Stephen Hess, a counselor to the President on youth relations, had spoken to the student leaders earlier in the day. When I arrived at the hotel, a group of ASG organizers came to me and said they were very alarmed. "The Laird and Hess speeches were 'bombs,' " they said. "All they did was parrot the Administration line, and slip and slide during their short question and answer periods. We hope you will be more candid."

I was, although I didn't change a word of my prepared remarks. I told about 700 students and university officials that I rejected the "rhetoric of polarization." In discussing campus violence, I declared: "To be negative is to divide. It turns us against each other and keeps us small. Demonstrations do not, by themselves, solve problems. Of course, rioting and violence are negative. So is the rhetoric of polarization. Some people fear an economic depression. I fear more a depression of the spirit. *As hard as we try, we cannot tear the nation together."*

At almost the same moment, Vice President Agnew was addressing a $150-a-plate Republican banquet in Milwaukee. He exhorted his audience: "A call to intellectual combat cannot be issued by a flute; it needs a trumpet."

I was not aware of what the Vice President was saying in Milwaukee, but it was probably natural that the press assumed the next day that I had been talking about Agnew when I referred to "the people who demand law and order, but refuse to concern themselves with why there is hatred, frustration and violence in the land."

My remark to the student leaders — that we could not "tear the country together" —touched a sore nerve. John Whitaker called Pat Ryan the next morning and complained, "That was an unfortunate remark." But the phrase stayed in speeches I continued to give around the country.

Despite Whitaker's complaint to Pat

Ryan about my speech to the student leaders, it seemed to me that speculative news stories about Hickel leaving the Cabinet, or being in trouble with the White House, were appearing less regularly—at least for the time being. I thought I knew the reason.

Several weeks earlier, Nick Ruwe, an aide at the White House, had been designated to handle speakers and general scheduling during the upcoming election campaign. Ruwe had met with Pat Ryan, Dave Parker and me in my office. It was stressed that the White House wanted to make maximum use of me during the campaign as a traveling salesman for the Administration.

I had no objection. I welcomed the opportunity to get out and talk with all Americans. However, while I told Ruwe that I would be willing to travel extensively around the country, there was one place where I did not want to spend a great deal of time—Texas. If I went into Texas I would be expected to do "fund raisers"—that is, make speeches to the party faithful. I argued that if I went into Texas at all, "at least let me go down to the Rio Grande and talk to the Mexican-Americans; the poor, the braceros, the Democrats, the liberals—that huge bloc of Texans who are *not* on the Administration's side."

Working with Ruwe, Dave Parker began putting together an ambitious campaign schedule in a total of fourteen states. The President had made it clear earlier that he liked my style of campaigning. On August 26, 1970, I was in San Clemente for a Domestic Council meeting. At the end of the day I received a note from Bob Finch. It said the President wanted to know if I could stay over an additional day: "The President would like to see you privately." I made arrangements to remain in California another day, and the next morning I walked into the President's Western White House office.

We were joined by Finch, and as we sat down I decided to try to lay some of the persistent rumors of my pending departure to rest. I told the President, "I wish something could be done to symbolize the fact that we're all on the same team, and to dispel all these rumors." The President seemed a little startled, and he told Finch, "Call the reporters in; call the photographers in." This was done, and the wire services were soon relaying a photograph across the country showing Nixon, Finch and me smiling and chatting in the President's office.

After the reporters left and we returned to our private discussion, the conversation moved to the campaign. The President turned to me and said, "Wally, the thing to do is to get into a city — make a speech or something — and then find a way to get on television. For every person you reach in a speech, you can reach thousands more on television."

As in 1968, "get on television" was to be the guiding rule for the advance men and all the others involved in campaign planning.

In the final weeks before the election, we almost always were able to supplement "The Speech" with one or more appearances on local television. The whole effort was capped during the last week in October with a frantic and calculated down-to-the-last-minute trip that took me into Iowa, South Dakota, North Dakota,

Illinois, Missouri, Ohio, Connecticut and back to Washington, D.C. — all in three days.

There was only one jarring note during this period. On October 19 I flew into Colorado Springs for a few hours of rest after campaign appearances in New Mexico. I had just checked into the Broadmoor Hotel when I picked up a newspaper and read a wire story out of Washington that quoted "White House sources" as saying that "if we win the Senate, Hickel will be out as Secretary of the Interior." I placed a long-distance call to the Signal Corps switchboard at the White House, asking for Bob Finch.

When they found him an hour later, I said: "Bob, what the hell is going on? How can I be out here all over the country campaigning to try and elect Republicans to the Senate, when it appears that the White House is leaking stories that I'm going to leave if we're successful? That is ridiculous."

Finch said he also "considered the stories ridiculous. I'll check it out and get back to you, Wally." But he never called back.

7. 'That Son of a Bitch!'

The Republican rhetoric of the 1970 campaign, as the results proved on November 3, totally misread the wavelength of America. The country did not want to hear negative, divisive and "anti" talks from its leaders. Hammering on the issue of law and order, the Vice President gave our Administration an image of playing on people's fears instead of encouraging their hopes and aspirations.

As I campaigned I tried in my own way to emphasize the strength of our record and to speak of the promises I saw ahead. I still could not let myself believe that the President subscribed to the "Agnew approach."

On election eve the Republican National Committee ran a videotape of the President campaigning in Phoenix, Arizona, a few days before. The technical quality of the tape was pitifully poor, but even poorer was the quality of the rhetoric. The man I had believed in and sweated for, the man on whom I had staked my political future, was shaking his fist and inflaming his audience with a negative philosophy. He talked as if he were campaigning for the position of Sheriff in Maricopa County.

As we watched the show on television, Ermalee got up and walked out of the room, saying in a low voice, as if to herself, "I have lost my heart."

Election night was a nightmare. Ermalee, Pat Ryan and I went to dinner at the home of Frank Bracken, my legislative counsel at Interior, and his wife, Judy. Another of my assistants, Jack Horton, was there with his wife, Grace. After dinner Pat and I drove to the Sheraton-Park Hotel. I had been invited to join the Vice President and some of the other Cabinet officers to watch the election returns. Red Blount came by, along with John Mitchell and HEW's Elliot Richardson.

The overwhelming attitude was not one of victory and joy, but rather of revenge. When one of the television networks reported that Senator Charles Goodell, a Republican, had been defeated in his bid to return to the Senate from New York, Agnew strode over to the TV set and said: "We got that son of a bitch!" He was far more elated about having helped defeat Goodell than in winning in some other area of the country. Such an attitude was completely contrary to the whole way I had approached the campaign — to work *for* something and *for* somebody.

I left the room as quietly and as quickly as I could and went back to the Bracken home. I told Ermalee what I had just witnessed at the Sheraton-Park and said that I thought the election had been a disaster.

Two days later, on the morning of November 5, the Cabinet assembled at the White House for a post-election briefing from the President. He said he was pleased with the outcome of the election: "It was a victory." He recited statistics on the Senate races which he felt supported his argument that we had "at least made philosophical gains."

Then he said something that absolutely astonished me. Someone mentioned that a total of eleven Republican Governors had gone down the drain in the election.

The President tossed that aside with a quick wave of his hand. He said: "Governors aren't important in national elections. The only people left who can deliver big blocks of votes are people like Daley," referring to Chicago Mayor Richard J. Daley.

I was glad that no one asked for my opinion.

There was no way that election could be viewed as a "victory." I thought to myself, "The American people won't believe it either."

I felt that the White House could not continue to follow the policies and rhetoric of polarization if it was to survive its own test at the polls in 1972.

8. Fire Behind the Smoke

Two days before the election, on November 1, the Washington *Evening Star* observed: "In the halls and on platforms that make up the campaign trail, Interior Secretary Hickel—who was out of favor at the White House not long ago—has been doing yeoman work in the GOP effort this fall.

'He has turned out to be one of our stars; he's in heavy demand around the country,' said one party strategist."

But it did not take long for the tide to turn once the election was over and I had returned from the campaign trail. By November 20, the *Star* was editorializing:

Anyone who has been paying even partial attention to his newpapers these past few days must be aware that some new faces are expected around the President's Cabinet table almost any day now. And anyone who has been around Washington for more than 24 hours will realize that it is no coincidence that the name Walter J. Hickel heads just about everybody's list of presumed expendables. This ubiquitous highly reliable anonymous official has been at it again, whispering sweet somethings in the ears of selected pundits.

In this case, where there was smoke there *was* fire, and I had started smelling it even during that Cabinet meeting on November 5, right after the President's analysis of the election. As the meeting broke up, I walked over to John Mitchell and asked if I could meet with him later in the day at his office. He told me to come right over.

As I sat down in the Attorney General's office, I said, "John, I'd like to get to the bottom of a problem." I explained that I was already aware of a new resurgence of speculation that I was going to be dismissed, or edged into a position of such political and public discomfort that I would resign rather than continue under such conditions.

"John," I continued, "all these rumors coming out that I might get fired or relieved are upsetting my department something terrible. You know yourself how difficult it is to run a department when your people, especially the heads of bureaus, think that their boss is going to be fired at any moment. All sorts of political games get going."

"I haven't heard anything about it," Mitchell said. "I know nothing about it. I haven't heard any conversation about you being fired or asked to leave."

I ended the conversation by saying,

"Well, John, check it out. Because they've got to stop putting out those statements from the White House and kill them once and for all. This isn't doing anyone any good."

Mitchell said he would check it out. But despite our talk, it appeared that some wheels had already been set in motion to deal with me. Earlier, Pat Ryan had received a call from the White House asking that I meet with Fred Malek at 10:45 A.M. on the morning of the election. Malek, a former staff member at HEW, had been transferred to the White House as a personnel troubleshooter. In the cloakrooms he was described more accurately, if more colloquially, as "the hatchet man."

When I met with Malek on November 3 he said, "Now we're going to solve our personnel problems; at this time we can stand the political heat." Then, a few days later, one of Malek's assistants, Richard Ferry, met with Pat Ryan and said that he wanted to "review the files on all of Hickel's key people."

I tried to dismiss the whole problem of the future from my mind as I flew to New York for a speech on November 16 before the lawyers division of the Federation of Jewish Philanthropies. I also had scheduled a meeting with the editorial board of *The New York Times,* and another with Mayor Lindsay to discuss the Street Scene program to block off selected city streets from automobile traffic.

My remarks to the Jewish lawyers organization, outlining some of our accomplishments at Interior, were well received, and I also was given one of the most gracious introductions of my career by New York's Senator Jacob K. Javits: "In this town, Wally, we admire you . . . for the heart, the spirit, the patriotism of the highest kind which dictated that famous Hickel letter. Probably what you should be most proud of is to be a member of the Cabinet of the United States, but not to have checked your conscience at the door."

My meeting with Mayor Lindsay also went well, and I felt great Tuesday night, November 17, as I walked along Madison Avenue with the Mayor and Secretary of

Agriculture Cliff Hardin. The mood was festive, and John Lindsay rose to the occasion with his infectious and warm personality.

Hardin had come to New York for a speech of his own, and earlier that day, during a visit to Gracie Mansion, Lindsay had invited him to join us for the Street Scene walk. During our tour Hardin apparently noticed that the Mayor and I were good friends, because on the plane returning to Washington that night he asked, "But what will you do if Lindsay announces tomorrow that he is changing parties?"

I laughed at Cliff's expression when I replied, "Then I'll announce that I think he's a great Democratic mayor!"

Back in Washington I was again exposed to a barrage of speculation about my future. And now there was very good reason for the speculation, even though I had made a decision, while I was in New York, that I would not give up my fight to try to get the Administration to turn a corner.

On November 12, four days before I went to New York, John Mitchell had called, asking for a second meeting — in my office. This time, the Attorney General did know what was going on. He said, "Wally, your relationship with the Administration is just not compatible." He made it clear that it was thought best that I resign and "just go away."

I said: "John, I'm sorry to hear that. I don't agree with it. But at any time the President asks me to leave, I'll put on my hat and go." I talked about 1972, how the Republican Party would need everything possible in its favor to win, and how I thought I could be of help.

We talked for fifty-five minutes. When the conversation was over, Mitchell had not changed his attitude. But after my remarks about the 1972 election, he concluded the meeting by saying, "Wally, sit tight until you hear from me."

9. *Arrow in the Heart*

Word of my second meeting with Mitchell, and "reliable source" leaks about the nature of our conversation, churned up the press even more during the week that followed. And on November 18, Mike Wallace was on the phone again, trying to get me to agree to do another appearance on the Columbia Broadcasting System's "60 Minutes."

My staff was split on the idea. Some said that if we were ever to make peace with the White House, we absolutely could not consider such an appearance. Others thought that we had reached the fission point. I did not agree with either argument, so I decided to do the program. We could only go forward.

At two o'clock in the afternoon of November 20, I sat down in a leather chair in the Yellow Room, a guest reception area just down the hall from the office of the Secretary, on Interior's sixth floor. Don Hewitt and his CBS crew had been there for three hours setting up, and they were ready to start filming. Pat Ryan, Dave Parker and Joe Holbert followed me into the room. Ermalee was already there. I told Dave to lock the doors. I said I wanted a closed set, with no distractions. I reflected on the past twenty-two months, and I felt proud of the new confidence and vigor we had brought to the Interior Department.

Before the cameras started to roll, Mike Wallace grinned and said, "Anyone that gets fired because of this show can have a job with CBS."

"Let's get down to business," I said, and the cameras started. Wallace kept trying to penetrate my last meeting with Mitchell. I would only acknowledge that the Attorney General and I had had a talk, and that Mitchell had told me to sit tight until I heard from him again.

I repeated that I had come to Washington to do a job for the President of the United States, and as long as the President wanted me doing that job I would remain as Secretary of the Interior — "But when the President asks me to leave, I'll put on my hat and go."

Actually it came late in the filming, but CBS used one of my comments at the opening of "60 Minutes" the following Tuesday night, November 23:

"If I go away, I'm going away with an arrow in my heart, not a bullet in my back."

10. Thanksgiving Eve

My schedule was very busy for Wednesday, November 25, the day before Thanksgiving. I had an early-morning staff meeting lasting until ten o'clock, followed by a long and tough session with Mitch Melich, Bill Pecora and a group of Justice Department lawyers regarding an oil pollution case. At noon I met with Ambassador Glenn Olds, United States Representative to the United Nations Economic and Social Commission. At one o'clock Hilton drove me to the Luxembourg Embassy on Massachusetts Avenue for a reception honoring the Apostolic Delegate, Archbishop Raimondi.

I had hardly returned to the office at two o'clock when I went into a meeting with Inge Bengtsson, the Swedish Minister of Agriculture. That meeting was supposed to be followed by an interview with Miss Bridget Lay, from the Voice of America. But I told Yvonne to postpone that one because we were running late.

All day long Pat Ryan had been getting calls from John Whitaker insisting that I shuffle my schedule so that I could come to dealing with the environment and pollution. He said he had no criticism of my handling of Interior.

Then he turned and said, "Wally, you're a strong man, and so I'd like to be just as strong when I tell you what I'm going to tell you. I believe that's the way you'd want it."

He said that he felt that "there's a mutual lack of confidence." He wanted me to go.

I thought, "Mutual means both," but I kept quiet. He was doing the talking and I was doing the listening, and he had the right to say what he wished.

He said he wanted a quiet transition. I did not know what he meant by that; how can you quietly fire a man?

I refused to plead my case. I said, "Mr. President, I will stand on my record, and I'll let history decide." I told him about the tremendous problems and difficult decisions we had faced at Interior, such as going to the grand jury in the Chevron case in the Gulf of Mexico. I said that I felt that I had avoided getting the White House involved in a decision that might have embarrassed the Administration politically.

Throughout the meeting, Ehrlichman

said nothing except when I referred to our difficulties with the oil companies. I said, "John, you remember me talking to you about this early in the Administration." "Yes, Mr. President," he said, "the Secretary did."

I got up to leave. I did not shake hands with the President, but not out of bitterness. I didn't think of it. I felt so clean and totally free.

11. 'I Had to Do It My Way'

It was twenty minutes before six. As Ehrlichman and I walked out of the President's office and into the hall, we passed Ron Ziegler. He looked white. John and I went into Ehrlichman's office. I said: "John, I don't want anymore of this crap about leaks and maybe this or maybe that about me being fired. I want it announced right now."

I added: "John, it's been a great two years. It could have been greater."

Then I left.

Hilton Coleman, my driver, was the first person on my staff to find out what had

happened. I told him as I climbed into the limousine. He began to weep and cried out: "No, no, Mr. Secretary! This just can't happen! It just can't be!"

We drove back to Interior and I took the private elevator to the sixth floor and my office. I called Ermalee, but she already knew.

Apparently Ziegler had already laid the groundwork for the announcement, because the networks had the news of the firing shortly before six o'clock.

Helen Ryan had called Ermalee after hearing it on the radio. It would be a long night, and most of my closest staff ended up at the house in Kenwood, trying to fend off reporters, neighbors and telephone calls. Later in the evening about a dozen neighbors would show up at the door to sing "For He's a Jolly Good Fellow," and my second youngest son, sixteen-year-old Joe, would storm out of the house crying, "Nobody can fire my dad!"

But for the moment, as I sat in the office of the Secretary of the Interior, at 6:30 on Thanksgiving Eve, my only concern was to meet the press with a brief statement and then go home to my family.

Joe Holbert heard the news over the radio as he was starting on his evening commuting trip to his home in northern Virginia. It was 5:55 P.M., the height of the rush hour, but he instantly jumped his car over a concrete divider, made a spinning U-turn in the middle of the Theodore Roosevelt Bridge and headed back to the office.

All three networks had camera crews in the lobby of the Interior Building by 6:30, and by 6:45 the fifth-floor conference room was jammed with forty to fifty reporters.

While efforts were under way to get the press conference in order, I sat in the Yellow Room with Harrison Loesch, one of my best assistant secretaries—and one of my best friends. Mitch Melich and Pat Ryan were there. Others started to trickle in within minutes.

Shortly after seven o'clock I walked into the conference room and stepped in front of the floodlights. It took me only a minute:

The President terminated me about two hours ago—and there's really nothing

I can say to help the situation—and nothing I would say to hurt it. Given the hostility toward me when I first arrived—and some of those incredible decisions I had to make immediately thereafter—and trying to do a job for the President and all Americans and still survive as an individual—I had to do it my way.

The adversary is really a searcher, seeking out the naked truth.

CHAPTER **12**

The Searchers

On December 16, 1970, I was driven to Friendship Airport for the last time by my chauffeur, Hilton Coleman. I had stayed in Washington for the interim sixteen days since the President had fired me, because I was required to testify in court. Pauley Petroleum Inc. was suing the federal government and me personally as Secretary of the Interior for our actions in Santa Barbara. They contended that we had violated their rights as defined in their offshore oil leases.

Pauley's attorneys were probably sorry they put me on the stand. When I finished answering their questions, I said to the judge: "Your Honor, I would like to make a request. When this case is wrapped up, let

502

me return and be the last witness." The suit was for $230 million. With that kind of money at stake, a company's legal staff can usually drag a case on for years until those who were in government at the time have moved on. Eventually there is no one who cares about defending the public interest. "I'll fly back from Alaska at my own expense to testify," I said.

Waiting for the plane at Friendship, I was buoyant. Everyone was asking what I was going to do now. My answer was simple. I was going home.

I had escaped the danger of contracting Potomac fever. The white-tie dinners, limousines, the pomp of White House receptions, the opportunity to sit in the highest board room of the nation: I respected all of those things. But they had not become more important than getting a job done.

A few nights earlier, my staff had come to my home in Kenwood. I called them over to thank them for the spirit they had helped generate in the Department, and for the long nights of work and extra effort they had put in. As always, there was an Alaskan boisterousness and good-natured leg pulling throughout the evening. Morris Thompson, who had been my special assistant for Indian affairs, presented me with a large plaque with a heart mounted on it, pierced by an Indian war arrow. I laughed and said, "Well, if I had it to do over again, I'd take the bullet in the back."

Then I said: "I came to Washington a free man. I served the public as a free man. And I leave as a free man."

I was not bitter. I was disappointed, true. I had hoped that I could turn the Administration away from the direction Vice President Agnew had come to represent, and get the President back on the track of his Inaugural Address. But I was in complete agreement with his prerogative to dismiss any of those whom he had appointed, including me. I was convinced in my heart that I had done the best job I could and had not compromised the trust the President and the public had placed in me.

Above all, I was not disillusioned with the system. I was convinced the system could work, because we had made it work for twenty-two months.

I said good-by to Hilton, boarded United Flight No. 41 and began my trip home, across the great continent and mixing bowl that comprises America and its blend of people and dreams. I looked forward with anticipation to returning to my own life in Alaska. I was reminded again of what I had said many times in Washington: "You'll never be happy where you're going unless you were happy where you're from." But I also wondered, as the vastness of America swept beneath our wings, about the path that lay ahead for all those below. Is America destined to be led forward or backward in the decades ahead? Will our children, and our children's children, be led by "computerized men"? Or will they be led by men of heart?

1. The New and Untried

I believe that the people are looking for something new in leadership. They are fed up with being represented by those who only play the partisan political game, using their positions for personal benefit. Politics as we have known it is becoming more and more out of touch with the people. It is less and less able to respond to the opportunities of the times we live in.

The frustration felt by Americans — whether airline pilots, plumbers or housewives — stems from the fact that they are busy coping with their own problems. They can only hope, as far as government is concerned, that someone will care enough to see that the country is run properly.

Our world changes at the speed of global electronic communication. This demands a new breed of national leader, a "searcher" who ferrets out and explores the new and the never-tried-before. He never puts a ceiling on his expectations, and he refuses to let his thought become inflexible and locked into the past. A searcher is a man who wants to improve upon the solutions for problems he finds while searching.

As early as 1956 I began looking for that type of man and woman to invite to Alaska, to help our young country. I spoke in Fairbanks in October of that year, saying: "There is only one thing we need—people to come to Alaska who care. My definition of a searcher is a man who, no matter what he accomplishes or what he might do, isn't satisfied. He is a combination of the dreamer and the doer, the contented man and the ambitious man, all molded into one."

The searcher is never contented with the system, but instead of discarding it, works to find ways to improve it. Above all, a searcher's vision is not bound by limitations. He is free. He is free to find and follow great purposes. He is free to act. Leaders must be free to respond to their intellect, their heart and their conscience without having to qualify every decision according to a previous commitment or promise. They must be free to make decisions for the benefit of all, rather than the few.

As Secretary of the Interior, I had no special interests backing me up with a powerful lobbying effort. Some would argue that this was my weakness, but I would not have had it any other way. Being free of entanglements to an industry, to a certain segment of the financial community or to some other interest group meant that I was obligated only to make decisions on the basis of what I felt was best for America as a whole. Special interests and their lobby groups exert great influence in Washington.[1] This is not necessarily bad. It is a question of intent.

A special interest may be a resource industry such as coal and oil, a conservation organization, a banking and investment firm, a corporate structure like General Motors or IBM, or perhaps nothing more than a society to preserve tennis courts. All of these groups deserve to be represented in the nation's capital, and their needs should be known. But the decision-makers should not give them more than their due. The American public, from ghetto child to corporate president, needs that new breed of leader who searches all avenues so that every interest has an audience, but no one has a claim.

[1] *The phrase "special interest" has come to mean "evil interest" in the connotation it is given. This is not fair. It has been warped through overuse and misuse.*

2. Ten Cents for Freedom

How can a man get elected in a country our size and remain free? How can he finance his campaign without hopelessly compromising his freedom? The men who seek the presidency of the United States, if they are to wage any sort of effective campaign under today's circumstances, must solicit huge sums of money to finance their efforts. How beholden must they be to the individuals, the giant corporations, the unions or whoever is responsible for their major donations?

Administrations, the Congress and candidates have long sought a solution to presidential campaign financing, especially in recent years when television-oriented campaigns have become so costly. But what if every person in America, from the poorest slum dweller to the wealthiest corporate executive, gave only ten cents a year to a public fund to finance the campaigns of the major presidential candidates? We used dimes to cure polio; why not politics?

Every four years, with our existing

population, we would have available more than $80 million — surely an adequate sum to permit all citizens of our nation to receive an accurate evaluation of the candidates' qualifications. Such a program would require regulation to ensure that the fund was not misspent, but regulations are not that difficult to write and implement. The attractiveness of such a proposal is its simplicity, and the fact that it would give every individual in America, regardless of his status, a chance to be an active part of the system, a dues-paying "member" of America.

Any family of five could become directly involved in putting into government those people whom they regard as the searchers, and the total cost to that family would be just fifty cents a year. We must not say that the poor cannot afford it: They cannot afford *not* to do it. And what a difference we would see in our candidates if instead of depending on the $100,000 contribution from an individual industrialist, those same dollars came from 200 million Americans. We would see a swift change in priorities.

Our two-party system is great, but it has one major weakness. The general public has no direct role in the selection of the nominees for President, the man who sets the tone and the direction for the nation. That man is a vital concern for every American who cares.

A citizen can become involved and have an impact on the selection of a city councilman, a mayor, a congressman, a senator or a governor. But the choice of who is to represent the two major parties in the presidential race is left up to a tiny minority of Americans—those who manage the conventions of both parties. This is a source of enormous frustration to more and more concerned Americans. And think of the frightening possibility of one small group controlling both conventions!

It may be time for a people's party to emerge every four years to offer an alternative candidate for President, to break the hammerlock that the leaders of the two major parties now have on presidential candidate selection. It could breathe new life into the entire system. In effect it would be a third party within the two-party system. The Senate and House would still be organized in the customary manner, but the President would be the nonpartisan representative of all the people. I believe that instead of receiving the hate or opposition of Congress, he would get the heart and hope of both parties to work with him.

America is ready for the leadership of an individual who steps forth and unites the people by working with both political parties, an individual who represents the whole instead of the special few. The opportunity for this type of truly democratic leadership to emerge is especially great in the years just ahead. There are potentially twenty-five million new voters coming into the system in 1972. There are at least that many citizens who just never bother to vote. Add to these two groups the growing force of independents and those of both parties who are not satisfied with their own candidates. The sum total of these elements in America is where the solution lies.

The overriding importance of the success

of this approach is that the President would be as independent as the judiciary, and his constituents would be all the American people. If the President cannot be free, who owns America?

3. Speak with the Heart

Those in the White House in any administration, at any given time, must represent everyone in the country, not just those who elected them. Otherwise those who have operated within the free system, but did not choose to vote for those in power, are frustrated to a degree that encourages them to go outside the system for answers. The nation is almost instantly fragmented — essentially paralyzed — when an administration chooses to declare in reference to the black, the young, the labor movement, the farmers, the bankers or whomever: "They didn't put us here, so we don't owe them a thing."

To pretend to represent all of America and to ignore the needs of what is considered an unfriendly voting bloc is the worst form of hypocrisy. We will never solve our problems if we continue to divide the nation into little ideological sections, caring only for those who share our political allegiance. Americans do not like political double-talk, and they are far more aware than many of our public figures realize.

There are too many men in government who do not remember why they got there. Not "how," but "why." These are the men who want to get a job rather than do a job. Once they reach their positions, they spend their efforts in keeping their jobs rather than solving problems. They often aggravate the very problems they were sent to Washington, the state-house or the county courthouse to solve.

The public can tell the difference between words spoken from the mouth and words spoken from the heart. America is tired of face-lifting; we are looking for reality in promises. We are looking for action and integrity — commodities no Madison Avenue public relations firm has been able to package and market. It takes one man to do something right; it takes 100 men to make something appear right.

We have been preaching in the schools of

America the need for greater involvement by the people. We have preached it, but unless our leaders will listen and respond, the preaching is useless and dangerous because of the frustration it generates. One man who cares is worth a million people just talking about the problem.

We seek men who are free enough to let their intelligence go to their hearts. The simplicity of acting in good faith is so clean and so acceptable. Instinctively the people want to believe. But if they do not see anyone ready to lead their battles with heart, the people begin to lose hope. They cannot look forward to anything changing or improving.

Words are free, and anyone can use them. Anyone can recite the Gettysburg Address, but the words change nothing unless they are spoken from the heart. Hope and care have motivated the great leaders of America. Thomas Jefferson cared; Abe Lincoln cared; Teddy Roosevelt cared. If they were here today, they would agree that what is needed is men who know the difference between right and wrong and have the guts to make decisions accordingly. *To turn your mind off from your conscience for political reasons, to make a moral wrong politically right, does not make it right.*

4. A Third of a Man

If America is to produce a generation of searchers, we must teach the young to be curious. It is no longer acceptable to have a sign around your neck that says: "I have a Ph.D.; I'm smart." There is a narrowness in our academic system that fails to prepare the total man. We have really thought about only a third of the man, the man of the mind. That system encourages only those who strive to be put into the category of the intellectual. The weakness of this is that often graduates do not know how to make their philosophies "happen."

A truly educated man knows how to use his hands and heart as well as his intellect. The ability to use your hands in some constructive way gives you the internal confidence that is so necessary to express your thoughts and knowledge in communicating with others.

516

The man who is going to govern most effectively in the future will come out of the total system and not just out of the university system. He will come out of the system of experience, with a balance of intellect, action and heart. Formal education by itself does not create the kind of individual who will put guts into the system.

I recall listening to a presentation to the Cabinet by a representative of the Department of Health, Education and Welfare. His statement was so full of technical jargon and so unreal that it was pathetic. Finally John Ehrlichman interrupted him and asked what he was talking about. His second nonexplanation was even more confused than his first. I leaned across David Kennedy and asked John Mitchell, "Doesn't anyone around here ever use the word horseshit anymore?"

Technology is moving the world so fast that what was absolute yesterday is obsolete today. We must upgrade modern education by changing its emphasis. The most important thing we can do for a young person is to teach him how to learn and how to live, rather than what to learn. In his curiosity he will continue to learn from the changes which are brought about so rapidly, and which affect the living of life. A curious and creative person will never stagnate.

We need education that sets you free — education that does not tie you down to the past, but frees you to use your imagination. We have placed too great an emphasis on the degree. What we really need to ask is to what degree we have motivated the person to be curious.

5. The Art of Compromise Isn't

"Politics is the art of compromise." If those words were carved out of solid granite in ten-foot letters up each side of the Washington Monument, they would be no more revered than they already are in the American capital. The expression has been used for generations as an excuse for selling out one's beliefs and "making a deal." The man who listens, who finds out the naked truth and goes forward without compromise, is a truly great leader. The real challenge for a leader is to sell those ideas he absolutely believes in from the heart. His greatest achievement is to gain support for those ideas that do not compromise his principles.

However, compromise in the sense of finding a common ground is something else. We need leaders who stick to their principles and, in making decisions, know that compromises should only be between genuine alternatives, not between compromises. But this kind of compromise can be achieved, with justification, only at the last stage of the administrative decision or the legislative process.

Unfortunately, it rarely happens that way. Compromise almost always begins at the first stage, not the last. In fact, the art of compromise is so built into politics in this country that in Washington nearly everyone who tries to draft a piece of legislation or a new administrative program dilutes his original draft with compromises. Instead of setting down, in simple English, what ought to happen, a bureau drafting a new law says: "Well, we must take Senator So-and-So into consideration when we write this section. And when we write this one over here, we must remember how we got shot down by the White House and the budget people the last time." When the thing is done, it is a mishmash of weaseled thoughts and qualifications. To make matters worse, two or three other people in other bureaus are probably drafting legislation on the same subject, and their drafts are just as full of compromises.

Therefore, when the final decision must be taken and a choice made between plans A, B and C, there is no clear-cut option at all. All three plans involve compromises accepted at lower levels and almost always for the wrong reasons, some of which are never clear to the man who has to make the decision. Instead there should be a positive plan A, a positive plan B and a positive plan C, all submitted by men who are prepared to defend them. Then we would have an adversary system in which compromises would serve a useful function and administrative or legislative action could be taken with reasonably good sense. This simply cannot happen when everyone is so conscious of compromise that he builds it into his initial recommendations.

When a department of government is preparing proposals for the White House, there should be no hesitation about coming up with honest, genuine answers to problems — rather than merely what someone wants to hear. This honesty should hold true from the lowest executive level of government clear up to the top. The assistant to the director should have the freedom to tell his bureau chief, "This is what you want to hear, but it's wrong. This other idea may not be what you want to hear, but it's right." The bureau chief, in turn, should express himself with equal force when he reports up the line to the Secretary in charge of his department. When the problem reaches the Cabinet level, its members should have the candor to be equally open with their President. They are not there to tell the President what a splendid fellow he is; they are there to help the President solve problems.

Harry Truman put it in a wonderful way when he said: "The President hears a hundred voices telling him that he is the greatest man in the world. He must listen carefully indeed to hear the one voice that tells him he is not." This is the foundation stone for the adversary system.

To make this system work in my department and to free the decision-makers all down the line, I tackled the problem head-on. Calling all my department heads together, I said: "People have been asking what our policy is going to be. It is simply this: If you know the difference between right and wrong, do what's right and you'll have no problems with me." From that moment they no longer had to worry about whose back to scratch, and they could clearly and cleanly act upon what they believed to be the truth.

I respect the precedents of the past, but I'm damned if we should be bound by them. "Politics is the art of compromise" implies a deal or copout. This need not happen. Additionally, there are those who think that "the first obligation of a politician is to get reelected." However, the best way for a man to get reelected and to earn the greatest constituency is to do those things that are in the best interest of all the people he represents.

There are many good men in the United

States Senate who are miles apart ideologically, such as Barry Goldwater and Mark Hatfield. But they are assets to the Senate because they refuse to compromise their principles just to get reelected. By the same token, any President, once he is in office, should put to one side the issue of whether or not he will be reelected. The only reason for a man to desire that office should be the compulsion to do a job for all Americans.

People respect a noncompromising leader—if he keeps an open mind. The distinction is very fine, but it is a great and important one. At the highest level of government, a President should always remember the difference between stubbornness and strength. The mark of a man who lacks an open mind is the lack of confidence, and a man without confidence does not want criticism. A person who has great confidence, and who is guided by his conscience, finds it invigorating to hear criticism. He is eager to learn from it. Only those who really fear themselves get isolated.

If you know, through some previous

commitment, that you cannot do what you know is right, then just to make your life tolerable you must become isolated from those who disagree. If you do not want to become isolated, you must not hide behind what you *hope* is the truth. You must have criticism from within to separate "truth" from Truth.

6. *The High Ground of Reason*

I boil government down to two basic types, based on what happens to the adversary. In this country I got fired. In a totalitarian state, I might have been shot. There is more than a subtle distinction between the two. A basic advantage of our system is that it permits disagreement — even bitter disagreement. But to interpret this freedom as a license for violence is to endanger seriously the greatness of a free society.

On a given issue, such as the war in Southeast Asia, the hawks want revenge, which is really hate, and the doves simply hate what happened. Both sides are saying things that are too small. The extreme on one side is barking, "We are the greatest";

the extreme on the other side is disdainful of its own society. And if it appears, on issues such as Vietnam, that "our side" is wrong or discredited, we should not automatically assume that the other side is right. To say that there are only "white hats" and "black hats" is a dangerous and careless assumption. Too often there may only be a choice between two shades of black. The searcher judges *all* the options critically and fairly, and he brings a new voice—a voice that is bigger than both, a voice of vision that brings the issue into perspective.

The protest that marked the end of the 1960's and the beginning of the 1970's would have occurred with or without the war in Vietnam. The basic protest we have witnessed was not so much against an event as against an attitude. It was a protest against the exclusion of the public from decision-making. This was the same reason for our stimulated concern for the environment, or almost any other area of public interest that we might mention. It just happens that the war was the obvious issue.

Hawks and doves are not restricted to

issues of military consequence. There are examples today throughout America of the hawk or dove approach to issues such as the environment.

We are rapidly approaching a civil war of priorities in our nation: neighbor against neighbor, man against need, over the preservation or use of our resources. Bitter voices are being raised — on the one side pleading, "Give us work, give us energy for our homes"; and on the other side shouting, "Stop the rape of our environment. Protect our wildlife and our wilderness." Somewhere in between there is a small voice saying that if we work together we can do it right.

We cannot undo all the wrongs of yesterday, but we can guide responsibly to meet the needs of tomorrow. All human needs must be taken into consideration — those of everyday necessity such as energy, and those of lasting beauty such as a wilderness. I am convinced that in dealing with this civil war of priorities, the searchers will find solutions on the high ground of reason.

Unless we reestablish a climate of reason,

we will continue to witness a swing of the pendulum toward the Right on the part of those who are in power, and an equally dramatic swing toward the Left on the part of those who are not. This is a frightening prospect. Without a new breed of searchers who can reconcile the two extremes, we are almost inevitably bound to end up with a nation of rulers at the top, with nothing underneath but a rebellious mass.

7. Locked In — Not Out

I will always consider government's major job to be the setting and administering of regulations. But this should come only after the public has had a full opportunity to comment. If the public understands that it is locked in, not locked out, then people will have confidence. But if they have no chance to make an input, they will be totally frustrated.

The American people should be able to ask "Why?" when something is done that does not seem to be in the public interest. Why the secrecy in government? Why the abuse of the confidential stamp? The overuse of the word confidential only complicates the situation—and in many cases the word is used to keep the public uninformed. Although there are times when the confidential stamp is necessary, there are more times when it is used to cover up bungling within a department or an agency. This can run from a simple thing, like the cost of a drainage ditch, to a billion-dollar overrun on a military contract. The only people being kept in the dark are the American public.

We hold public hearings on a lot of things in this country. The newspapers carry legal notices announcing hearings on zoning changes, where a new highway is going to be routed or how welfare payments are going to be altered or distributed. It would take a book thicker than this one just to list all of the things that are being "heard" in the United States on a given day. The hooker comes when we try to determine just how much the public knows about all these hearings.

The notices are tucked away in obscure column in tiny type. The letter of the law is met—and no more. About the *last* thing officials want is for anyone actually to attend and express an opinion.

I wanted to avoid this governmental trick when I told my staff at the Department of the Interior that I intended to schedule public hearings in New Orleans to take testimony and evidence regarding oil leasing in the Gulf of Mexico. I was determined to violate the Washington rule of thumb which says that if you are going to hold a hearing on a project in Peoria, hold the hearing in Washington, D.C., so that nobody will come. Then, after the hearing is held, the responsible government official can grandly announce, "The people had their chance."

We were not required by law to hold the New Orleans hearings. It had been the practice in the past to hold none at all. But we wanted the facts in the open. I could have held these hearings only in Washington, and from appearances they probably would have seemed thorough and fair. But few Louisiana residents would have been heard. I advocated taking the hearings to the people, not the people to the hearings. We must seek out the naked truth in places where it is convenient for the people to come and state their views.

Some say, "You can't beat city hall." *You can beat city hall*. But sometimes you have to get pretty noisy to do so. Noise will often be the only remedy that works against bad government.

8. *Do It in Style*

If you are going to do a job for America and do it right, do it with a sense of style. Perhaps it sounds corny when we are surrounded today by so much "cool" and cynicism, but I believe most Americans not only want good government — they want exciting government.

This sense of excitement could be physically felt in the Department of the Interior. Our determination to "make decisions — make things happen" had career employees hustling around with new ideas. In years past they had hardly made a move other than between their offices and the cafeteria as they tried to exist under systems that encouraged them only to "go along."

We developed positive programs. But we also tried, as we developed each program, to find ways to dramatize it to the public. I could have sat in my Washington office for months and made solemn pronouncements about the problem of extinction facing the alligator in the Everglades, and we might have attracted enough public attention to the issue to get a two-inch story on page sixteen. But by actually going to the Everglades, and by taking part in a mock poacher hunt, we dramatized the problem for the American people. Sure, some people laughed. And there were a few people at the White House who thought, "Wally's just showboating." But our midnight prowl through the swamps of southern Florida not only got laughs—it got results.

Laughter is a rare commodity in Washington, D.C. Many of those in government in responsible positions take themselves so seriously that they fail to see the lighter side of life. And that failure makes them less effective as leaders, because it forces them into a mold of blandness. They look at life and government through gray lenses that blur their vision and lead them to reach conclusions only as to why we *can't* do things.

Laughter has its place in government, and we provided our share, sometimes accidentally. I shall never forget a dinner party Ermalee and I gave at our Kenwood home, which turned into a headlined Alaska version of one of Lyndon Johnson's barbecues on the Pedernales.

On November 19, 1970, the National Broadcasting Company videotaped a special show at Ford's Theatre called "Festival at Ford's." The production was to be carried over the networks a week later, on Thanksgiving evening. I was involved because of Interior's responsibility for Ford's Theatre, an involvement I personally embraced with great enthusiasm. We were successful in lining up nearly a dozen of the top entertainers in the country who contributed their talents to a Thanksgiving salute to the music of America.

The night before the taping I invited several of the entertainers to my home for barbecued rack of lamb—one of the things I like to prepare as an amateur chef.

Everything was going along fine, and Jimmy Stewart, Bobbie Gentry and Tennessee Ernie Ford were among the personalities gathered in our dining room.

We had only one minor problem. Pearl Bailey arrived a bit late, accompanied by her manager, whom we welcomed but had not known was coming. I had my aide, Dave Parker, get a steak out of the freezer, which I put on the grill for Pearl's manager.

In every home that I have had, including the one in Kenwood, I have installed a gas-fired indoor barbecue grill. They are great appliances, but this particular night mine had a problem. I had just taken Miss Bailey's lamb and her manager's steak off the grill when I discovered that the gas valve was stuck. It would not shut off.

After several minutes, things got pretty warm. With no meat on it to absorb the heat, the grill grating and the fan hood above were beginning to smoke slightly. I called Dave Parker over, and told him to quietly—very quietly—call the gas company and have them send out a repairman. "Tell him all he needs is a wrench and to come quietly, and we'll let him in the back door."

Apparently the gas company was more alarmed than I. A few minutes later, Dave was standing nearby talking to Ermalee. She cocked an ear and whispered, "They better not be coming here." The wail of sirens, which was getting increasingly louder, sounded as if every piece of emergency equipment on the eastern seaboard was advancing down River Road toward Kenwood.

Dave had sent Hilton Coleman down to the corner so that he could direct the gas company repairman to the right house when he got to our neighborhood. Hilton was the first to spot a parade of eight fire trucks and rescue units screaming toward the Hickel house.

Our dining room happened to be curtained with very thin white draperies. There was no question something was going on when the first truck roared up—an emergency unit with two of the biggest searchlights in the world mounted on its roof. When they popped on those lights, the glare through the white draperies was blinding. I felt I was standing on the set of an old James Cagney gangster movie. All we needed was a guy in the front yard with a bullhorn shouting, "Come out with your hands up!"

Everything worked out okay. Jimmy Stewart must have examined every nut and bolt on each of the shiny red fire trucks. He was like a kid with a new toy. The firemen had a ball taking turns posing for photographs with Bobbie Gentry, passing around the camera they normally use for fire investigations. And Tennessee Ernie Ford, shuffling around our basement in an old windbreaker, was finally the one to discover the shut-off valve for the gas. Nothing ever did catch fire. But Pearl Bailey exclaimed: "Wally, when you throw a party, you don't mess around. Honey, that was the hottest time I've had in years!"

9. *The Time of Your Life!*

The kind of leader who is a searcher does not need to play old-fashioned party politics. The searchers are the young of all ages. They are not afraid of changing attitudes. They want to find solutions for problems regardless of whose idea the solutions might be. They want the opposition to become just as involved as the Administration itself. They put the burden of proof upon those who want to solve problems for humanity with goals that are attainable. And a leader who really wants to face the challenge of doing what is right will find the majority of Congress with him, regardless of political party, because the momentum of the public will be devastating to those who oppose solutions for the living of life.

Our leaders, both in government and in the private sector, must be willing to say: "We cannot make decisions just for partisan or monetary reasons, or for short-term gain. These decisions must be great beyond our lifetimes and not just for the moment." These men must be bold enough to face the challenge of change.

An example of keeping an open mind in industry about decisions made by government for the benefit of all was expressed by Fred Hartley, president of the Union Oil Company of California. He was one of my toughest opponents during the crisis in Santa Barbara over the oil blowout. But as the months passed, we came to share respect for each other. When I was fired, Hartley wrote a public letter. He said in part:

The sudden firing of Secretary Hickel and his six advisory associates is an unfortunate loss to our nation and a sad example of the kind of human behavior which should not be condoned in an enlightened democratic society. Unfortunately for him, he understood and had the fortitude to seek out the practical balance that must be achieved among environmental conservation, over-dependence upon foreign supply of crude oil, and the incredible energy demands of the people of this country. . . .

Progress was being made in establishing rules, regulations and policy objectives that would create a better working relationship between industry and government, compatible with the objectives of the rational conservationists, the security of the nation and the necessity of providing additional domestic sources of oil and gas demanded by the citizens of our creature comfort society.

It is encouraging to note that the replacement nominee for Secretary of the Interior, Mr. Rogers C. B. Morton, has commended Mr. Hickel's efforts. *Thus there is hope that this high office will not revert to being used for political purposes. . . .**

Hope is what people really count on from the time they are small children until they die. The searchers see life as an opportunity to care for people. Their job is people! If you treat humans as humans, instead of as votes, the great heart of America will respond. America will awaken; she will shake off her frustration and fear. And we will demonstrate to the world that it is possible to care for all the needs of *all* the people.

*Italics mine.

The vocation of the politician and the man dedicated to the social good has been ridiculed in the past and is still ridiculed today. But who suffers most when the best talent of a generation refuses to go into government work? That generation itself.

Mediocre men in government, by their performance, invite ridicule. They do not want men of dedication and ideals to dominate governmental life and make them look bad. Many times they do not stand up for their own vocation. We must reverse the sad thing I have found in the high schools and on college campuses, where the students mimic this same ridicule. They are parroting the line that profits the special interests.

The searcher will not get lost in a backwater of history by trying to change society without using the tools of government. The system can work. It is a great system, and those elements in it, like bureaucracy, can be made to work for the good of the public if they are directed by men of vision at the top. The searchers—the challengers and dreamers of all ages—openly question the values that have been the guidelines for generations before us. They want to make human values the guiding force in their lives of public service.

Government needs more than management. Government needs a conscience. It needs men and women who are excited about life and want to contribute something great. Government is where the decisions are made, to represent the greatest special interest of all, the American public. And to the new breed of leader who is considering government service, I say:

"Try it! You'll have the time of your life!"

What appears to be a breakdown in American society is in reality a breakthrough.

CHAPTER **13**

The Environment of Hope

In contrast to those who predict doomsday for America and the world, I believe that we are on the verge of the greatest era in our history. It is an exciting moment. It is a moment in which forces that began to take shape a century ago are pushing us into another phase of the American experiment. Our free society, a concept first fashioned in an agricultural era, is struggling to encompass the realities of a new age.

The 19th century, as far as America was concerned, was the century of agriculture and westward movement. The 20th century, as far as Western civilization is concerned, is the century of technology. The 21st century, as far as the world is concerned, will be the century of the human.

You can recognize an era by how it defines its priorities. The old age believed that America's role in the world was to be the No. 1 power. The new era adds a word and makes America the No. 1 *peace* power. From the beginning of recorded time, the most important thing to that first man, whoever he was, has been protection. This principle — protection — spread to man's family and then to the community. Up through medieval times, man built great forts with walls six feet thick, which are still standing today. Yet he would sleep on the floor with rats running around. The priorities were not for the living of life; they were for the protection and destruction of life. And so this rolled on, until we in the 20th century still spend about half of our time, energy and money on protection and destruction of life.

It was after World War II that we started to react to artificial fears to justify such things as compulsory military training and the creation of a "defense industry" dwarfing anything we had in the war. We were being led into the trap of no longer being the conscience of the world. In fact, in Vietnam we participated in the destruction of an ancient civilization.

I want America to be the conscience of the world again. I want Americans to lead the world in showing that the human being is the most important thing in existence, and perhaps we are just the people to do it. We are a mongrel people. One hundred years ago hardly anyone outside the United States believed that we would ever create a great nation. We are not German; we are not British; we are not Asian; we are not white; and we are not black. We are all of these things, and more. It may take a mongrel kind of people like ours to create an environment of hope for all people.

It is time that we switched the emphasis in America and showed the world how to live life. As long as national rivalries exist, we shall never eliminate altogether the need for national defense, or abandon the responsibility to defend our country. But our priorities are shifting, slowly but positively, to the problems of living a better life. If you went out and asked a fellow raking leaves on his lawn, "What are the problems today?" he would say, "We are spending too much of our money on war." And I would agree, because our challenge is to satisfy the yearnings of the inner man. We worry, and rightly so, about the problems of the inner city, but we will never solve those until we solve the problems of the inner man.

The only adequate response to that challenge lies in a totally new national approach to government in the United States, and a totally new involvement of the individual in determining his destiny.

1. *A Collective World — But So Private*

The belief that we have too much government has been accepted without question by what must be a majority of Americans of all political persuasions. I totally disagree. There may be too many people in government, or government may be misdirected, but I will argue until I die that there is not enough government in those areas where life is being choked from living: transportation, the cities and the general environment.

What we must now realize for the first time in America is that it is really a collective world, but one in which we live so privately. Without concern for the other person, for his desires and wants, activities for strictly private gain become destructive not only to others but eventually to oneself. No matter how great, how vast or how simple individual ownership might be, it must be looked upon as a passing thing. What good would it be if one owned it all and left an emptiness in passing? In reality, one has but a lease on ownership during one's lifetime. The success or failure of how something is used depends on how it is left.

How will we leave America? Will the heritage our generation leaves behind be an exhausted earth and a human who is degraded? Will the rugged individualism on which we have prided ourselves result in collective destruction? Not if we have a truly *national* approach to government.

We must have more men with the courage to accept responsibility for planning and implementing policies that will lift us as a nation into the next century, the century of the human. Government must be visionary in nature and be prepared to "return to us" those things that only national government can give back, such as clean rivers, unpolluted air and a free spirit in the inner man.

At stake is the living of life, and this is not a narrow or regional thing. It cannot be sustained by a government based on the principle that the blending of a conglomeration of special interests will produce a truly national policy. An individual or local government can take care of a problem in an individual or local way, but there are very few local splashes that do not make waves across the country. They are problems of the community called the United States. Decisions on where to put a freeway or how to dispose of municipal sewage have repercussions important throughout the land.

2. Enough Room for All?

Although there are limitations to the resources we have in our country, there is still a vast potential to be explored and wisely planned for. Our population is growing, and our urban centers especially give the impression that we are rapidly running out of space. In reality, there are still great regions of private and public land available for both the living of life and the restoration of man's spirit. Anyone who crosses the country can readily see that the immediate problem is one of distribution—not only of goods but of people.

If all the people in the world—not just the United States, but the world—were placed in the State of Texas, each person could be given 2,000 square feet of land, the equivalent of a good-sized home. Interesting though this example is, it would not be acceptable. There would be too damned many Texans! But it illustrates the reality of the situation: Our greatest lack has not been one of space but the lack of imagination to care and plan for all our property and all our people.

Is it right to give a cow 100 acres of public land on which to roam, while we pen up a ghetto family in 100 square feet? We can no longer address ourselves to our resources of the land without relating them to our people resources. And we cannot talk about wise use of our resources by the people without knowing what is there. That is why the time has come to look in detail at the entire country; to catalogue all those lands and assets the public owns, and decide how they will be used and conserved for the maximum benefit of everyone. We must have a national land inventory — a stimulating and exciting challenge, a task big enough to enlist thousands.

As in other areas of the environment, the development of a comprehensive land-use policy would mean jobs. And these jobs would demand the creative and imaginative talent of everyone involved, because it would be a pioneering venture. The aim would be to put a value — a value that cannot be measured in dollars and cents — on a mountain stream, a prairie, a forest or a wilderness. This would demand people who understand the balance between meeting the needs of our population for minerals, energy, and all kinds of resources on the one hand, and for esthetics and recreation on the other.

Perhaps by the middle of the next century

our land surfaces will be used primarily for the living and enjoyment of life, while the ocean, the ocean floor and the polar regions will be a major source of minerals and food production. In the meantime, the challenge we are confronted with is to live off the great resources of our land without desecrating it.

3. Green River Banks

What a magnificent nation we would have if the great rivers of America ran clean and blue—the Potomac, the Mississippi, the James, the Shenandoah, the Cuyahoga and the Missouri! Is this possible? Yes. As part of a national approach to the living of life, we should establish a network of national rivers throughout our country. Each of the great rivers should have its banks preserved as green belts to filter and purify the runoff from rains and agricultural irrigation. These forested banks would provide great park spaces for all the people. The waters could be clean and available for private use—but not abuse.

What will it cost? It is within reach. We

could pay for it over twenty years. After all, what does a war cost? We have marshaled men and materiel to destroy nations and wreak havoc on their environment; surely we can learn how to turn around that vast machinery to the construction and conservation of our nation.

When I was in Washington, I wanted to make the Potomac our first National River. With all the squabbling and bickering going on over cleaning up the sewage presently pumped into the Potomac system, I knew we were really fighting over only one part of the problem. If all the sewage were stopped completely today, the Potomac would still be dirty. The banks and shores at various places along the way have been bulldozed and developed, destroying the natural filtration system. Unless that basic problem is faced, the Potomac will never again be the great river it once was.

Some psychologists say that the drive in man that takes him to war is rooted in his need for stimulation. But they also say that stimulation need not be satisfied by violence, that it can be channeled into creative and positive action. We are stimulated by challenges, and the creation of a national land-use policy and a national rivers policy are two of the greatest challenges that I know.

4. *The Key to Ignition*

Another major question confronting America is how it will use its resources wisely and in the best interest of the American public, to take care of everyday needs and yet not abuse the air, the water and the land. One of the greatest problems we have to face is how do we use energy — whether that energy be water, coal, oil, gas or nuclear.

We cannot turn off the ignition of the world. Our concern is how we can better utilize the energy we have. The whole direction of utilizing energy has to be viewed on a national basis. This means the government is going to have to get involved in how this energy is used for the advancement of 200 million Americans.

As we look at our nation in the perspective of the next ten or twenty years, it is absolutely clear that we must coordinate our energy development and distribution so that no part of the country need suffer when faced by an emergency overload. Many small generating plants in a given area cause additional air, water and land pollution, to say nothing of the sight pollution, especially because of the duplication of power lines. In many parts of America there are dozens of different distribution systems providing energy to homes and industries. These companies have grown up in response to the rising demands of their separate communities. The situation is similar to the time when the railroads had different gauges of track, making it difficult to create a national transportation network.

Government must set down the rules by which industry can best meet the public needs. This means coordination and cooperation among the utility-providing companies. There is tremendous resistance to this type of national approach from the utility industries involved. This is partly because some companies want to manipulate rates in their areas. When energy supplies get low, they would rather construct new plants and raise the charge to the consumer than draw on a coordinated national system. The rate to the consumer is based on how much a utility has invested in its own system.

We must have government that cares for the total, that sees the nation as a whole in order to solve the problems on the broadest level. The airlines run by regulation. Everyone accepts the zoning of the lot across the street. Everyone accepts a stop light. This is not an infringement on a person's rights. This is the most responsible application of a free system. Rather than take individual opportunity away from the person, we must give the individual a choice. It is up to the nation as a whole to see to it that we conserve those resources that are limited in nature, and that we use them in the most efficient way to bring about the better living of life for the individual. This is not less freedom. It is more freedom.

While I was Secretary of the Interior, I envisioned a total North American energy policy. I set up a study group to find out what is the best use of all energy sources.

Can we collectively, with Canada, better utilize our resources of coal, oil, gas, water, tar sand and shale? We cannot look upon energy and the pollution-causing byproducts of energy just as one-country things. As pollution knows no borders, resources know no boundaries. Until we can start this international cooperation with our neighbor, how can we expect much smaller countries to cooperate on similar matters?

5. *The Disciplines of Freedom*

No other society on earth demands as much of the individual citizen as a free society. All issues relating to a national approach to the problems and opportunities of the decade ahead are related to the disciplines of freedom. Through personal decisions or the decisions of those we elect to office, we restrict ourselves from doing things that will hurt others. This is a paradox, because the more discipline we individually impose on ourselves, the freer we become.

This can be seen in a thousand everyday examples. We restrict ourselves to driving on one side of the street, and for this reason are able to travel much more rapidly and much more safely. We are freer because we are restricted. You are free to swing your fist at the end of your arm until it lands on someone else's nose. Although this appears to be a limitation on freedom, in reality it is part of what makes a free society work.

This does not mean that conformity and regimentation are necessary in a free society. Our strength will always come from the emergence of the new and the creative, and it is part of the challenge to the free man to know and honor the difference between self-discipline and regimentation.

There are very few purely private decisions anymore. Increasingly every private decision related to our society must also be considered a *public* decision, which cannot be undertaken without regard for its effect upon others. Continued indifference to the public today can only burden more severely the public of tomorrow.

What can we do about private decisions that are destructive? We can alert people, educate them and inspire them. There is no substitute for the motivation of millions of people. The power of people who are informed and committed to a great cause can achieve what billions of federal dollars cannot begin to do. Further, in those areas where individuals or institutions refuse to listen to the public's demand for a voice of reason, government has got to take a strong stand. For example, in dealing with the environment, a man should be free to produce a product for sale, but his freedom ends when his factory pollutes the air, contaminates the waterways, desecrates beauty or harms those around him.

Our nation fosters the concept that all men are created equal and should be so treated by their government. But too often government, on one level or another, has ignored the long-term good of one segment of its people to enhance the political advantage of another, thereby creating inequality of the worst sort.

6. *Hate and Heart*

The strength of our nation is that we can expose our weaknesses and try to change them in broad daylight. We do not have all the answers. Our problems of race, pollution, crime and poverty are national shames, and we should refuse to sweep them under the carpet. Let us admit that they exist, and fight in the open to bring about a cure.

The greatness of this moment lies in the monumental dimensions of what is at stake. The decisions we make now, or neglect to make, will affect the quality of life for generations to come.

This is a great responsibility. It demands sacrifice, but it is not something to fear. The American people resent living under a mantle of smallness. But when given a challenge, a sense of anticipation and the hope of undertaking something truly worthwhile, they rise to greatness. Calling on a nation to sacrifice is not punishing that nation.

I do not have such a low opinion of the American people as to think that they can only be motivated by war. I think it is possible to motivate Americans in the direction of the better living of life. In fact, this is what our nation longs for.

The two greatest powers for motivating people are hate and heart. Hate power is easy to generate. Nations can be rallied with it, wars mounted, universities and industries disrupted and civilizations destroyed. Heart power is most clearly seen in the approach to life of a small child. It is found in the openness and generosity of the average person in all corners of America.

The question is: Can heart power deal with the dirt and grime of pollution, the power and greed of certain vested interests, the lawlessness and crime in our cities? Personally, I believe no force can stand up to that power of the heart in people when it is wedded to tough, practical men of commitment in government.

When people care, there is hope and anticipation. Since the beginning of man, every person who ever lived on earth has lived his whole life "today." He goes through hardships knowing what happened yesterday. But anticipating a better tomorrow is what motivates him to solve the problems of today.

The hope of tomorrow inspires everyone: whether it is the student frustrated by academic training not being what he thinks it ought to be; whether it is the person who is bewildered because in the age of technology things are passing him by; whether it is a young married man with a family seeking what is secure and what is opportune; or whether it is the middle-aged man who knows he no longer can go back and do some of the things that he would have liked to do. All of these people can anticipate tomorrow just in the excitement and the curiosity of what could happen.

People fear an economic depression. I fear more a depression of the spirit. In the 1930's, although we had the worst economic depression in our history, we had hope. Today we have a depression of the spirit in a time of economic prosperity. This nation cannot stand an economic depression and a depression of the spirit at the same time. Something violent would happen, with consequences no man can foresee. Of course we must avoid an economic depression, but first and foremost we must rebuild the spirit of all Americans—and restore the element of hope. Then, if we are ever so unlucky as to experience another great economic depression, we will be able to cope with it.

Hope was what enabled us to survive the bad times of the 1930's, for all the individual hardship and the poverty and the bread lines. People still had hope in their minds, and there was no true depression of the spirit. Every day a man who had no job hoped that tomorrow would be better. Hope not only got us through a time of economic misery but through the greatest war in modern times, a war won by free men who fought with the hope of tomorrow.

Today, perhaps for the first time in our history, enormous numbers of Americans live with little or no hope for tomorrow. Why are our leaders unable to motivate Americans to raise their spirits? This is what the young are asking. We have an affluent society, but if that is all government cares about, then we have a decadent society, and one that will fail.

It is imperative to cool the hatreds that have flared throughout our country during the last decade of rapid change. But to throw a wet blanket on the problems, in order to cool the country, is not to solve the problems. It will only postpone them for another generation. To put off solving a problem because you do not want to face the challenge of it is to burden future generations with our problems as well as their own.

We must not cool the spirit, cool the anticipation of hope, cool the desire to care, cool the ambition to make society better. Men must be free, free to work and free to try something new. *Only the small and fearful want a controlled society.* They prostitute patriotism and morality in a futile attempt to keep the lid on what they do not understand—the new, the original, the unique. Change does not frighten a people or a nation that is youthful, growing and learning. Great leadership does not suppress change but welcomes it, guides it and directs it.

America must not cool its passions out of fear, but rather redirect them from hate power to heart power, so that those things that need to change are changed in a responsible, imaginative way. I do not ask the young to be quiet. I ask them to be committed—committed in terms of a lifetime to improve all areas of a free society.

More and more of our people are learning that change is not an instant thing. They know you cannot "add water and stir" and solve the ingrained prejudice and indifference of people, the cruelty of the inner cities and the desecration of our natural environment. Maturity, in the sense of effective social change, has very little to do with age. When change is found difficult, the immature turn to violence or they drop out. The mature dig in.

Of course we would all prefer an instant cure to our problems. We would like to be able to relax and settle back into our private pursuits. But the great vocations of the new age we are entering lie in the architecture of change and the engineering of change. These callings are not easy or always comfortable — but they are great. They attract men and women bold enough to say, "This will be great beyond my lifetime and not just for the moment"; people who will risk the fury and the pressure of the special interests. *There is nothing to fear in these tasks if your security lies in your freedom and your principles.*

7. *The Power of One*

In the area of the environment, immediate survival is at stake for certain wild creatures and plant life. Man's ultimate survival is at stake as he realizes that the earth is a closed system. We cannot create resources. We can only alter them. They cannot be destroyed, but they can be wasted and irretrievably lost. Environmental responsibility is a way of life, an attitude toward our habitat, an ever-present awareness of the interrelationship and interdependence of all living things on this earth.

With this sober awakening has come the joyousness of a morning. Values that were forgotten—the poetry of an untouched mountain stream, the philosophy of a lonely wilderness, the majesty of a mountain range or a great ocean's expanse—these simple sides of life that have been man's companions from the very beginning are returning to enrich the individual and shift the world back into balance.

This awakening brings an awareness that the individual cannot live without his neighbor. Life styles of consumption and extravagance must change, and the individual can no longer remain isolated. His personal decisions affect his neighbor. His neighbor's decisions affect him. Even when the community you live in is absolutely free of air and water pollution, if your neighbor is prejudiced the "atmosphere" in your neighborhood is in a very real sense polluted.

The individual, who has appeared to be becoming more and more impotent in a vast society, is now discovering that he alone is the key to survival, to the improvement of life for humanity. To accomplish a worldwide change of values, so that our resources are not squandered and our surroundings destroyed, challenges the imagination of all the people on earth.

A young environmental activist once said to me, "There is no survival value in pessimism." He and thousands of others like him are aware that the job before us is to inspire the people to change their life styles.

You do not inspire people by being negative. You make them insecure and afraid. A positive approach to people does not mean a lessening in the intensity of the feeling that there has to be a drastic change. Rather, it is a deepening in the understanding of how a redirection must be brought about.

The individual has the capacity and the opportunity to make a positive contribution. There are many things the government cannot do and the individual can. For instance, the government could spend billions on the litter problem and not solve it. Unless the private citizen becomes concerned and corrects his tendency to be the world's messiest animal, the streets and countrysides will increasingly look like helter-skelter junkyards.

8. *The Wheel of Life*

We are beginning to see the need to make decisions based on a wider range of values — all those things that have to do with the living of life.

Everything that has been accepted as right and good and American is being reevaluated and rethought. The old era made its decisions mainly for the economic gain of the moment. We confused free enterprise with free society. But free enterprise is only part of the wheel. Enterprise means some kind of business, and that is right and good. But business is not the total man—75 percent of most people's time is *not* devoted to earning a living.

Free enterprise left alone without government regulation can destroy itself. It can dominate the rest of the wheel of life. In a completely unregulated competitive system, the most economical approach is to put everyone into slavery, feed them a little less each day, and when they die throw them to one side. Total freedom to exploit can lead to total slavery. This is why the free enterprise system needs tough government guidelines from the top.

Freedom implies a series of choices. If you have no options, you are not free, and this is particularly relevant to the management—or mismanagement—of money in our country. There are very few options when you need money in a hurry, and usually they are unnecessarily painful.

Money is, or should be, just another consumer item in a credit society. And the manipulation of the economy in a credit society can no longer be successfully based on making money "tight," as was true in our old cash society.

This thinking was behind my firm conviction, expressed in one of the first Cabinet meetings I attended as Secretary of the Interior, that pushing the Federal Reserve Board's prime interest rate to higher and higher levels made an inflationary situation worse. When the federal government offers a safe high-interest haven for "idle money," there is no incentive for a bank to make money available to individual borrowers, for business or personal reasons, except at inflationary rates of interest — which people have to go right on paying because they have no choice. For example, thousands of individuals, while waiting for a better day, overuse their credit out of desperation and find themselves paying interest rates of up to 18 percent while trying to regain solvency. Yet the largest bank in the world really "owns" nothing. We found this out in the Depression 1930's, when people took their money out of banks and the banks went broke.

Because money is a consumer item, banks really need to become shopping centers. The day of being able to solve the world's problems in the board rooms of the money establishment is over. A million-dollar loan to some corporation is becoming a smaller part of the total picture. It is the home owner, borrowing a few hundred dollars to landscape his lawn, who puts people to work. A man starting up a laundry, which hires three or four men, also helps solve the unemployment problem. He is part of a structure in which one American hires another American to do a job.

Something is very wrong about a free enterprise system in which we bail out a huge corporation with enormous sums of government money, but a poor fisherman often cannot go to the bank and get $500 to repair his boat. There always seems to be money in the hundreds of millions to rescue companies that have ceased to perform a useful public service, and people should object to this. If we are going to use huge sums of public money to keep a company like Lockheed or the Penn Central out of bankruptcy, we at least ought to get a public stock interest out of it. These big corporations are not propping up government: the government is propping up the corporations. With all our computers and technology, why can't we demand that these corporations be more accurate in calculating the cost of a new airplane?

The people who make a practice of belittling the bureaucracy and inefficiency of government, the people who criticize government most, are the same people who always come back to government with their hand out for financial help. Meanwhile they say, "The poor should help themselves, but our companies should be helped by the government because it's in the national interest." Bullshit! In the long run the laziness of a million-dollar "bailout" might open up less opportunity than the liveliness of a one-buck loan.

Technology is freeing man from being a machine. It is freeing him from spending all his waking hours working for the necessities of life. He has more and more time to think and create. The full wheel of life can be completed. Man's imagination, his creative ability and his capacity for humanity are now what count.

This need exclude no one. You can be creative in anything you do. In the past we have characterized success only by monetary achievement. We have not figured out what it is that makes a man happy.

All professions are equally important, whatever they may be. You can be just as successful with yourself and your family and your relationships with people as a creative craftsman as you can be being President. If you really love what you are doing, it is a satisfying profession. Watch a great cabinet-maker at work, for example, and you will see how something can be done with total commitment and love.

In the next twenty years proportionately fewer people will be involved in the production of goods and proportionately more people in services requiring personal contact between buyer and seller. Because the service professions, unlike a power plant or a factory, cannot substitute automation for manpower on a large scale, I think it possible that by 1980 the service industries will account for 70 percent of *all* jobs in the United States. I also think it possible that in many professions, if not most, the mandated workweek is on the way to becoming obsolete. In the future a man will get paid for doing his own thing, whether it is part-time or all the time.

We are breaking into a new era of how to live life. In this new era, work will be the fulfillment and satisfaction that comes with accomplishment. You can be totally free working around the clock. You can be enslaved doing nothing. What good is a full stomach and an empty heart? The man who lives is the man who works because he enjoys it. It completes the total man. I am concerned when a person thinks only about security and misses the great opportunities that involve a certain amount of risk. There is no crime in making a mistake or failing to attain a great goal. The real crime is in mistaking the safe and the mediocre for the greatness of life.

Real wealth is not money. It is productivity and taking care of the needs of people. Do a thing because people need it, and you will be wealthy. Do a thing *just* to make money, and you will eventually consider yourself a failure. There are ways to make a living in whatever you want to do, if you sincerely want to do it. The world will fall in step with a man who is committed in his mind, his heart and his soul.

Looking back on the 1970's and 1980's from the next century, the future will say it was during this period that people found the vision to demand a new direction. It was then that people began to see that the monetary glitter was not all that there was to life. Success was not judged by material things acquired in a lifetime. It was based upon those who gave, not just those who received. It was the giving and not the receiving that made greatness.

9. *An Iron Curtain of Fear*

We are in the midst of a dangerous variation of the nationalism game in this country. A great isolation of spirit has collided with the feeling that we are the chosen people, a people who triumphed because of the justice of our cause and the virtue with which we "prosecuted" it. The youth of our generation have dared to strip aside the curtain of national virtue and look at the consequences of our actions. They see the desecration of the environment for strictly monetary reasons. They see that our national priorities are selected for short-term gain. And they feel frustrated because they see the uselessness of dying in a useless war.

The credibility of a nation is at stake when it tries to justify at the same time both war and peace, setting a priority on neither and losing both.

We shall gain nothing if we simply withdraw from Vietnam and then withdraw into America. For all our needs at home, the world desperately needs an America that is *outward*. Our youth, normally outward in their feelings, are beginning to turn more and more inward. Now it is time for us to lead the world in showing that instead of being guided by artificial fears, created for artificial reasons, we can plunge ahead to create an environment of hope.

The great fallacy in our national priorities after the end of World War II lay in the fact that we poured our wealth into "protection" and neglected the heart of the global issue — communication. As we built a great wall of defense around us, we unrealistically hoped that somehow the international threat, the misunderstanding, the hate and the rivalry would magically disappear. How much have we spent in terms of man-hours, monetary investment and physical energy without trying to "reach out"? How much have the endless debates across negotiating tables helped turn our enemies into friends? How much of our budget has gone into researching the root causes of our international differences?

Are we truly a peaceful nation? Yes — at least we mean to be. Yet we still preach and live by a philosophy of artificial fear. The need is for trust, and trust is certainly not a one-way street. But until we communicate, we will never understand. Who will raise the iron curtain of fear if we don't? The Russians and the Chinese are both a part of the environment of fear. They could be a part of the environment of hope. Trust your friends and cultivate your enemies.

An individual, a society or a nation as a

whole cannot be respected unless it in turn respects. This is where we must start. Somewhere, somehow, a nation will emerge—a nation that cares about the needs of the human everywhere, not just within its own borders. That would be the finest kind of leadership any nation could give to the world.

Our foreign aid has generally been poorly managed in the past. Does that mean we should cut it off? Of course not. But we must stop using it to satisfy the political whims of some governments, and start trying to solve the human needs in those countries.

The challenge of freedom still ahead of us is to break out into the freedom of the heart, the mind and the soul. This *is* a great nation. But a great nation, standing still, decays and falls under its own weight. If we pause now to bathe in the glory of our rhetoric, then we are on the road to failure. That need not happen.

I see a mood building in this country, and around the world, among the young and those who think young—the *searchers* and the *new voices*. Together we can let our imaginations go. Don't be afraid to dream. Dream big dreams. With big dreams we can achieve big things and little things, but with little dreams we can only achieve little things. The young thought, the free thought — that is what is important. The anticipation of tomorrow is the excitement of living. Together we can create the kind of world that was meant to be.

The searchers in nations around the world must pool their knowledge and join a common effort. There is no other way to protect our great oceans, our atmosphere and the total environment of the only planet we have to live on. There is no other way to build trust among men.

Think about it — three and a half billion people arriving at a unity of purpose. What a challenge! What an opportunity!

Acknowledgments I would like to thank those who helped make this book possible: the members of my staff who gave this project long hours of untiring attention, Malcolm Roberts, Josef Holbert, Dr. Carl McMurray and Miss Yvonne Esbensen; and Gene Farmer, a *Life* senior editor, who took a leave of absence to contribute valuable technical assistance.

Walter J. Hickel